The
ROGER FEDERER
Effect

The
ROGER FEDERER
Effect

Rivals, Friends, Fans
and How The Maestro
Changed Their Lives

**Simon Cambers
& Simon Graf**

First published by Pitch Publishing, 2022
Paperback edition, 2023

Pitch Publishing
9 Donnington Park,
85 Birdham Road,
Chichester,
West Sussex,
PO20 7AJ
www.pitchpublishing.co.uk
info@pitchpublishing.co.uk

A CIP catalogue record is available for this book
from the British Library.

ISBN 978 1 80150 447 8

Typesetting and origination by Pitch Publishing
Printed and bound in India by Replika Press Pvt. Ltd.

Contents

INTRODUCTION

*Roger Federer just may be the most famous
sportsman of his time.*

THE SWISS has captivated audiences ever since he first
hit the headlines as the Wimbledon boys' champion and a
junior world No 1, progressing at speed to become one of
the greatest players ever and dominating men's tennis with
a seemingly effortless playing style which many have tried
to emulate, to no avail.

In a career that spanned four decades, Federer won 20
Grand Slam titles, including eight at Wimbledon, collected
more than 100 tournament victories worldwide and thrilled
crowds all over the planet as he became the most popular
player of his or any generation.

How has he done it? Through more than 40 exclusive
interviews, we tell his story in a new way, through the eyes
of those whose lives he has impacted the most – and those
who shaped and experienced him early on. From his biggest
rivals, like Rafael Nadal and Novak Djokovic, who made
him improve again; to his childhood friends; to his coaches,
like Sven Groeneveld and Paul Annacone, who helped to
steer him on the right path; to his peers.

His super-fans explain why they changed their lives to
follow Federer, spending thousands of pounds to follow him

all over the world. We learn how he turned from a goofy, pony-tailed talent into a man with so much style many call him James Bond.

Above all, this is the story of how Federer transcended sport to become a true icon and why so many people, from other sports and from all walks of life, including politics, music and film, were inspired by him and want to be close to him.

In talking to those whose lives he has touched, in so many different ways, his sheer joy for playing tennis, even into his 40s, shines through.

It is a love that has never wilted. It helped him become one of the best tennis players in history and it has impacted the lives of millions more.

ROGER, THE FRIEND

AT THE origin of every great sports career is play. Those who love to play as children will also want to express themselves creatively later on, in very different ways. Playing is invaluable. You may do it even as an adult.

Young Roger loved playing anything that involved a ball. When his head was barely higher than the table, he played table tennis, then tennis, football, squash, basketball. His favourite playmate became Marco Chiudinelli, whom he met during tennis training and shared with him the joy of playing, the urge to move and the desire to compete. They kept on playing when everyone else had already gone home. They also played for hours on the PlayStation or PC.

Federer dreamed of Wimbledon at a young age, even though he found a nemesis in Danny Schnyder early on. His first rival prepared him for the later challenges of Rafael Nadal and Novak Djokovic. Schnyder never turned pro, but he achieved what Nadal and Djokovic never managed to do.

As a teenager, Federer was introduced to the tough professional world by Marc Rosset and Wayne Ferreira, among others. Rosset was happy to welcome another Swiss to the ATP Tour. Ferreira, as a South African – Federer's second home – felt like a mentor to him. The two were also there for him in his darkest hours when he was first confronted with death.

Wrestler Urs Bürgler gave a helping hand at the Sydney 2000 Olympics when the shy Roger didn't know whether to make the first move on Mirka. That's what friends are for.

Marco Chiudinelli, childhood friend

And the winner said: "Sure, let's play again!"'

As childhood friends, Marco Chiudinelli and Roger Federer were at times inseparable. Their friendship lasts to this day, and Chiudinelli can still remember a lot from their carefree youth. They were eight or nine when they first met. The 'Association of Tennis Clubs of Basel and Surroundings' organised a weekly training session for the most talented juniors. 'We were a mixed bunch, ten or 12 kids. But I only remember Roger,' Chiudinelli said. 'We clicked right away.'

The training sessions took place at the Van der Merwe Center in Allschwil, a centre for racquet sports, fitness and health. After the practices, when the three tennis courts were occupied again, Marco and Roger continued to let off steam on the squash court. 'At first, we played with our racquets and tennis balls,' Chiudinelli recalled with a smile. 'They were spiking wildly like in a pinball machine. At some point, we got a squash ball from the reception and played with it. But it wasn't perfect either. We kept hitting the wall with the big tennis racquets. At Christmas, we got squash racquets from our parents, and then it went better.'

The urge to move and play and their sporting ambition united the two, who otherwise would hardly have met. At least, not so early. Although their birthdays are only 33 days apart (Roger is older), they did not go to school together. At that time, the Chiudinellis lived in the centre of Basel near the zoo, the Federers in Münchenstein. Not a round-the-world trip, but still a few kilometres away.

Marco and Roger showed so much talent that their joint training sessions soon became more. In a now more exclusive group, they were allowed to train three times a week: Marco, Roger and Frank Frey, the son of the president of the association. 'Those training sessions brought Roger and me closer together. Thanks to tennis, we now met three times a week. Our parents were happy that we had fun together and were out and about in the neighbourhood as a team of two. That calmed them down.'

At that time, they also played their first official match against each other at the Bambino Bären Cup in Arlesheim. 'It was played to nine games and I won 9-7,' Chiudinelli said, remembering very clearly. In the beginning, he was down 5-2 and was comforted by his friend, then he took the lead and had to build Roger up mentally. But that didn't help anymore. That victory against Federer was to remain the only one for Chiudinelli in an official match. It was the semi-final, and in the final he lost to Enzo Aresta, Chiudinelli recounts, adding jokingly: 'That defeat still torments me today.'

Their joint training was suspended at some point and Chiudinelli can no longer say why. Their parents had become friends in the meantime and the Federers encouraged the Chiudinellis to send their son to the TC Old Boys as well. A good decision. 'There was a completely different atmosphere than at the Basel Lawn Tennis Club, where I had been before,' Chiudinelli recalled. 'We had a lot of kids at a similar level at the Old Boys, and you always found someone to play with.'

As chance would have it, the Chiudinelli family moved very close to the Federers in Münchenstein at the time. So the two sons went to training together by bike. On the way back, they stocked up on all kinds of treats at the kiosk with their pocket money: sour tongues, snakes, and Coke florets. 'We got back on the bikes, rode on and stuffed our mouths full of the sweets. That's how we filled up our sugar reservoirs again,' Chiudinelli said. The bags of sweets were empty before they got home, so their parents didn't notice. They invested two francs each in their sweets. In those days, you got so much sweet and sour for that money that your tongue burned.

They were coached at the TC Old Boys by the Australian Peter Carter, who later moved to Swiss Tennis to continue personally coaching Federer. 'At that time, we were of a similar level, the same age and both ambitious,' Chiudinelli said. 'We had this competitive spirit. We always wanted to play games and sets. Others had less of this intrinsic motivation. The loser always wanted a rematch, and the winner said: "Sure, let's play again!" At the Old Boys, we had a big group of juniors; Roger and I always stayed the longest and kept challenging each other in a good way. We could play with each other for hours on end.'

Besides that, they still played football intensively: Chiudinelli at FC Basel, Federer at Concordia Basel. And the two rival clubs played against each other again and again. 'We always had trouble with Concordia,' Chiudinelli recalled. 'We were very structured at FCB; they were not at all. They had only dribblers, but individually they were very skilled and unpredictable. They were all street footballers, most of them sons of immigrants. And they had good cohesion. Roger was the strategist in his team, probably the only one. He had a strong right foot but no left.' Chiudinelli smiled: 'He only needed the left one to keep from falling over. But he had a powerful shot with his right foot and was dangerous with headers; he had good timing.' Chiudinelli was a sweeper for many years and later a full-back and Federer was always a striker. He lived out his attacking spirit in football as well.

What Chiudinelli remembers most from football are the duels at the indoor tournaments in the region, in which FCB and Concordia always took part. 'In the hall, it was challenging to cover Roger. There you score goals from the halfway line. They had another one with a monster shot, Roberto Canosso, he shot with his left. When those two were on the field simultaneously, it became difficult for us. Nobody wanted to be hit by a shot from them.'

At the prestigious indoor tournament in Möhlin, a 30-minute drive from Basel, FCB and Concordia Basel duelled twice in the final. 'The first time, it was 0-0 or 1-1 and we won in a penalty shoot-out, but Roger sunk his. The second time we lost 2-0, we had no chance. After that, Roger stopped playing football and concentrated on tennis. I continued to play for two more years. Roger played football for five or six years; I played eight.'

Soon they went their separate ways. Federer moved out to the National Training Centre in Ecublens in 1995 when he was 14. 'For me, it was not an option,' said Chiudinelli. 'After all, I didn't even qualify for the Swiss Junior Championships every year. Roger always played for the title. But I missed him at Old Boys. I was certainly better than those who only played regionally but not good enough to dream of earning a living with tennis one day. I wrote "computer scientist" in the friendship books as my dream job. That's what my parents did. In tennis, my goal was to achieve an N ranking [to be among the top 150 active players in the country] one day.'

Chiudinelli feared that their friendship might break up when Federer moved to Lake Geneva. But the opposite was the case. When he came home at weekends, they always spent time together. The Friday or Saturday evening they spent together looked like this: with 20 or 30 francs in their pockets, they took the 10 tram to Steinenvorstadt in Basel, where there was always a lot going on, strolled through the alleys, ate at McDonald's, gambled away the rest of the money in the amusement arcade or watched others play games. The big boxes with the video games, quite simple by today's standards, exerted a great fascination on the two boys. Chiudinelli remembers a game where you had to circle a dragon and be careful not to get hit by the fire it was breathing. To find the right strategy for the different levels, they would hang around the box for hours and watch how others did it.

When the amusement arcade closed at 1am, there were no more trams, so they walked the four kilometres home and talked about everything during that hour. Then they continued to entertain themselves on Chiudinelli's PC at home until three or four in the morning. 'We mostly played NBA and FIFA. In basketball, he was the Phoenix Suns; I was the Chicago Bulls when we played each other.' Because Chiudinelli had a basketball hoop in his childhood room, they also duelled with a real ball. Not at night, though; that would have been too loud, but when they met during the day. 'It was an intense, beautiful time,' he said, reminiscing. They were not yet very interested in parties, alcohol or girls. They, the two pronounced gamblers, only wanted to play: on the court with racquet and ball, on the PlayStation, on the PC or in the amusement arcade.

Chiudinelli did not ask his friend much about Ecublens. At least, not about tennis. 'It didn't even occur to me that

I could go there one day, and that's why I wasn't very interested in what was going on there tennis-wise.' That was until he received a letter from Swiss Tennis at age 15 in early 1997, telling him he could show his skills at the National Tennis Centre. Probably Peter Carter had put in a good word for him.

'I travelled to Ecublens in awe. Ecublens was the holy grail of Swiss Tennis at the time, even though the hall was old and almost collapsed. That day I played big, and everything worked out. I only failed in the 12-minute run at the end. They told me I was nominated for Biel.' That year, Swiss Tennis moved from Ecublens to Biel in the ultra-modern new National Tennis Centre, and from then on, Chiudinelli also pursued a tennis career. 'If Swiss Tennis hadn't nominated me for the national squad, it would never have occurred to me to train more,' he said, shrugging his shoulders. Sometimes luck finds you.

In Biel, however, Chiudinelli and Federer didn't see each other that often. They were in different training groups and hardly ever played together. And Federer, 16 by now, was often travelling to tournaments. On 22 September 1997, after his first victories in a series of satellite tournaments in Bossonnens, Fribourg, he appeared in the ATP world rankings for the first time, as No 803, five spots ahead of a certain Lleyton Hewitt. 'When he was 15, 16, it was clear to me that Roger would become a professional tennis player and succeed,' said Chiudinelli. 'But I didn't think at that time that he would win Grand Slams.'

Gaming didn't leave the two of them entirely in Biel either. Federer had moved into a flat with Yves Allegro, and he and Chiudinelli once played all night on the PlayStation. Again and again *Tekken*, which was a fighting game Federer mastered like no other. 'We played maybe 200 times, he won 198 times, but I kept trying,' Chiudinelli recounted. Despite the long gaming night, Federer got up in the morning and went to practice on time. He let his friend sleep a little longer, which caused him a lot of trouble. When he woke up around noon, everyone was in an uproar, at school, at Swiss Tennis, at his host family, because he hadn't shown up. Chiudinelli's mother smoothed things over but demanded that her son tell his father the truth about the night they had spent together gaming.

While Federer won the junior tournament at Wimbledon in 1998 and made his debut on the ATP Tour in Gstaad at 17, Chiudinelli was still far off. But he, too, was now focusing on tennis. He turned professional in August 1999 at 18, soon won a satellite tournament and climbed straight into the top 500 in the first few months. Nevertheless, they were travelling in different worlds; Federer had already played his way into the top 100 by then. Chiudinelli can still remember where he was when Federer beat his idol Pete Sampras in Wimbledon on 3 July 2001: in Montauban in southern France. 'It went badly, I was playing in qualifying for a Challenger tournament and I couldn't hit a ball.'

While Federer celebrated his moment of glory and was cheered on Wimbledon's Centre Court, Chiudinelli was outclassed by the Argentine Walter Larrea, a local club player: 'I lost the first set 6-1, went into the dressing room, smashed a racquet and said to myself, "That's Walter Larrea, he might have earned one ATP point in his life. Now you go out and fight!" I went out and fought like crazy and lost the second set 6-0.'

Of course, he was happy for Federer, 'but I was mostly preoccupied with myself at the time. I was in Montauban, thinking about flying to Tbilisi [Georgia] and playing two Futures tournaments because I didn't know how to win a match anymore. I was completely down, had no more support from Swiss Tennis, and he beat Sampras at Wimbledon.'

Was Chiudinelli never jealous of his childhood friend and his career? He smiled: 'I often hear that question. No, I have no trace of envy. Because I never saw myself on the same level as Roger, not even in my junior days. He usually won the national championships; I often got stuck in the regional eliminations. As well as I know Roger, I never compared myself to him. That question never came up for me. You have other people in all professions who are more successful than you. But that doesn't mean you constantly compare yourself with them. Otherwise, almost everyone would have to be unhappy in their job.'

So Chiudinelli tried to gain a foothold on the professional Tour while Federer rushed from success to success. Chiudinelli can't remember Federer's first Wimbledon victory on 6 July 2003 in the final against Mark Philippoussis. Or, more precisely: he slept through it. He was also at Wimbledon initially that year, qualified in the doubles with the Croatian Lovro Zovko, but lost in round one.

In those days, he had problems with his left wrist and could only play the backhand with a slice, i.e. one-handed. While surfing the internet, he discovered that two of his favourite bands would be performing in Montreal at the same concert, one after the other: the progressive rock bands Dream Theater and Queensrÿche. He had signed up for the Challenger Tournament in Granby, near Montreal, but was supposed to cancel because of his wrist. But then he decided to fly there anyway and attend the concert beforehand to combine fun with his job and get his mind off things. On the plane to Montreal, he met Maximilian Abel from Germany, who was also competing in Granby. They joined forces, attended the concert in Montreal on Saturday, 5 July, and wandered around until early in the morning. When Chiudinelli woke up around noon, Federer had become Wimbledon champion 5,000 kilometres and five time zones away.

The fact that they both became tennis pros helped keep their friendship alive, even though they played in different spheres. 'If I had a question about an opponent, I knew I could always call Roger. We saw each other at several ATP tournaments and the four Grand Slams. There he always arrived early, and I was there for the qualifying. We met there four times a year. In Basel, too, we always trained together before the tournament.' And when it happened, they would go out to dinner together.

Wasn't it always hectic around Federer? Chiudinelli shakes his head. 'He was able to shield himself well. When we went out to eat, he usually had his corner, so we still had our privacy and could talk without everyone listening.' He says Federer hasn't changed due to the hype surrounding him anyway. 'I have no comparison. I don't know anyone else since childhood who became a superstar afterwards. But I'd say he's a role model in how he's dealt with it all.'

How does Chiudinelli explain Federer's durability and professionalism? Thinking for a moment, he says: 'He had a good situation with his parents, who knew a bit about the sport and supported him but still held back. And he had a golden hand in choosing the people who surrounded him. First and foremost with Mirka, who manages his life and the whole trappings. Other partners and women on Tour bring more chaos than calm. She is enormously valuable to him. Pierre [Paganini, the fitness trainer] was essential to him from the beginning, also in terms of mindset: setting goals and sticking to them. He also found a constant in Seve [Lüthi, his coach]. And with Tony [Godsick, his manager]. Roger understood how to build people around him who protected and encouraged him and brought their input so that he got better and better. Many people don't know what it takes in terms of teamwork in tennis to perform as an individual athlete on the court. You need a good group of people so that you can deliver 100 per cent on the court and not get stuck at 93 per cent. He lived this teamwork very distinctly and proved to be a good judge of character when he chose his people.'

Chiudinelli, on the other hand, often travelled the globe alone and was repeatedly set back by injuries. But he kept at it, and at 27, after an 18-month break following complicated knee surgery, he made a remarkable comeback that even earned him the ATP's Comeback Player of the Year award. In October 2009, he broke into the top 100 for the first time, and at the beginning of November, he played big at the Swiss Indoors, challenging Federer in the semi-finals. For the first time, they, who had experienced so much together in their younger years, played against each other in the pros. And their encounter delivered what it promised. Chiudinelli played boldly, missed three break points to lead 5-3, led 4-1 in the tiebreak and had a set point at 7-6, which Federer fended off with a brilliant backhand passing shot. The favourite then went on to win 7-6, 6-3.

'It was a beautiful and bitter moment for me,' said Chiudinelli. 'I had my chances, so it was disappointing.

But it was beautiful for me to walk onto the court, a full stadium, and the sympathies were similarly distributed. Half for Roger, half for me. That hardly ever happened in Basel. It was extraordinary to share that with him.' He would have preferred to leave the court immediately after the defeat; he was so disappointed. But he had to stay for the joint on-court interview. 'That was good because I regained my composure more quickly.'

It was not a game like any other for either of them, 20 years after they first hit balls together. Chiudinelli told his friend before the match that he likes to take his time between points. He knows that Federer wants to play fast. But that was not to provoke him, he said. 'And against anyone else, after losing the first set, I would have gone out to the toilet for a moment to process that. Against Roger, I didn't do that. Because of my respect for him. I promptly conceded the only break of the match in the first game of the second set. That annoyed me. But after the on-court interview, everything was okay again.'

Together they celebrated the Davis Cup title in Lille in November 2014 with a 3-1 win over France. Federer and Stan Wawrinka got the necessary three points, and long-time Davis Cup players Chiudinelli and Michael Lammer were also on the team. 'It was an extremely nice moment for me,' said Chiudinelli. 'When we talked after the win, Roger made me feel that he had played for us too. He knew: this was the only chance for Michi [Lammer] and me to win something of this magnitude. We couldn't have done it alone. We are eternally grateful to him and Stan for that. This is one of the top three highlights of my career.' He sensed that a huge weight had fallen off Federer because he had given the Swiss fans and Swiss Tennis this title after all those years in which he had also occasionally declined to play in the Davis Cup. 'He could now tick all that off.'

While Federer launched his magnificent comeback in 2017 and went on to win three more Grand Slam titles, Chiudinelli's career ended that year. His body no longer played along; knee and Achilles tendon problems constantly plagued him. He went on his farewell tour, played one more time at the places where he had particularly enjoyed it, and then retired in October at the Swiss Indoors in Basel.

Two weeks earlier, when they had dinner on the sidelines of the tournament in Shanghai, Chiudinelli had told Federer of his retirement plans. 'We had a good conversation, later went to his room and discussed it further. He had advised me to inform the most important Swiss journalists beforehand and give them interviews. Maybe one of these articles would open a door for me for life after my career if someone read it. So that's what I did.'

On a Monday evening at the end of October 2017, Chiudinelli gave his farewell at the Swiss Indoors with a defeat to Robin Haase. Federer was in the front row, shedding tears during his lap of honour and hugging his friend. 'I'm a fan of yours,' he breathed in his ear. 'Roger being there meant a lot to me,' Chiudinelli said. 'He was present at the beginning and until my last match.'

Their bond will always remain, even if they don't have as much contact at times. And tennis doesn't let go of Chiudinelli either. He now organises camps for ambitious recreational players on courts in Switzerland, Spain and Germany; even on the grass in Halle, where his childhood friend triumphed ten times. And every now and again, a participant asks him a question or two about a certain Roger Federer.

Danny Schnyder, first rival

He did what Nadal and Djokovic couldn't

Nobody beats Roger Federer eight times in a row. Not even Rafael Nadal or Novak Djokovic. No one? Well, one man has done it: Danny Schnyder.

Young Roger despaired of his tennis colleague from the Basel area. The two were the best players in Switzerland, born in 1981, clashed regularly at junior tournaments between eight and 14, and became friends. Danny, the younger brother of Patty Schnyder, who would later become a professional herself, grew up in Bottmingen; Roger, in the neighbouring village of Münchenstein. Sometimes they went to a Football Club Basel match together or watched a movie at home and on free weekends they often met on the tennis court and got up to all kinds of mischief. But in official matches, they were dead serious. 'That's when we no longer knew of friendship,' Schnyder said. 'We were both very ambitious, and that showed. It always became very emotional.' In the first few matches, it was mainly Federer who got loud and sometimes had a racquet slip out of his hand.

Schnyder, who was just over six months older, was initially just as unpleasant an opponent for Federer as Novak Djokovic was later to become for him. He committed hardly any errors, had a stable double-handed backhand and exploited Federer's vulnerable one-handed backhand. 'I was very solid from the baseline, made few mistakes,' Schnyder said. 'He was always the more risky player, even tried to play serve-and-volley, which didn't pay off at such a young age. With his forehand, he tried to force. But he made too many mistakes and his backhand was a huge weakness. That's where I nailed him.'

The first five or six times, it wasn't even close, Schnyder remembers. 'Rogi was frustrated; he hated to lose.' Schnyder won the first eight times but once Federer broke the spell, he only lost to his teenage rival once more. 'The balance was narrowly positive for Rogi at the end,' Schnyder said. He remembers how they consoled each other when the other wasn't doing so well. More and more often, Federer was victorious. Like in 1993 in the final of the Junior Swiss Championships in Bellinzona. Together they won the doubles. In a photograph, they are both beaming as they hold their two medals each to the camera, three gold and one silver.

'When I see Rogi's successes over all these years, it seems like a dream that I was once able to keep up with him for six years,' Schnyder mused. Their times together as ambitious juniors have kept them linked to this day, even though they hardly see each other anymore. In March 2015, Schnyder, living in San Diego, visited his childhood friend at the tournament in Indian Wells. 'I thought he might have 15 minutes with his packed schedule. But we sat together in the Players' Garden for more than an hour, chatting about old times, our current lives and our families. Of course, I'm proud of him for having such a great career. But even more than all the titles, I'm pleased that he's remained the same easy-going guy he was 20, 25 years ago.'

They refreshed memories like the one when they went to a junior tournament together in Annecy, France, and just goofed around. 'We'd shoot balls around and the one who hit the other would get a lollipop. We laughed so hard when we remembered that. What I find insane is that Rogi can still remember every detail of our matches, and he even knew some of the scores.' Then Federer drove his childhood friend to the hotel by car.

But why did Federer become a tennis superstar and his first nemesis didn't? 'I'm often asked that,' said Schnyder, who pursued an academic career instead of one in sports. 'I think even if I had gone full tennis, I wouldn't have gotten further than the top 600, 700 in the world. I didn't have the body and the talent to get any better. And more importantly, I lacked the absolute passion that you need. I didn't want to devote more than six, seven hours a week to tennis. The touch was there, but you can't make up for the huge lack of passion.' It was a passion Schnyder sensed in Federer. 'He wanted to compete and win. He loved the game and he loved to win even more. His will to win was huge.'

Schnyder saw from his sister Patty, who is a good two years older and was to advance to No 7 on the WTA Tour and win 11 professional titles, how much you have to invest in a professional career. 'When I was 15, 16, I preferred to do things with my friends. And I was a big fan of FC Basel and attended all the games. Then when I was 17, 18, I was going out more often, and tennis took a back seat.' He made it to 67th in the national rankings in the end.

What amazes him most about Federer is the straightforwardness with which he drove his career onwards. 'We were similar as youngsters, not very diligent in training and had a lot of fluff in our heads. We didn't warm up for long when we played together, but we soon played for points. Playing balls longline or cross-court for hours on end wasn't our thing. I think it's incredible how Rogi changed in that respect, how he managed to achieve this discipline and coolness. I would never have thought that. I always knew he had talent. But I was surprised that he would put in this gruelling work every day. And that he would become such a model athlete and the dream of all mothers-in-law. I rather thought he would become a character like Gaël Monfils. Playful and not always so disciplined. A charismatic artist who plays with the audience and occasionally smashes a racquet. Roger had a mind of his own and was a rascal in a good way.'

The two parted ways when Federer moved to the National Tennis Centre in Ecublens in the autumn of 1995. 'Rogi developed rapidly there. After just six months, I noticed a big change. He didn't let himself get rattled so quickly on the court anymore,' Schnyder said. 'He no longer looked at what people were doing around him. The decision for Ecublens was groundbreaking for his career. He now had much more time for tennis. And he probably also felt more pressure. If he took this risk and didn't go the normal school route, he would now have to succeed in tennis. I had the feeling he was much more focused on everything he did from then on. And I soon had no chance against him anymore.'

Schnyder studied Spanish as a major and political science and communication as minors in Basel. In 2003, he emigrated to Mexico, where he studied international affairs with a focus on business at the college in Monterrey. After receiving his master's degree, he soon relocated to Houston for professional reasons and later to San Diego. In 2018, Swiss building materials producer Holcim poached him, and he returned to the greater Houston area as its Head of Sales. He is satisfied with how his life has turned out. Now the father of a daughter and a son, he is very rarely in Switzerland. From his 20s to 30s, he rarely picked up a racquet but now he plays tennis regularly again in the USA, even competitively, and at a reasonable level.

Schnyder admits that he now prefers to watch baseball rather than tennis. But he has always tuned in during Federer's big finals. 'I'm a big sports fan, but not a tennis fan. I only watch tennis when Rogi is playing,' he said. 'Everything looks so fluid and natural with him. That's what I like most about him – that ease. When I watch Nadal, I feel like he's always suffering. With Rogi, everything is so smooth. It's beautiful to watch.'

Does he still occasionally mention that he once beat the great Roger Federer eight times in a row? Schnyder grins. 'It's not like I come up with it on my own,' he said. 'But when I mention I'm from Switzerland, I'm often told, "Ah, like Roger Federer!" And then I say I know him and even played against him in the past and beat him.'

Of course, many wouldn't believe him immediately, so when he met Federer in Indian Wells in 2015, he recorded a short video in which the 20-time Grand Slam champion confirmed it. The atmosphere is relaxed as Schnyder says, 'We are here now, with Roger.' Federer interjects, 'In Indian Wells.' Then he says with a mischievous smile, 'and it's a nostalgic time. And we realised that the only player who beat me more often, as often as Nadal and Djokovic, is Danny Schnyder. There he is!' The camera swings to Schnyder, who makes a Victory sign. And Federer concludes, 'Cheers to that!'

'This video has earned me a lot of free beers,' Schnyder said with a smirk. 'It's won me a lot of bets in bars.' And he doesn't hide that his relationship with Federer has also worked to his advantage in business. 'With certain CEOs who are tennis fans, I immediately had a good foundation for conversation. You're already starting on a different level.'

Danny Schnyder did not become a tennis pro. But his years as a successful junior and Roger Federer's first rival still mark his life today.

Marc Rosset, Swiss mentor

'And Roger? He was as relaxed as one can be'

Marc Rosset has to smile when he talks about his first encounter with Roger Federer: 'He was 14 or 15 when he came to Geneva to practise with me. I was told he was very talented, and I was curious to meet him. When I was a teenager and got to hit balls with the great Henri Leconte for the first time, I was totally tense. I wanted to present myself at my best, gave everything, to the brink of exhaustion. And Roger? Not a trace of nervousness! He was as relaxed as one can be. He didn't move much on the court; his balls flew in all directions. I had to laugh; he was so different from me, once with Leconte.'

But didn't it annoy Rosset that this teenager was not in awe of him, the Olympic champion? 'Oh, on the contrary. I immediately took Roger to my heart.' He noticed that Federer was gifted. 'But that wasn't so important for me. At that age, you can't tell if someone will become a great player or not. That is impossible. What impressed me was his easy-going nature. I just liked this boy. I always liked those who are a bit different. That's why I became friends with the likes of Marat Safin or Goran Ivanisevic.'

When their paths crossed for the second time in mid-July 1998, Federer had just become junior Wimbledon champion and had made his professional debut in Gstaad. Davis Cup captain Stéphane Oberer took the youngster to the quarter-final against Spain in La Coruña as the Swiss team's sparring partner, as a reward for his success.

'I asked if Roger could have the room next to me in the hotel,' Rosset recounted. 'It was important that he felt welcome as part of the team. We then even got rooms with a connecting door. I first opened it and asked him if he wanted to come over and play PlayStation with me.' Federer didn't have to be asked twice. And so they repeatedly had heated duels with the game *Formula 1* in those days. 'Roger felt so comfortable that he was often already sitting in my room playing PlayStation when I came back from training,' Rosset recalled. 'A couple of times, I had to say, "Sorry, I've just practised for two hours, and I need to rest for a minute." But that was easy for him. He then just kept playing. It was completely relaxed with him.'

Rosset slipped into the role of big brother for Federer and helped him establish himself with the pros. Despite an age difference of more than ten years, they hit it off immediately. 'We had the same sense of humour; we always made little jokes. I didn't see him as a rival; on the contrary. I wanted to support him. It's not easy when you come on Tour at 17, 18. You travel a lot; sometimes, you're alone. I was happy that a young Swiss came up.'

Rosset was not only Federer's companion but also a trailblazer for him. With his Olympic victory in 1992, the sensitive giant achieved the greatest success for Swiss tennis up to that time. It should be noted that the world's elite competed in Barcelona, from Jim Courier to Stefan Edberg and Pete Sampras to Boris Becker. It was the second Olympic tournament since tennis had been reintroduced into the Olympic programme in 1988. A few months after his Olympic victory, Rosset also played in the 1992

Davis Cup final with Jakob Hlasek against an American dream team with Courier, Sampras, Andre Agassi and John McEnroe. Although the Geneva native stunned everyone by beating Courier in the second singles in Fort Worth, Texas, the Swiss lost 3-1. When Federer and Stan Wawrinka won the Davis Cup title in Lille in 2014, it was a late satisfaction for the 2.01-metre (6ft 7in) man. 'Swiss tennis deserved that,' he said.

Rosset was the first Grand Slam semi-finalist from the small Alpine country, in 1996 at Roland-Garros. Björn Borg and McEnroe, in their stylish outfits, had once inspired him to take the path of professional tennis. His most fateful decision, however, had only marginally to do with tennis: after his first-round exit at the 1998 US Open, he booked a ticket on Swissair flight 111 from New York to Geneva on 2 September. At the last minute, he changed his reservation on a whim and thus escaped the plane crash off the coast of Halifax [Nova Scotia], in which all 229 passengers and crew members died. Rosset says that the memory of this tragedy, which he had skidded a hair's breadth past, did not haunt his dreams in the aftermath. 'For people who have survived a plane crash, it is certainly different. But life didn't want me to get on that plane.'

Fortunately, Rosset's journey continued and Federer's career gradually picked up speed in 1999. They competed more often in the same tournaments and played doubles together a few times. Their friendship soon extended beyond the daily tournament routine. After returning from the Australian Open in 2000, Rosset asked Federer if he would come up to Crans-Montana for a few days of skiing. Federer spontaneously agreed. In the Valais mountains, he initially struggled with the effects of jet lag. During a dinner in a Chinese restaurant Federer even fell asleep at the table, Rosset recalls with amusement. But on the slopes, he did not hold back. 'You know it,' he recounted. 'On the first run, you still have respect and ride a bit more cautiously. On the second run, you're more confident. By the third, your inhibitions are gone.'

Especially if you are a daredevil like the 18-year-old Federer was back then. They chose the slope of the women's downhill race, where two hills follow each other. 'All of a sudden, Roger roared past me as if he were Peter Müller,' Rosset recalled. But Federer was unfortunately not as steady on his skis as the former Swiss downhill world champion. 'Roger went full speed towards the jump, made a huge jump, lost his balance in the air and fell backwards. At first, I shook my head, then I got scared. What if he broke his leg now? I felt responsible. I drove down to him, saw him lying in the snow, and asked, "Roger, are you okay?" When he nodded, I was very relieved. Today we laugh about it but I was terrified at that moment.' Federer took that fall as a lesson and confined himself to après-ski for the rest of his tennis career.

A few weeks later, the two friends met again on the court – in the final of the Marseille indoor tournament. The up-and-coming Federer was in his first final on the ATP Tour on 13 February 2000, but experience prevailed: Rosset won by the razor-thin margin of 2-6, 6-3, 7-6. The youthful loser initially held it together after the match but he could no longer hold back the tears of disappointment during the award ceremony. 'I was relieved to win because I felt like I had a bit more pressure as the older one,' said Rosset, for whom it was the second to last of his 15 professional titles. 'But I couldn't be euphoric because I saw Roger's sadness.

I felt for him. He probably thought at that moment that he had missed perhaps his only chance to win a professional tournament. During my victory speech, I tried to cheer him up: "Roger, it's not the end of the world. Don't worry; you're going to be a great player and you're going to win many more tournaments. No question about it.'" At the time, Rosset could not have known that the loser on that day would go on to win 20 Grand Slam titles and more than 100 tournaments.

Rosset believes that a tragic stroke of fate was groundbreaking for Federer's successful career: the death of his ex-coach Peter Carter on 1 August 2002 in a traffic accident on his honeymoon in South Africa. 'Sometimes you need painful experiences in life to mature,' said Rosset. 'I was also there at the funeral in Basel. It was terrible. I had known Peter Carter too, but never as well as Roger. Carter had been a fantastic person. Seeing Roger at his funeral so sad, so destroyed, hurt me. I wanted to hold and comfort him, but I knew that wasn't enough. Everyone deals with such tragic events differently. With Roger, I had the feeling that it made him grow.' When Federer met Carter's parents in person for the first time in September 2003 on the sidelines of the Davis Cup semi-final in Melbourne, Rosset accompanied him. It was a challenging walk for him, the Geneva native sensed. 'I had the feeling that it helped him that I came along. I was just there in case Roger needed me.'

Eleven months after Carter's tragic death, Federer celebrated his first Grand Slam title at Wimbledon in 2003. Rosset's career was gradually drawing to a close at the time. He watched the historic Wimbledon final against Mark Philippoussis on television in Geneva, having lost in the first round at the All England Club. Rosset remembers how he and Federer had practised in Wimbledon in 2001 before the tournament. They put their 30 minutes together to be allowed to practise for an hour on a match court. 'Roger played unbelievably; I didn't see a ball,' said Rosset. That year, the young tennis virtuoso with the ponytail beat his idol, Pete Sampras, in the round of 16, in their only duel on the professional Tour. Two years later, Federer made his big breakthrough at Church Road.

Did Rosset sense that the first Wimbledon title was the prelude to Federer's winning streak? 'Yes and no. Of course, you want to win more Grand Slams once you've done it. But then, Roger was not yet the complete player he later became. In 2003, for example, his backhand was not very mature. He still had many things to improve on. And he did. It's one thing to win a Grand Slam. And quite another to dominate the sport. He developed extremely well in all areas and how he channelled his emotions. When you win a big tournament like Wimbledon, it brings enormous pressure. Roger was able to handle it; he became a winning machine.'

But how does this development fit with the 14-year-old who was so relaxed, so easy-going at the time? 'Yes, Roger is a very easy-going guy and he has an inimitable ease on the court,' Rosset admitted. 'But there is a lot of work behind it. And he was lucky enough to meet many good people along the way. Like Pierre Paganini, for me the world's best fitness trainer for a tennis player, or his coach Severin Lüthi. But the most important meeting was with Mirka, his wife. I always say: he owes 50 per cent of his success to her. Without her, his career would not have been possible. She always had his back. Even when their family grew and the covetousness around him. When you have four children, nannies, and your team, that's a lot of people. You have to organise many things when travelling around with such an entourage. Still, he could always concentrate on tennis because Mirka took care of everything for him. You can't have that kind of career if your wife isn't fully behind you.'

How important was it that Federer's wife had been a tennis pro herself? 'It's certainly helpful because she knows what it takes in this sport. But it's not the decisive factor. Jelena Djokovic, Novak's wife, hadn't played on the Tour. The most important thing is that you have a stable woman who always supports you and sometimes puts her interests aside for yours. If you have a girlfriend who always wants to party, that can mess you up.' You can't separate Roger Federer, the tennis pro, from Roger Federer, the private person, he said. 'He is a pronounced family man, never wanting to travel around without his wife and children for any length of time. Mirka made it possible for the family to come along.'

Rosset sees the work-life balance in such an extraordinary job as the secret to Federer retaining the joy of the sport for so long. 'It was important for him to be able to return to the hotel at the tournaments and see his children. That way, he could clear his head and think about something else. He took his time for tennis but also for his family. Time and again, he took himself completely out of the sport. You can't think about tennis 24 hours a day. Of course, he did that before the big finals. But otherwise, he lived a more or less normal life on the Tour and did other things that were good for him.'

For years Federer beat his fellow players over and over again, yet they repeatedly voted him the most popular tennis player on Tour. How does Rosset explain this apparent contradiction? 'Because Roger is a likeable person. I don't find anything negative about him. It didn't get into his head; he never forgot where he came from and all who helped him along the way.' And no matter with whom, Federer always made time for a chat on Tour, rarely appearing stressed. 'He has an incredible memory, remembering everyone he played with on the junior tour. And the stories from back in the day. Do you know anyone who doesn't like Roger? Maybe one says: "I prefer Nadal." But I don't know anyone who doesn't like him. He's friendly to everybody. Not because he has to be. It's just the way he is. Because he loves people. With his empathy, he reminded me of Andre Agassi.'

After his retirement in 2005, Rosset followed Federer's career as an expert co-commentator for French-speaking Swiss television and a trenchant newspaper columnist. What fascinated him most was Federer's rivalry with Rafael Nadal – and how he dealt with it: 'In the beginning, Roger perceived Rafa as an adversary who kept him from winning everything. That annoyed him. But then he accepted the fight, and a great rivalry developed. At some point, Roger realised that they were very similar. When someone asks me the difference between Roger and Rafa, I say none. Of course, their tennis is completely different. But the way they love and live tennis, the way they respect this sport, in this regard they are like two brothers to me.'

One match, in particular, stands out for Rosset: their 2017 Australian Open final, a classic that Federer won in five sets. 'The way Roger played there, the way he attacked and took risks, also with his backhand, was pure joy for me.' Federer also played courageously at Wimbledon 2019 but missed out on the title against Novak Djokovic despite two match points. Rosset wrote in a column in the French-speaking Swiss newspaper *Le Temps* at the time: 'It reminded me of the films I watched as a child in which the hero died at the end. Alain Delon was a specialist in this genre, and I hated it; it made me sick. I felt the same sense of injustice then.' But Rosset found a conciliatory conclusion: 'If Roger had won, we would have been delighted that he had won a 21st Grand Slam title. But would we have liked him more? Our admiration is now joined by empathy for heroes and the defeated. We want to comfort him, hug him, tell him we love him.'

These are words from someone who has known Federer for a long time, since the latter strolled onto the court as a teenager to hit a few balls with him for the first time. What role does Rosset see himself as having played for Federer? As his mentor, his big brother or simply his friend? 'Oh, I don't know. It's not so important what you call it either. I know my feelings for him, and I know his feelings for me. I admire the way he played tennis. But what interests me more is that he is happy, smiling and loves life.'

Urs Bürgler, wrestler and matchmaker

'Now, Roger, this is your chance!'

Urs Bürgler tells with a smirk how he met Roger Federer for the first time at the beginning of the Olympic Games in Sydney in 2000. 'We opened the door to our house in the athletes' village and Rogi sat at the table and had a puzzle with 3,000 pieces in front of him. Mountains, lakes and a bird in the middle. He sat there in peace, all alone and absorbed in his task. You have to have patience and nerve to solve such a huge puzzle. Especially a nature puzzle where almost every piece looks the same.'

The wrestlers and the tennis players shared a semi-detached house during those Olympics. Greco-Roman wrestler Bürgler, 1.90 metres (6ft 3in) tall and weighing 100 kilos (15st 10lb), a mountain of a man, but amiable and with a good sense of humour, laughs: 'The people in charge at Swiss Olympic perhaps thought, the tennis players need protection, we'll assign the wrestlers to them so they can keep an eye out down below.' So the wrestlers slept on the ground floor, where there was also a social room; Federer, his coach Peter Lundgren, Mirka Vavrinec and Emmanuelle Gagliardi were upstairs. It was a spacious house with seven or eight bedrooms, Bürgler remembers. Later, beach volleyball players Paul and Martin Laciga also moved in for a few nights.

'Rogi was only 19, a youngster, and I was almost ten years older. But we connected right away. I was still a child at heart back then, and I still am today,' said Bürgler. 'Rogi was also up for any mischief. He was completely relaxed; you could have stolen horses with him. That's how we became friends. We were always on the road together for those two weeks, and I watched all his matches. My competition was only towards the end of the Games, so I had time for that.' He also liked Federer's coach, Lundgren, said Bürgler. 'He knew exactly how to take Rogi. I thought it was a pity when they parted ways later.'

Federer was not yet a star, 'But people already thought that he could become one someday,' Bürgler said. 'He was already No 36 in the world at the time.' In Sydney, he played his way to the semi-finals before losing to Tommy Haas and the bronze medal match against the Frenchman Arnaud Di Pasquale. 'He should have beaten him,' said Bürgler, who finished seventh in his competition. But the grand finale, which would shape Federer's life much more than his sporting performance, was still to come.

Bürgler soon realised in Sydney that the latter had his eye on Vavrinec. 'Mirka was very open-minded; you could talk to her about anything,' he recalled. 'At one point, Rogi asked me: "What do you think of Mirka? I think she's great!" I said, "She's a good one. If you have a chance with her, you have to strike!" They had fun together, but he was hesitant to make the first move. He was so shy, so decent. You could tell he came from a good home. And he didn't have that much experience in these things either; he'd only had one girlfriend before. Mirka was more mature. She had experienced more in terms of relationships.'

When Federer missed his second chance to win a medal against Di Pasquale and was bitterly disappointed, the Swiss Olympic flatmates went out in the evening. 'Mirka, Rogi, Peter and I went to the Holland Heineken House, which was always the most happening place. But that evening, it was still a bit early. We stood at the bar and had a drink; next to us was the emergency exit. It was warm inside, and the door was open. At some point, Mirka said she was going outside for fresh air. I grabbed Rogi and said to him: "Now, Roger, this is your chance!" And he: "Do you think so?" Me: "Yeah, sure, now you have to go for it!" Him: "What should I say?" "Tell her you were warm too. I'll shut the door, and you'll be out there to yourselves."'

No sooner said than done. Federer also went outside; Bürgler closed the door after 30 seconds. 'Then they gave each other their first kiss. They were outside for half an hour. When they returned, they were both beaming. The next morning he told me every detail. But I keep that to myself; it's too intimate. Before Rogi left, he wrote me a little letter. Unfortunately, I didn't keep it. He wrote: "Dear Urs, thank you very much for these two weeks. They were the best two weeks of my life." I still get goosebumps when I think about it.'

While Federer continued with the indoor tournaments in Europe, in Vienna, Basel, Stuttgart, Lyon, Paris and Stockholm, Bürgler travelled alone for three and a half weeks as a backpacker through Australia after the Olympics. 'I said to myself, if I'm already there, I want to see the country as well. In some places, I met other athletes who did the same. My flight back was from Sydney again.'

Federer and Bürgler continued to maintain contact after the Olympic Games. 'I had only followed tennis on the side before,' said the wrestler. 'But Rogi brought me to tennis.' After Wimbledon 2001, where he beat his idol, Pete Sampras, he invited Bürgler to the tournament in Gstaad at the beginning of July. Bürgler quickly realised that Federer was now moving in a different sphere: 'I asked him, "Do you have a room for us?" He said, "Just come, and I'll take care of you. Pull up at the bottom of the Hotel Palace, and you can come up to the third floor."'

When Bürgler and his girlfriend at the time knocked on the room door Federer had given him, Mirka and Federer opened it. 'They greeted us and showed us around everywhere. The living room alone was 100 square metres, it had TVs everywhere, even in the bathroom, and the whole thing existed twice. Two flats were connected, one of which we were free to use. We spent three nights in Gstaad, watched tennis, and played cards with Rogi. And when the weather was bad, I went to a spa with him and Marat Safin. He was also totally relaxed.' Federer lost in the opening round to his future coach Ivan Ljubicic in the singles, but in the doubles, he advanced to the final with Safin.

With Ludwig Küng, the national coach of the freestyle wrestlers, who had also been in Sydney, Bürgler visited Federer at the Swiss Indoors in Basel in 2001. At his home tournament, Federer always used to sleep in a hotel to keep up the routine. He put up his Olympic colleagues at his home in the terraced house in Münchenstein, with his mother Lynette, father Robert and sister Diana. 'Ludi slept in a guest bed and I slept in Rogi's children's room. Next to the bed, there was a huge pile of tennis magazines.' Lynette made breakfast for the two hungry wrestlers; Bürgler raves about Roger's parents and how down-to-earth they are. 'Lynette is a real mummy, warm, caring, but also one who says what she thinks. I like that.'

In return, that November, when the tennis season was over, Federer and Mirka visited the wrestlers at a team competition in the multipurpose hall in Eichberg in the Rhine Valley of St Gallen. In Sydney, Federer had watched some wrestling matches on TV, so he already had some prior knowledge. 'I had the feeling he liked it,' said Bürgler. 'Man against man, like tennis.'

One day he also visited Bürgler in the latter's wrestling flatshare in Oberriet in St Gallen and spent the night there. 'After the disco, we ended up in a bar at two in the morning. We were drinking a beer when a colleague of mine, already quite drunk, came up to us, examined him closely and said: "Hey, you look like Federer!" Rogi replied with a mischievous smile: "Yes, many people have mentioned that to me." When he later told his colleague that he had not been mistaken, that it had indeed been Federer, the latter could hardly believe it. The young tennis pro was well on his way to becoming a celebrity in Switzerland.

The contact remained, and at Federer's chalet in Valbella in the Grisons mountains, Bürgler, a trained road builder, asphalted the driveway. And he followed Federer's career intensively, often got tickets from him and travelled to the Grand Slams. At Roland-Garros, he once ended up in David Ferrer's box on Court Philippe Chatrier before Federer's match because the usher had read 'Ferrer' instead of 'Federer' on his tickets. Bürgler most enjoyed travelling to Paris or Wimbledon and was often present at the World Tour Finals in London. The most impressive match he experienced on-site was the 2012 Olympic semi-final at Wimbledon against Juan Martin del Potro. Four and a half hours, 19-17 for Federer in the third set, pure drama. Bürgler's bladder almost burst, but he didn't dare go outside to the toilet for over an hour because he didn't want to miss the decisive break.

But Bürgler emphasises that it was not like he always followed Federer around. 'I couldn't make a living from sport; I worked so that I could practise my sport.' He was not only a two-time Olympic participant in Greco-Roman wrestling but also very successful in the Swiss national sport of schwingen, Switzerland's traditional variant of wrestling. He won 18 competitions and, in 1996, almost captured the legendary Kilchberg Schwinget, which only takes place every six years. As different as their postures are – on the one hand, the bulky wrestler and schwinger; on the other, the slender, lithe tennis player – as humans, they always got along well with their roguishness. But Bürgler regrets that they don't see as much of each other as they used to.

Would he have thought back then in Sydney that Federer and Vavrinec would be such a good match? He shrugs it off. 'In this age, relationships come and go, and you're not yet thinking about getting married and having children. What has become of it is amazing. They have never had a scandal or anything! And she manages his whole life.'

He is proud that he became the midwife of this relationship, which has produced four children and probably many sporting successes. He said: 'Maybe it needed me. Maybe they would have gotten together without me. But who knows, after the Olympic Games, they would have gone their separate ways again if Rogi hadn't gone on the attack that night.' He paused and said: 'Maybe I was the last piece missing from his 3,000-piece puzzle.'

Wayne Ferreira, South African mentor
'I'm never going to hit another ball with him'

The Swiss Indoors in Basel maintains the wonderful tradition of the two finalists hanging medals around the necks of the ball kids after the final – in recognition of their work that week and to inspire the next generation. In Roger Federer's case, it worked. He was chasing balls in the St Jakobshalle in 1993 and 1994, receiving the medal from the winners, Michael Stich in the first year and Wayne Ferreira in the second. Ferreira triumphed on his debut in Basel, where he met a fellow South African: Lynette Federer.

Roger's mother worked for the tournament and, because she handed out the badges, had contact with the players. 'With her being South African as well, we immediately felt connected,' Ferreira recounted. 'We were friends for a bunch of years before Roger started doing well. Every time

I'd go to Basel, I would see her and hang out with her. She's really, really sweet. I would always look forward to meeting her. When I first saw Roger, I didn't know much about him, except that he was Lynette's son. That's how I knew him. I didn't even know he was playing tennis. Lynette didn't tell me. So when he started doing well a few years later, somebody brought up the picture of me giving him a handshake at the trophy ceremony.'

When Federer came on Tour at 18, Ferreira saw himself as a mentor for him: 'Because of that interaction that I had with Lynette, and I was very good friends with Peter Lundgren at the time, who was coaching Roger. So I spent a lot of time with them. I practised a lot with him. Even though he was much younger than me when he started, we spent a lot of time together. We were good friends. I was trying to help him out a little bit. But nobody knew he was going to be as good as he was. We knew he was going to be good. But we didn't realise he was going to be that good.'

When they started to practise together, Ferreira immediately saw the young Swiss's potential and striking weakness: 'He wasn't able to hit topspin on the backhand. So everyone was like, "Oh, this guy's good. But he will never be great until he can go over his backhand." He struggled on Tour for the first few years that he played. I played him a few times, and I remember him having a hard time against me because he had no topspin backhand.'

The two friends squared off three times on the professional Tour, all three times in 2001. Ferreira vividly remembers one encounter: their round of 16 meeting at the clay tournament in Rome. 'I beat him relatively easily in two sets because I exploited him very heavily on the backhand. My game was designed to get around my backhand and hit forehands, and I stayed in the backhand corner and hit to his backhand. I don't think I hit more than maybe four backhands in the whole match. I believe it was a big eye-opener for him because he realised then that if he doesn't improve his backhand, it would be tough for him to be good.'

Ferreira is probably exaggerating a bit, since Federer was already a top-20 player at that time – as was the ten-year-older South African. In any case, Ferreira is one of the few with a positive record against Federer: he won the head-to-head 2-1. 'And I'm going to keep my winning record forever,' he said, smiling. 'I'm never going to play him again. If I were ever invited to just a social match against him at the club one weekend, I would not be going. I'm never going to hit another tennis ball with Roger ever again. I'm going to keep that victory. That's it.'

Ferreira was also an excellent doubles player and played with the young Federer. 'We decided to play together a few times because we were friends. But it was more for fun and to play to hang out rather than being a team looking to do well. I would have loved to play more with him, but I don't think he played as much doubles as I did. But we always used to joke around and talk about it.' However, Ferreira still regrets one missed opportunity: when they withdrew in doubles after two wins at Wimbledon in 2001 following Federer's triumph over Pete Sampras in singles.

'He beat Pete and was having a little bit of a problem with his hamstring and was a little tired after the match. So I said to him: "Let's pull out of the doubles." He said: "No, I want to play; let's play." But I said: "Look, the singles is way more important; you want to build your career around your singles and don't want to waste it on doubles." As I did consider myself a little bit of a mentor, I looked at him and what I would have done at that stage. In retrospect, this might have been the one mistake I made with him. Not for him, but for my benefit. We would have possibly had a good chance of winning Wimbledon.' And although rested, Federer then lost to Tim Henman in the quarter-finals of the singles.

Ferreira also accompanied Federer in his darkest hour when, while in Toronto, he received the tragic news of the death of his ex-coach Peter Carter at the beginning of August 2002. Federer had already lost in the opening round in Toronto when he learned the devastating news, but he continued to play alongside Ferreira in the doubles. For the match against the Australians Joshua Eagle and Sandon Stolle, he wore a black armband in honour of Carter. 'Because of his personality, never wanting to quit and never wanting to give up, he wanted to play anyway,' Ferreira said. 'But it was a shock for him. He had such a close relationship with Peter throughout the years, and it was very tough for him.'

They lost that doubles match in Toronto and even though his head was no longer in the game, Federer travelled on to Cincinnati. He was probably not a big help at the time in coming to terms with this loss, said Ferreira. 'I hadn't gone through an experience like that. So it was hard for me to understand exactly how he felt. I tried to support him and be there. But I didn't know what to tell him.'

In the singles, Federer again lost in round one in Cincinnati; in the doubles, he won one more match with Ferreira before forfeiting the next round and travelling back to Basel for the funeral. 'I think he was trying to hide his sadness in the wrong way, trying to just sort of play tennis around it,' said Ferreira. 'That lasted a little over a week.

People around him were telling him, "You've got to take a break and go back. You have to go to the funeral."' Which Federer eventually also realised.

'Peter's death affected Roger for a long time,' Ferreira is certain. 'It was very, very tough for him. Even today, he probably still feels sad and has difficulty getting over it when he thinks about it.' What does Ferreira say about the theory that Federer only matured as a player because of this stroke of fate? 'Let's put it this way: it didn't hurt his career; if anything, it helped him in the long run. But I wouldn't say that was the most important part of making him the player he became. I'm sure that what happened to Peter was something that inspired him to want to go out and do better. But as I mentioned earlier, him working on his backhand and getting a better backhand was the difference between him being a good tennis player and a great tennis player. And he spent a lot of time doing that and fixing that.'

Ferreira retired after the US Open in 2004, at the age of 33. The former world No 6, a 15-time tournament winner on the ATP Tour, turned his back on tennis for a long time until he returned in March 2020 as coach of the American, Frances Tiafoe. 'I wasn't around tennis for a very, very long time,' he said. 'Occasionally, I would go to Wimbledon or the Australian Open to do some commentary and play in the legends event, and I would always make an effort to go and see Roger. We have good memories, and our friendship never changed. So even though he got really good and moved to a different level in his life, he didn't change. Whenever I saw him, he was very nice, hugged me and talked and spent time with me.'

Are people in South Africa proud of Federer, their lost son? Do they regard him as their own? Because he has lived in the USA for over 30 years, it is difficult for him to judge, said Ferreira. 'People love him anywhere in the world. I don't think that they think of him as a South African. He was born and grew up in Switzerland. So I would say no. But I think people in South Africa respect him as a tennis player and admire him as everyone else worldwide does. He's really good to give back there. There are a lot of people that benefit from his foundation, and they appreciate that. But I mean, he's just really loved everywhere.'

Although he wasn't involved in tennis much anymore, Ferreira followed Federer's career closely. 'I watched every match of his when I could, and I always enjoyed watching him play. Roger is the best tennis player because he has every aspect of the game: the serve, the forehand, the chip and charge, the slice, the topspin, and the volleys. He is what you would consider being as perfect as possible as an all-round tennis player. He's the last of the dying breed of the great all-rounder. And his longevity is amazing, that he's been able to stay healthy and play as long.'

There are many reasons why he felt so close to Federer even after his career, said Ferreira. 'Apart from being an amazing tennis player, he's just a nice guy. He's charming and kind; he's nice to everybody. He's very likeable; there's nothing that you can dislike about him. And since he was very young, I've followed his career. I felt like we were friends; I got to know him well. I always wanted him to do well. I picked him above anybody throughout his whole career.'

Who would have thought that on 3 October 1994 at the Swiss Indoors in Basel, when Ferreira shook the hand of this teenager who smiled at him in awe?

ROGER, THE STUDENT

NO SPORTSMAN or woman gets to the top on their own. Only by surrounding themselves with the very best people, learning from each one, do they fulfil their potential and achieve everything their talent makes them capable of.

Roger Federer had the uncanny knack of having or finding the right people to be around him, from Annemarie Rüegg and Pierre Paganini to Peter Carter, from Sven Groeneveld and Peter Lundgren to Severin Lüthi, Tony Roche and Paul Annacone, to Ivan Ljubicic and everyone else in between. Not forgetting: his parents.

Each of them brought something different to the table, offering him the insight he needed to navigate his way on the ATP Tour. Many of them helped him win Grand Slam titles, all of them offered him their expertise and even those he didn't hire as coach, like Darren Cahill, who was Carter's best friend and the coach of Lleyton Hewitt, played a role in his development.

As a teenager, Federer needed guidance. Occasionally he needed disciplining, but as Groeneveld discovered, there was a unique way to do it without ruining his love of the sport. As a young player on the ATP Tour he needed someone who'd been there and done it, which Lundgren took care of. Together they won Wimbledon. When he was looking for someone to regain supremacy after Rafael Nadal translated his clay-court success to grass, he turned to Paul Annacone. And when he needed a reboot, in late 2015, he hired Ljubicic, with whom he won his last three slam titles.

Each of them played their part.

Annemarie Rüegg, school coordinator

'He had put his head on his arm and fallen asleep'

A few days after his 14th birthday, Roger Federer set off for new horizons. As No 1 in his age group in Switzerland, he was determined to take the next step at the National Tennis Centre in Ecublens. In the canton of Vaud, however, he also had to complete the last two years of his compulsory schooling at Collège La Planta. 'Roger is not the most diligent at school,' father Robert told the *Basler Zeitung* when his son passed the tennis entrance exam. 'But thanks to the individual support and contact person Annemarie Rüegg, responsible for school matters, there shouldn't be any big problems there.'

Rüegg has to smile at this quote. 'Robert sums it up pretty well,' she said. In the 70s, Rüegg, who grew up on Lake Constance, was one of the first Swiss women to play tennis semi-professionally. In 1977, she even faced Chris Evert in the Fed Cup in Eastbourne and took three games from the world No 1. Later, she studied English, French and Latin and graduated as a Gymnasium teacher. Pierre Paganini, who later became Federer's fitness coach, brought her as school coordinator to the new Tennis Etudes project in Ecublens in 1993, which combined school and sport. There she would also look after the young Federer.

These were two formative, character-building years for the budding tennis star. When Federer came to Lake

Geneva, he spoke only a few words of French. 'It was a tough start,' said Rüegg. She helped him mainly with the language and was the contact person when there were problems. 'I remember one or two phone calls from school when Roger dozed off during class. He had put his head on his arm and fallen asleep. They were worried at school whether we were pushing him too hard physically. I interpreted it more like this: he wasn't that awake yet, and the subject didn't interest him much either.'

Federer was not the most diligent, but he also had lighter moments in the classroom: 'When something did interest him, he was very awake and focused. When he wasn't, he could shut down without a problem. Everything that had to do with a drill, grammar exercises, for example, bored him. But he was happy to contribute if you had to read a text or discuss a topic. Orally, he made rapid progress in French. He enjoyed expressing himself creatively, always picking up expressions and incorporating them. English he spoke excellently anyway, thanks to his mother, so he was sometimes excused from lessons. Later, I followed with interest the press conferences he gave in different languages, even as a young boy. That made me particularly happy as a language teacher.'

Rüegg also noticed something else: 'Roger had exceptional perception; he could process many things simultaneously. That also helped him as a tennis player. On the court, you must be aware of many things: Where is the ball? Where is the opponent? How is he moving? Where could he play? How is the ball rotating?'

Moreover, Federer's characteristic of completely switching off when it comes to things that don't interest him has helped him in his career, Rüegg believes. 'Then he doesn't waste any energy on it. That is an important reason for his longevity; he is an energy artist.'

Especially in the first months, homesickness plagued the young Roger in Ecublens; sometimes, he cried. But he didn't show it much to Rüegg or at school. 'It was important that he had a good host family in the Christinets, where he felt safe,' said Rüegg. 'His parents had chosen them and maintained close contact with them.' And it helped that the mother was Swiss German, and Federer became friends with their son Vincent.

For Rüegg, how his parents handled their son was exemplary and groundbreaking for his career: 'They gave him a healthy dose of self-responsibility. They didn't patronise him; it always had to come from him. Today, parents often project something on to their children. Lynette and Robert said: "Hey Roger, you have to want it!" After all, he had decided to come to Ecublens. They didn't overwhelm him with too high expectations. But they didn't under-challenge him either. They gave him a certain framework within which he could move. And when they realised that he had exceptional skills, they put all their eggs in the tennis basket.'

Was Rüegg surprised by his transformation from a teenager who fell asleep at school and threw racquets on the courts to a model personality? She shakes her head. 'There are people who think Roger is too perfect. They think he's annoying with his flawless image. I find his appearance impressive, and it doesn't surprise me. Even in his adolescence, he was always decent; he had good manners. His underlying attitude towards other people was always respectful. He had had a good upbringing, you could tell. He wasn't boringly good, but he was funny and always friendly. I never got any complaints from the teachers. For me, the natural continuation is that he has retained this respect as an adult and as a superstar.'

Federer completed his compulsory schooling in Ecublens in 1997. After moving from Ecublens to Biel, where Swiss Tennis now had its new base, he focused entirely on tennis. He became increasingly aware of what it would take to become a professional player, says Rüegg. She remembers an episode from the 1998 Orange Bowl when she travelled to Miami with the Swiss Tennis delegation: 'One evening, we all met outside to cool off and do a few exercises. Roger played the clown; he deliberately jumped awkwardly with the skipping rope and promptly sprained his foot. The foot swelled up and became a big lump. That was in the middle of the tournament, and Roger was already in the quarter-finals. Now he was threatened with elimination.'

But Federer certainly didn't want to rob himself of his title chances because of this silliness. 'He put all his focus on getting his foot ready to be able to continue playing. Our physio Paul Dorochenko only looked after Roger. And indeed, with tapes, treatments and exercises, he managed to pull it off despite the sprained foot and win the Orange Bowl.

'That was an amazing performance by him, also mentally. Through that episode, he started to think: Where is this going? What am I doing here? What does it take? He was a hilarious guy. We often had fun. But we couldn't let it get to the point where he was fooling around too much and putting obstacles in his way. Those days leading up to the final of the Orange Bowl were impressive when we could watch how he nurtured himself, how focused he was, and how he channelled his energy only towards this goal. That was an important step for his young career.' It was the first, but far from the last time, he played with an injury without showing any signs.

Rüegg is convinced that his girlfriend Mirka Vavrinec became an essential factor in his career. She got to know her when she was still a member of the Swiss Tennis squad. 'Mirka became the ideal complement to Roger. She didn't have it easy as a young tennis player; she had to assert herself. She had a lot of stamina, and she needed it to succeed. She is ambitious and persistent, a tough personality, but she also has charm. The fact that Roger found a relationship with her early on, which solidified him, was essential.'

Rüegg followed his career closely, was occasionally on-site at tournaments in Switzerland, such as in Basel or Gstaad, and otherwise sat in front of the television. 'I also occasionally got up in the middle of the night to watch him play in the night session of the US Open. His gestures and facial expressions are still familiar to me from his youth. And it's just a pleasure to watch how he moves and acts on the court. I don't like players who constantly clench their fists and make a grim face, who even show their fists to the opponent. That's not my thing at all. The way Roger behaves, that's what we want to teach our youngsters.'

It is not only his victories but, above all, the approachable manner that has made him so popular, Rüegg believes. At Swiss Tennis, she is responsible for the 'School and Social Affairs' department, but she also looks after juniors from a sporting point of view. When they hand out questionnaires, she said Federer is almost always mentioned as a role model. 'A few write Nadal or Djokovic. Women are hardly ever mentioned. Maybe [Martina] Hingis or [Belinda] Bencic once or twice. But most girls take their inspiration from the men.' That's probably because the Swiss success story in tennis has been mainly male over the past 20 years. At least until Belinda Bencic won Olympic gold in Tokyo in 2021.

Federer has had a lasting effect on tennis in Switzerland, but probably also globally, believes Rüegg. 'With him, you see how fun it is to play tennis. What a cool sport it is.' She, too, has never lost the joy of tennis in all these years. In 2023 it will be 50 years since she was sent alone to London as a 15-year-old to play in Wimbledon's junior tournament. The coach did not join her until two days later. She boarded the plane with a piece of paper with the address of Crystal Palace College, where she was to stay. 'I survived it,' she said. 'And it didn't do me any harm.'

Sven Groeneveld, coach
'He's still the clown'

Sven Groeneveld has known Roger Federer longer than most people in tennis. As the then head coach of the Swiss Tennis Federation, he first met him in 1997 when Federer was part of a camp in Geneva. His impact was immediate.

'Everybody spoke about him,' the Dutchman said. 'He was technically so sound already at a young age and the ball-striking was so clean, when he actually was in the right position. You could see that there was a certain element of relaxation in his shots that allowed him to have an incredible acceleration, that you cannot really teach, that is a God-given talent. That's what I think everybody saw, that there was so much room for him to grow into. The only limitations that we all saw were his flare-ups and his temperament. He got very impatient. I guess you can also say that his standards were very high. He expected a lot from himself and he expected to be able to handle certain shots. I guess because of those moods that he would get into, that also pushed him to excel. You cannot just be somebody that doesn't have that type of self-judgement and critical judgement in that sense. Otherwise you are satisfied even if you are making some errors. That was not the case with Roger. Roger just didn't accept any really terrible shots, it's something that he couldn't do.'

When many people think of Federer, they think of a man completely under control, someone able to produce his best in a seemingly effortless manner, someone who has made a very difficult sport look easy. All of that is true, but before he became a world-beater, Federer went through the kind of development issues all top young players do. As a teenager, Federer was a perfectionist, someone who would not settle for good, when brilliant was possible. It led him to great heights, like becoming the world's top-ranked junior, but it also led to frustration when things didn't go his way. His release was to throw his racquet and get angry.

After one incident, Groeneveld had the task of disciplining Federer. Intuitively he knew that there was a particular way to do it. 'We did see that if you would try to discipline him, that was not always the way to go about him getting the maximum out of himself,' he said. 'But sometimes you do have to. I disciplined him one time when he threw a racquet from the back of the court through some sponsors' thing in a new facility in Biel, at the National Training Centre. So I had him ten days cleaning the court and helping me with the groundsman, basically. But we didn't ground him so that he couldn't practise. He didn't mean to [do it] but just sometimes he couldn't help himself.'

Like many of those involved in Federer's life and career, Groeneveld saw the Swiss's playful side, too. 'When he's with someone that he feels he can be himself with, when he's among his trustworthy group, or even in the players' lounge or the locker room, he's still the clown,' he said. 'He's still messing around. He's still coming up with things that, you know, an 18-year-old would do. I think that his play ability was not only on court, but also as an individual, he just likes to have a good laugh. He likes to have fun. He doesn't want to take things too serious, because he's a sensitive person, so laughter and joy and messing around was very important to him. He was and he's still the clown. If you give him a chance, he likes to have fun and part of the fun is also some explosive fun, he can explode.'

At the Swiss Tennis Federation, Federer had been looked after by Peter Carter, an Australian player-turned-coach, who became a mentor, coach, friend and second father all in one as Federer negotiated the tricky teenage years. Peter Lundgren, a former Swedish player who coached Marcelo Rios, a future world No 1, was also an integral figure in his development. When the time came to decide who should travel with him as he made his way onto the ATP Tour, Federer's parents asked Groeneveld if he would do it. Realising the impact it would have on both Lundgren and Carter should he take the job, he said he was not the right person, so the parents asked his advice on who to take. Groeneveld told them that though Carter was 'such a strong, important voice for Roger' he could still maintain that role whenever Federer was at home. Instead, he felt Lundgren had the greater track record, as a leading coach and having been a top 25 player himself.

There was another reason Groeneveld suggested Lundgren. 'I also felt that Peter Lundgren would have a little bit stronger backbone for the press,' he said. 'I expected that it would be really difficult for Roger, because with the expectations of being No 1 in juniors and winning the Wimbledon Junior Championships, the pressure would be upon Roger's shoulders and he would need somebody next to him that could actually take some of the heat.' Carter, he felt, might have been given a harder time because he did not have the same experience as Lundgren. The plan was for Carter to eventually become Switzerland's Davis Cup captain, as he was applying for citizenship at the time. 'So they would still be involved, I did say, you know, both of them are such an important voice.'

Federer and Lundgren began an odyssey that would lead all the way to the Wimbledon title, his breakthrough Grand Slam title, in 2003. A year beforehand, Groeneveld, who used to attend his matches and considered himself a sort of unpaid advisor, made a decision after Federer's first-round loss at Wimbledon to Mario Ancic.

'Roger was going through a tough time,' he said. 'I said: "Roger, listen, you're very dear to me, but I'm no longer going to come to your matches. I'm no longer going to come to dinners. I'm going to withdraw myself because you just have too many people with you already." I was also working with [Greg] Rusedski at the time but it was a time for Roger to get more tunnel vision, in my opinion, because there was so much uncertainty at that time.'

Groeneveld said he and Federer never spoke about the possibility he might become his coach, at any stage. Instead, the Dutchman, who has also coached Maria Sharapova, believes Federer's choice of coaches throughout his career has been exceptional. 'I was so happy to see what he was doing. I still have a great relationship with him, but that's just more of a personal relationship. I think that the road that he has taken and the coaches that he has had, I believe he's done phenomenally well in all his transitions, even without a coach for some time. And then Tony Roche, I thought it was a great, great decision. I even thought José Higueras was a great decision. Paul Annacone ... you can see that with his transition and his growth. I think he's made an incredible choice in his coaches and his loyalty towards them.

I believe with Ivan [Ljubicic], probably he made the biggest improvement in his career after Peter Lundgren, in my opinion, just because he was finally stepping into his backhand. He started to play more like a single-handed player because I felt always that his backhand was hit almost like a double-handed backhand, instead of like a single-handed backhand. The one-handers that are really dominant with the backhand, like Ivan himself, stepped into the court, and I thought that really put him again at the level where he was challenging for the slams again.'

Federer listened to Groeneveld when he had advice to give, except once, which turned out to be the best choice he ever made. At the Sydney Olympics in 2000, Federer had met Mirka Vavrinec and asked Groeneveld and the other coaches if he should begin a relationship with her. 'He was devastated that he didn't get a medal,' Groeneveld said. 'I can only speak for myself. I felt that maybe, just because of this disappointment, he really wanted to start a relationship. He asked, "Should I or should I not?" And I said, "Well, I think it's maybe a little bit too early for you. You're just starting your life as a young guy on Tour. It's going to be very difficult and challenging." But obviously, he made the right choice. I think because of Mirka, he was able to really excel when he did finally get through that point, where he did win Wimbledon. The years prior to that, he was struggling. But Mirka and Peter Lundgren were such steady voices for him. I think because of the coaching, but also because of Mirka, he was able to overcome a very difficult time where a lot of expectations were on his shoulders and he could not really live up to that. He felt a lot of pressure.'

Mirka was also crucial in helping Federer after the shock death of Carter, who died in a car accident in 2002. 'Roger was a guy that looked for stability in everything he did,' Groeneveld said. 'And you can still see that he looks for that support system. He needs to have people that are around him for a long time, like Severin Lüthi, who has been with Roger for so long. That's why the loss of Peter Carter had such a great impact. Because he was a steady voice for Roger. So Mirka came more into the picture in 2000 during the Olympics. And that's when they started off their relationship. And here we are, 20, 21 years later, they're still together and have four kids.'

The death of Carter also had a big effect on Federer on the court. Realising that he needed to focus, he improved his behaviour and began the transition to the dominant player he would become. 'He really, I believe, started to realise that it was up to him,' Groeneveld said. 'He needed to make some changes. It was a gradual evolution. It was not from one day to another but obviously the death of Peter Carter had a big impact on him. But I think the biggest impact, you would have to say that is Mirka. Mirka was a couple of years older; obviously as a female, she was more mature and she just was able to have a really, really positive impact on Roger, on the court and off the court and gave Roger almost like a security blanket. That's what he needed. He needed this feeling that people were looking after him, especially after the loss of Peter Carter.'

Groeneveld has seen Federer come through from cheeky junior to world No 1 and arguably the greatest male player the world has ever seen. Through more than two decades, he has watched him evolve and mature. What makes Federer so popular, he says, can be explained in one particular way. 'I believe Roger is the most empathetic person that I have met,' he said. 'I still see Roger as I saw him when I was in Switzerland working with him. He is just real, you know? He was true to his own identity. Of course, he has matured and he's a father and he has unbelievable responsibilities towards his sponsors, and he's such a great spokesperson for our sport. But he's just very empathetic. He always thinks about other people. It's not about pleasing others, but respecting others. I think his biggest strength is his true love for the game, it's the history and the legacy that others have laid before him. I think that's what makes him so special. It's great to see him create the Laver Cup. That means the world to him. He wants to be in the footsteps of others, and he feels he has a responsibility towards that, as well. I think that empathy also translates in the coaches that he has had.'

Groeneveld recalled a story about an organisation – he didn't want to reveal what it was, and it never came to fruition – which wanted to do something about mastery. 'Since Rembrandt is a master and Roger is a master, they felt that there were similarities on how to look at mastery between Roger and Rembrandt,' he explained.

'I believe that people recognise a certain element of mastery. This is nothing about the best or the GOAT

[Greatest of All Time]. I believe mastery, an artist at work, I believe that's what people recognised. Whether it's Francis Bacon or Damien Hirst or Rembrandt or Bach, people recognise something that has nothing to do with the result but see an artist at work. And I believe that puts him on a pedestal ... where individuals recognise this incredible mastery that he produces. Some people will say: "I don't like Dalí but I love Francis Bacon." In tennis, we tend to look at results. But Roger has taken us to another level. And that is mastery and artistic talent that we rarely see. That's what it is.'

Darren Cahill, former coach of Lleyton Hewitt and Andre Agassi

'It's the little things you do that define you'

Had things turned out differently, Darren Cahill might have experienced what it was like to coach Federer, too. Having guided both Lleyton Hewitt and Andre Agassi to the world No 1 ranking, the Australian was in high demand and Federer was interested.

'In my eyes, I was pretty close,' Cahill said. 'I went across to Dubai for about ten to 12 days [in 2009]. I had just started with ESPN and I'd just started with Adidas, with the player development programme. If you take on that particular role with Roger, you have to be all in, there's no doing anything else. And I was committed to that. But one of the things that I wanted to make sure of was that, OK, after ten or 12 days, it has to be absolutely certain that this is what Roger wants and certainly what I want as well. And if there's any indecision on either side, then it's probably best we don't do it.'

Though the pair did not end up working together, Cahill got the chance to see the Swiss up close, see how he worked, where the genius came from. 'I enjoyed those ten or 12 days. I thought it was really eye-opening too,' he said. 'I think a lot of people see Roger at the majors and see his training routine, the way he goes about things and how lackadaisical he can be at times. But he's the complete opposite when he's away from the eyes of the public. He works the way you would expect him to work. He's put in an enormous amount of work, not only on the tennis court but also to protect his body. I'll always go through my life, I think, [wondering] what would have happened, what if, but I don't look at it that way so much as I look at it more as the fact that whenever I see him play, I see a reflection or a part of Peter Carter out there doing what he's doing. And I get a lot of pride and satisfaction from that, just seeing Roger do his thing.'

It was Carter, Federer's formative coach, who first alerted Cahill to the young man he was bringing through the junior ranks. The two South Australians were best friends, junior players together and then pros, although Carter's career had been interrupted by injury. Cahill first set eyes on Federer when he was in Basel, having flown to Switzerland to see Carter. There, his old friend, who had originally gone to play club tennis at TC Old Boys, was keen to know what he thought of this youngster in whom he had so much belief.

'He was super-talented back then, about 12 or 13 years of age,' Cahill said. 'Super-talented, made the game look pretty easy. He had a really fast arm, really whippy forehand actually; that was the one thing I remembered. And Peter, at the end of it, he was showing him off a little bit and putting him through his paces. I stayed and watched for about an hour or so and at the end of it we went and got dinner and

Carts was asking me what I thought. I started talking him down and then I said: "I reckon I've got someone better back in Adelaide that I'm working with about the same age." He said who's that and I said: "Lleyton Hewitt.'"

Two or three years later, Cahill was back in Switzerland with Hewitt, this time taking on Federer in the World Youth Cup in Zurich. Federer beat Hewitt 7-6 in the third set and, according to Cahill, both boys were not exactly the best behaved.

'Both Lleyton and Roger were as bad as each other on the court, bouncing their racquets, a few four-letter words were coming out and I reckon tears were coming out of both guys,' he said. 'And at one point, I reckon Lleyton threw his racquet into the back fence. They both knew of each other because of all the hype surrounding their junior careers.'

That was the start of a rivalry Cahill would witness as Hewitt's coach, the two men playing against each other 27 times in all. In the early days, Hewitt had the upper hand, winning three of their first four. By the end of it, Federer led 18-9 but the two men had plenty of respect for each other, in part because of Cahill and Carter.

'The first time they ever played as pros, we sat together,' Cahill said. 'If you go back to their record, you see the first pro match they played and he and I sat together in the stands, right next to each other. Roger and Lleyton actually became pretty good friends because of the relationship between Carts and I. They practised together quite a bit and they actually played doubles together. While they had a healthy rivalry with each other, they certainly were good friends and respected each other and I knew that both of these guys were probably going to run into each other a lot throughout their playing careers. And I actually still think that respect remains today, which is pretty nice.'

Federer has often explained the influence Carter had on him, guiding him through those important formative years. When he died in August 2002, Federer was distraught, the man he thought of almost as family, suddenly gone, just when he needed him. Cahill, too, was bereft. 'Carts really looked at him like a younger brother, even though there was a considerable age difference,' Cahill said. 'He took him under his wing. He cared a lot about him. I've got a great friend, Todd Viney, who we grew up playing junior tennis with. We went to Canberra at the Institute of Sport for a couple of years. There were four of us: Peter Carter, Anthony Lane, who was the 18s national champion in Australia, Todd Viney and myself. Todd ended up giving up and going back and playing Aussie Rules football, had a really successful football career, and even to this day, I just got a message from Todd, reminiscing about a story about Peter years ago.

'We called Carts the "Great Procrastinator" because he could never pull the trigger and make a decision,' Cahill said, laughing. 'All his decisions had to be so well thought out. He had to think about every single bit of execution as to what might play out if I choose this. It was so anti-Aussie because we're so black and white. Like, mate, just make a choice.'

But what made his friends laugh was a perfect foil for Federer, who took in everything Carter said, a sponge to his friend. That Carter died just when Federer's career was really taking off seems doubly harsh but Cahill said his old friend lives on in Federer. 'You see Roger a little bit, not so much being a procrastinator, but sort of thinking through scenarios, situations and weighing things up,' he said. 'I'm sure he and Peter got into these long conversations about what was the right thing to do and what happens if I do it this way, what do you think the outcome will be? There's so much of Peter that comes out in Roger, even today.'

For Cahill, who was so close to Carter, that has its positives and negatives. But he wouldn't have it any other way. 'I love it. I feel like he's a replica of the personality that Peter was,' he said. 'I also struggle with it a little bit as well because I struggle with the fact that Peter's not here anymore. I think about Peter every single day. So every time I do see Roger, it's a reflection of Peter and a reminder of Peter and there's good to that and there's bad to that as well. I just know that Peter would be super-proud, not even worrying about what he's accomplished between the lines on the court, but super-proud of the person that he's grown into. That's what he would be most proud about.'

What was Federer like when Cahill first met him? 'A little goofy. He was gangly, pretty loose with his game,' he said. 'He had an air of confidence that he walked with, he was always smiling, always cracking jokes. His practices I wouldn't say were super-intense, when he was a junior, [but] he turned that around later in his career or even early in his career, that's part of the reason why he became so good. But he was a really down-to-earth, nice kid, even back then.

'I think one of the most remarkable things about him is that you can look at Federer, 39, 40 years of age, then wind the clock backwards to when he was 18 or 19 and there are not too many differences in the kid from back then to what he is now like. Life is completely different for him now but when you go up and you have a conversation with him now, the same 19-year-old Roger Federer comes out in conversation.'

Federer remained close to Carter's parents throughout his career, arranging for them to fly down to Melbourne every year for the Australian Open, sorting out tickets for his matches and making the time to catch up and doubtless reminisce about their son, his old friend. Cahill said the way Federer looked after them each year speaks volumes about his character.

'What Roger did for them, bringing them to the Aussie Open, they looked forward to it every year and it made their year,' he said. 'That's the person he is. And that's kind of what made him so well respected and so well loved. It's the little things, you know. People talk so much about [how] you can do some big things in your career, which is great, but it's the little things that really define you. And Roger is the master at making sure that he's always looking after people and those people around him.'

On the court, Federer's brilliance also hastened a change in Cahill the coach. Instead of trying to figure out how he could be beaten by watching, looking for patterns, Cahill began to embrace the technology and statistics that, in 2008, were only really entering the game.

'I reckon we used the analytics a lot more after he came along because he separated himself so much from the game,' he said. 'We're talking 2005, 2006 and 2007 when he was completely dominant, when there was a massive gap between him and everybody – until Rafa [Nadal] closed that gap. That's when we started to dive into the analytics, because just going through your normal eyes and working out strengths and weaknesses and patterns and that sort of stuff, it wasn't working for anyone and it was actually getting further away. So people started to work out, how can we break this guy down?'

Cahill said he showed Federer the impact that statistics could have, when he went over for his trial in Dubai, asking him how he thought he'd played on the big points in the then-recent Australian Open final of 2009, the match where he lost to Nadal and ended up crying in the on-court trophy ceremony.

Cahill recalled: 'He said, "Well, I was really aggressive and went for it on the first return to see if I could get to his backhand. I don't think I did much wrong." And then we went through the tape, went through those points, went through where he was standing and he goes, "Woah, that's a little bit different to how I remember it." I think a lot of people started to dive a lot more into analytics when he started to dominate the game.'

Cahill has also seen just how popular Federer is all over the world, from fans to famous faces, how something about him just resonates with people. 'I think there's a little bit of mystique about him,' Cahill said. 'I can only really relate it to tennis because that's all I know. I grew up in the Borg–McEnroe era, and Borg had that swagger on the court, that [made you feel], I'd love to get to know this guy, get to know about him. I reckon Roger's got that as well.

'It's a different world now, of course, because Roger is much more accessible than Borg was back then and much more media-friendly. So we get to know and we get to see Roger a lot more than we got to know Björn back then. But the way they played the game was incredibly graceful. We all look at Roger playing and go, jeez, I wish I could play tennis like him. You don't necessarily say that about Rafa because it looks such damn hard work, the way he plays. You respect it just as much as you respect Roger but it doesn't feel real to a normal tennis player to be able to play like Rafa, whereas it does feel real to be able to play like Roger. We can all get on the court and swing the racquet the way Roger swings it – it's not going to come off the same, but we can't do what Rafa does.

'I think he's got a real connection to the tennis public. He's got a real connection to just the general public that don't even like tennis, about the way he played the game. The fact that he was so successful for so long makes him relatable to everybody. He kept doing what he loves. It's all got to do with how much you're enjoying the sport and doing what you love. And that's the most important thing for any athlete.'

Paul Annacone, former coach
'He's on the magician side of the spectrum'

When Paul Annacone first saw Roger Federer in action, he was already coaching the best player in the world, Pete Sampras. Annacone, a Grand Slam champion in doubles and good enough to be ranked No 12 at his peak in singles, had helped Sampras become world No 1 and dominate the ATP Tour and was always on the lookout for dangers to his man.

'I think it was 1998, I remember watching him when he was just getting ready to turn pro,' the American said. 'I didn't know him at all. I just remember watching him play somewhere and thinking how talented he was.'

Two years later, he saw him up close for the first time when he played in Miami and he was struck by one thing in particular. 'Just how easy the game looked to him. You look at players and you see how hard someone has to work to play at a high level. Well, for me, it didn't look like he had to work very hard to play at a high level. And what I mean by that is, there's no shame in working hard. It's just that all of his technique and everything was so sound. It wasn't going to take a lot for him to have a high ceiling.

'I have a kind of measure for athletes on a scale, on a spectrum from a mechanic to a magician. And he's all the way on that magician side, he is way over there. I didn't know him but I figured if he had a good head on his shoulders, he was going to be a big problem for everybody else on the Tour.'

And so it proved. Federer began making waves on the Tour quickly but it was at Wimbledon in 2001 that Annacone, and the world, really got a taste for what Federer might be capable of. Seeded No 15, he had already beaten two established players in Xavier Malisse and Jonas Björkman to set up a fourth-round meeting with Sampras. Though everyone was curious to see what Federer was all about, Sampras was the defending champion, had won seven of the past eight Wimbledon titles and was considered unbeatable on the hallowed turf of the All England Club.

Annacone had the best seat in the house to see the changing of the guard. 'I'd seen him play and Pete knew how good he was,' he said. 'The question with a young, talented guy like that is how does he hold up under pressure, you know, against Pete or whoever the next great player is? And what happens in the big moments. And so, to me, that was kind of the first time I saw Roger really step up and manage that moment and just play a little bit better than Pete in the biggest times, which had not really happened at Wimbledon before.'

Though it took Federer another couple of years to win his first Grand Slam title, at Wimbledon in 2003, he had already had an effect on Annacone, who knew that the Swiss was something special. In the years that followed, especially when he was working as the coach of British player Tim Henman, Annacone spent more time around Federer and learned what made him tick.

'I first met him when I was with Pete and he was being coached by Peter Lundgren. I know Peter and [Federer] just seemed like a shy, happy-go-lucky kid. And then when I started working with Tim back in 2003, I got to spend a little bit more time with him. He was just a fun-loving, really optimistic kid. He was not one of these kids that was very cynical or had a lot of baggage or entitlement, he was just really happy. He just really seemed to love tennis and really love life. And I was amazed, just watching how he operated, because it's very hard to be that established and accomplished as an athlete and still have a relatively stable footing on the ground of who you are as a person, prioritising life's real issues. It's all credit to Robbie and Lynette Federer. He was pretty darn grounded. His parents, I've had the good fortune of getting to know them and have meals with them. And they're just wonderful people. They understand life and priorities. And I think that's rubbed off on Roger really well.'

Staying grounded when you are world No 1 and everyone wants a piece of you is far from easy. Federer seemed to embrace his status, without ever getting away from who he is. That, Annacone said, goes some way to explaining how popular he became.

'I think people like to look at great athletes and wonder about them and wonder who they are and what makes them tick,' he said. 'When you see Roger, what you see is what you get. He's just a great guy that happens to be a tremendous tennis player. I think it's really refreshing to a lot of people. And I think they look for that and it's very appealing because, sure, they want them to be superstars, but they also love that they're approachable and Roger, if anything, is too approachable.'

It was 2010 when Annacone got the call to become Federer's coach, a role he would carry out until 2013. In that time, Federer won his seventh Wimbledon title and won the ATP Finals twice, along with many more titles around the world. It was an eye-opening experience for Annacone in many ways.

'The thing that was most appealing to me was how open-minded he was,' he said. 'He's interesting because he's interested – he doesn't want someone to tell him everything he likes to hear. He's interested in different perspectives. He's interested in a lot of stuff. He loved to play tennis and still loves to play tennis. So when we started together, I was amazed at his willingness to be open-minded about discussing and then trying different things to try to get more excellence from an already off-the-charts career. And he does it in a way that's very optimistic, it comes from a place of interest, not fear. It comes from a place of I'm curious, not from a fear of failure and I think that his ability to differentiate allowed him to play at this level for this long. I think it really let him just kind of embrace being out there and enjoy the game. He has a very empathetic heart. And he's not just interested in the super-elite of the world. He's interested in people and what makes the world go round. And I think that, again, just gives you a solid perspective on life.'

Having coached Sampras to world No 1 and several Grand Slam titles, Annacone already knew that listening was the key to success in his job. He was also always willing to change. 'If you listen to a lot of people and you don't change, then either you're unbelievably arrogant or you're perfect. And I don't really believe in perfection.'

Working with Federer, one of the most talented players in history, changed him as a coach, too. 'I wasn't so sure you could be as approachable and I wasn't so sure you could be as, I guess the word is, "open" to so many different things and still be at the level that he is at,' he said. 'I was never around anyone that, you know, during the US Open would go to a museum during the day with their kids for an hour and a half and then go play the night match. Pete never did that. Tim didn't do that.

'So at first I was nervous about it. And this is where Severin [Lüthi] and Pierre Paganini helped me a lot. Just helping understand how these things keep Roger relaxed. They keep him very much at ease. They keep him enjoying his life. And it doesn't take away from his athletic performance. I never saw him lose a match because he was tired. I never saw him lose a match because he just wasn't focused. So, he helped me understand and build even more of my philosophy about coaching now, which is that every player is different. You have to understand how to manage different [people]. If Pete Sampras travelled like Roger, he would have been nothing. He could never have done that. If Roger had Pete's life, he would have been bored to tears and never wanted to play tennis. They're just very different. And neither of those things are right or wrong. They're just about their own personalities.

'There are some parameters, there are some guidelines. Roger's not going out and staying up all night and partying until five in the morning. But he'll go to a museum, he'll have dinner with a group of friends and he'll come home at 11.30. He doesn't live like a recluse. I think that he really educated me as to [how] life is different for different people and the things that you do to help relax you actually allow you to be a better performer in the biggest moments if you manage them the right way. And that's what he did.'

As Federer's success on the court continued, Annacone saw how many famous people flocked to his matches and identified as a Federer fan. They were attracted by his talent and seemingly effortless style of play, of course, but also, Annacone feels, by something else.

'People are very curious. I am, too,' he said. 'I'm curious about excellence and I'm curious about genius in all different areas. And when you see an artist that's a genius and has excellence, I think human nature is to figure out what those ingredients are that make that, so maybe you can bring it to your life. And I know that I look at it, how can I help coach other people to get them to have some of these traits? You can't teach someone to have a God-given talent that some of these people have, but the way they operate, there tend to be some traits, some commonalities that allows this excellence to flourish. I think it's a curiosity about excellence and it's a curiosity about the execution in what they do to kind of shine.'

Watching him deal with the media in press conferences both at good times and in difficult moments, Annacone was struck by how even-tempered Federer usually was, how he rarely lost his temper, instead always thinking about the question and searching for a good answer, even if it was almost always something he's been asked before. 'He's very honest,' Annacone said. 'I mean, he doesn't take things personally, generally, unless you really attack him, in the press room. He's contemplative, right … so I think he does use it as a cathartic experience to kind of get a different perspective as to what's happened and why, whether it's positive or negative.

'I think it works well for him because the one thing that is a lot like Pete Sampras is that neither of them waste energy on stuff that they don't control. I mean, they're the two most amazing people I've ever been around about letting go of stuff that just either they don't control, or just doesn't matter. So if somebody thinks a certain way about them or gets accusatory about a bad performance or asks a nasty question, it doesn't make their pulse go up, they just let it go, they don't waste emotional energy on stuff they don't control. That's the biggest thing that Pete and Roger really have in common.'

But when Annacone thinks about the effect Federer had on him, personally, he says it's 'more generic and existential'. 'It was really just, do the best you can with what you have but boy have a good time doing it,' he said. 'Chasing dreams doesn't have to be misery and all sacrifice. It should be enjoyment. And I think the macro effect on everybody was, you actually can be pretty darned normal and a pretty darned good person and still be a sports icon, which is interesting. It's very interesting to me in today's day and age with social media. He's handled it pretty well.'

ROGER, THE RIVAL

AFTER TURNING professional in 1998, Roger Federer's career spanned four decades at the top of the men's game, during which he took the game to new levels.

In that time, he's played Andre Agassi and Pete Sampras; taken on the great clay-courters like Gustavo Kuerten and Guillermo Coria; stared down Marat Safin and Lleyton Hewitt; and, most famously of all, locked horns with Rafael Nadal, Novak Djokovic and Andy Murray. And he's beaten the lot.

Few players can say they have a winning record over Federer and some that did either 'got lucky', as Pat Rafter admits, or perhaps played most of their matches against him when he was already closer to 40 than 30. Others, like Andy Roddick and James Blake, could be forgiven if they really disliked Federer for all the defeats he inflicted on them at the height of their powers.

But it is no slight on the others to say that Federer's career has been defined, in many ways, by his clashes with Nadal and Djokovic.

Federer and Djokovic played each other 50 times; Federer and Nadal met 40 times; and at the time of writing, Djokovic and Nadal had gone head-to-head on 59 occasions. All three have contested iconic battles, dramatic finals.

Between them, the trio have dominated men's tennis like in no other era, mopping up the Grand Slam titles and leaving very little room for anyone else to get a look-in. Together, they have inspired each other to unrivalled heights.

Toni Nadal, coach and uncle of Rafael Nadal

'Federer always did things nicely. His hair was very beautiful. But his work also'

Rafael Nadal played his first Wimbledon in 2003, reaching the third round as a just-turned 17-year-old, which made him the youngest man to do so since Boris Becker in 1984. Few people knew then that he would go on to become one of the three greatest players of all time, or that he would begin a rivalry with Roger Federer that will go down as one of the best ever.

While Nadal was making his debut in a Grand Slam event that year, Federer won his first Grand Slam title, beating Mark Philippoussis in the final to win the first of his eight Wimbledon crowns and 20 slam titles. As he made his way through the draw, unbeknown to him, a man who would become an integral part of the rivalry with Nadal was watching in the stands.

'I think the first time that I saw him play was at Wimbledon in 2003,' said Toni Nadal, Rafa's uncle and coach, the man who steered him to glory throughout his career. 'I saw his match on Centre Court against the American Mardy Fish in the third round.'

Federer won that match in four sets – he dropped the third – but Toni, who was there with Rafael for the tournament, was immediately impressed, not just with the Swiss's game, but something else too. 'I saw a guy who played really well, who played with unbelievable technique,' he said. 'I love tennis and I love how he played. I love not only where the ball goes but how you put the ball there. Federer did things always very nicely. His hair was very beautiful. But his work also.'

They didn't play each other on the ATP Tour until the following year when Nadal shocked Federer in straight sets in Miami. 'I think the first time when Rafael beat him in Miami, he didn't play high to his backhand, he played normal. He played aggressive, he played with higher speed because he knew the only possibility to beat him was like this.'

That tactic soon changed as Nadal, who won his first Grand Slam title, at Roland-Garros in 2005, quickly spotted the weakness in the Federer game. The Swiss had won three slams in 2004 but on clay, especially, hitting hundreds of one-handed backhands from the baseline was something which, at the time, he was not ready for.

'In the first years, where we put the focus was to put the ball in high over his backhand,' Toni said. 'Because we knew, at this time, Federer moved the wrist a little too much to play the backhand and then with the spin [from Nadal], he had more problems.

'On clay it was always to play over his backhand and on hard courts was to play a little fast sometimes. I remember in a match in Dubai, the final in 2006, and Rafael lost the first set easily, 6-2. And I said to Rafael, play slower over his backhand and make the serve slower and okay, then Rafael beat him; 6-4, 6-4 in the second and third set.'

Nadal dominated the first meetings against Federer, winning six of the first seven encounters, four of which were on clay. Toni knew why. 'I think it was a mistake of Roger

Federer,' he said. 'Because many times when I spoke with Rafael, I said Federer plays not too smart with you. The problem for Federer, in my opinion, was that he normally played the return very easy to us. He was not aggressive enough. And then Rafael can take the initiative.'

Though Federer maintained his edge over Nadal on hard courts and on grass for a while, Nadal was coming, fast. After taking a set off him in the 2006 Wimbledon final, Nadal pushed him to five sets in the final the following year and then, in 2008, he ended Federer's five-year winning streak at Wimbledon by claiming the title for the first time after an epic final, including two rain breaks and which finished in near darkness. For Federer, it was a heartbreaking loss; for Nadal, and Toni, it was a massive breakthrough. 'The best memory is Wimbledon 2008,' Toni said.

Federer and Nadal played each other 40 times in all, with Nadal leading 24-16, 14 wins to ten in finals. Nadal leads 10-4 in their slam meetings (6-0 at Roland-Garros) and they met at least twice in the final of three of the four slams, with the US Open the only place they never faced each other. Righty v lefty, style v power; their match-up had all the elements people love in a rivalry.

'This rivalry had everything,' Toni said. 'It was the number one against the number two, then it changed, with number one for Rafael. It was a player that played with unbelievable technique, very elegant and another with passion, it was different styles. But at the end, there always was a very good respect. Both, I think, were very correct on court. It was one of the biggest rivalries in sport history, in my opinion.'

Though Nadal has played more matches against Novak Djokovic than against Federer, and though Federer and

Djokovic also met more often, the rivalry between Nadal and Federer seems to hold extra-special status, within the sport and for both players.

Rafael Nadal agrees. 'I mean, we shared a lot of important things together, no?' Nadal said, when we asked him at Wimbledon in 2022. '[With] all the things that we achieved, [it is] difficult in some way to think [of] tennis in the last 15, 20 years without thinking about the rivalry that we have because we have been playing in every big stadium – not in New York, that's the only thing that bothers me a little bit, that we never played in New York – but in the rest of the most important events of the world, we shared court, fighting for the most important things.'

Tennis has been blessed with great rivalries throughout its history. In the past 40 years alone, we have had Martina Navratilova–Chris Evert, John McEnroe–Björn Borg, Stefan Edberg–Boris Becker, Pete Sampras–Andre Agassi, all spurring each other on. Without their main rival, they may never have reached the heights they did. They make each other better, forcing them to improve if they want to remain at the top. Without Federer, Nadal may have won more titles but he would not have needed to improve; without Djokovic, they each might have won more but neither would have needed to keep on adding things to their game.

'I think in some way we push each other,' Nadal said. 'When you have somebody very good in front – I can talk about myself – I always wanted to think that my motivation never comes to me because of the others; it's a personal motivation. But, of course, with somebody like him, like a rival, that's amazing good, helps you to know the things that you have to do to be better.'

Federer readily admits that Nadal made him change his game. He was the only one whose natural style meant that his own natural game was not always good enough to win. The match-up was problematic. That, for Toni Nadal, is what makes Federer even more impressive, how he turned things on their head.

'Everything changed in 2017 when Federer started to hit the ball faster on the first ball [the return],' Toni said. 'You know, this moment in 2017, Federer said he didn't want to be the one to play more rallies. He wanted to play with the return, very fast and everything changed. On hard courts, it was very difficult for Rafael to beat him because he played so fast.'

Toni Nadal is referring specifically to the 2017 Australian Open final, when Federer, who had been off Tour for six months as he recovered from knee surgery, came from a break down in the final set to win his first Grand Slam title since 2012. It was an iconic moment and not a good one for Team Nadal.

'The worst memory was Australia 2017 because Rafael could win this match. He was winning 3-1 in the fifth set,' Toni said, pinpointing the moment when he felt fate went against his nephew, when, at 3-2, advantage, Nadal could not close out the service game to maintain his lead. 'He touched the net [with a forehand] and it goes out. And OK, we lose. This match I think Rafael could have beaten him.'

While their style of play is different, in many ways Federer and Nadal are quite similar. Passionate about their tennis, they play with courtesy, something Toni Nadal, in particular, admires. 'They showed to the people that you can have a very intense rivalry, but at the same time to have a good respect. And you can be a friend of your opponent.

Normally this doesn't happen, and with these two guys it happened and that was [special].'

In more recent years, Federer and Nadal have both helped each other out off the court. When Nadal opened his Rafael Nadal Academy in Manacor in 2018, Federer made the trip to lend it a bit of extra razzamatazz. Nadal returned the favour when he travelled to Cape Town in February 2020 to play Federer in an exhibition match in front of a record crowd, which raised $3.5 million for the Roger Federer Foundation.

Even in the heat of the battle, Federer and Nadal always got on and their families shared some incredible moments together, both in victory and defeat. 'I think they have a good relationship because it is unbelievable when during many years, you have the same job, bigger tournaments, you follow the same goals,' Toni said. 'The normal thing is to have a good relationship. And I think that the parents of Federer are very correct. His father is very kind too, so it's normal to have a good relationship.'

Rafael Nadal agrees. 'Our relationship has been, I think, always very positive, very friendly,' he said. 'Even our rivalry on court never bothered our relationship outside of the court.'

Marian Vajda, long-time coach of Novak Djokovic
Right in the middle of the greatest era

Marian Vajda is a true tennis enthusiast. He coached Novak Djokovic for 15 years, leading him to 20 Grand Slam titles. But after their collaboration ended in 2021 after the ATP Finals in Turin, he didn't stay at home in Slovakia for long. He soon took on a new challenge with his compatriot Alex Molcan, a talented left-hander.

At the 2022 French Open, he had already coached his first match against his long-time protégé. But his bond with Djokovic will always remain and when he talks about Novak's rivalries with Roger Federer and Rafael Nadal, his eyes sparkle. When all three have put their racquets aside, this era will probably be considered the greatest in tennis. Vajda was right in the middle of it.

When he saw Federer play for the first time in Indian Wells in 2000, he was not yet Djokovic's coach but that of the Slovak Dominik Hrbaty. Federer and Hrbaty, who was a good three years older, played doubles together, as the Swiss often did at the beginning of his professional career. In singles, then 18 years old and No 159 in the world, Federer had failed to qualify. In doubles, he and Hrbaty reached the semi-finals, beating, among others, the Australians Mark Woodforde and Todd Woodbridge, who were to win the French Open and Wimbledon that year.

'Already, back then, many predicted that Roger would one day become No 1,' Vajda said. 'He already played great, but he was not a complete player yet. He was very fresh on Tour. But of course, I saw his potential. Great volleys, excellent serve, but most of all, I saw that he enjoys tennis. He enjoyed every ball. I liked his attitude; he was like a kid that just wants to play.'

When Vajda introduced himself to Djokovic and his parents at the 2006 French Open as they were looking for a new coach, Federer had already won seven Grand Slam titles. 'After Paris, I agreed with Novak on a five-week trial period. During this time, he won his first ATP tournament [in Amersfoort, the Netherlands], after which we embarked on a longer collaboration. At that time, Novak was already in the top 50 but still far away from Roger and Rafa, who had won the French Open for the first time in 2005. But Novak started to set his sights on those two.'

Vajda continues: 'The effect of Roger on Novak was immense. He drove him to be better. We saw him as the most talented player because he makes everything look easy. Everything is in flow. His strokes, his serve. His serve is just amazing. It is not a big serve like [Taylor] Fritz's or [John] Isner's. But so precise and so consistent. And he gets a high percentage of balls in. Amazing rhythm, amazing technique. For Roger, everything comes naturally; Novak had to work for that. But he was committed to doing it. He improved by working more. Novak didn't have a serve like Roger at the beginning. But he improved it, and now he's serving great. That proves that talent is only 20, maybe 30 per cent, but everything else is hard work. And Novak was committed to putting in the hard work to be able to challenge Roger.'

And he was doing better and better; 2007 was a groundbreaking year for Djokovic: in Miami, he beat Nadal for the first time, and in Montreal, he beat Nadal and Federer in succession on his way to the title. He reached a Grand Slam final for the first time at the US Open, which he lost to Federer. In 2008, at the Australian Open, Djokovic won his first major title.

But the doubts remained, as Vajda recounts: 'I remember that one time Novak said to me, I think it was in 2009, that he thought he could never overtake Roger and Rafa. It was not a complaint. He just realised how good and consistent they were. They had won so many Grand Slams, and he had just won one. But the more matches he played against them, the more he started believing. By 2011, he had gotten used to their games and learned how to play against them and prepare for them. So he won three Grand Slams that year.'

One match, in particular, had strengthened his belief that he could win big matches against Federer: the spectacular semi-final at the US Open in 2011, when Djokovic had his back against the wall when he was down 5-3 and 40-15 in the fifth set on the Swiss's serve. He hit the line with a powerful forehand return on the first match point to turn the match around. 'He got a lot of confidence by winning that match,' Vajda recalled.

Every match between the Big Three had a unique flavour to it, he said. 'It's the same theatres, the same actors, but they always perform a different play. You never know what's going to happen. Of course, you have a certain strategy; you know how you want to play. But then, something unexpected happens, creating momentum and turning the game around. Whatever happened in those matches, they were always special.'

And each of the three, Djokovic, Federer and Nadal, constantly improved and adapted. 'Roger has a weaker backhand, for instance. But amazingly, he used his weakness in the next match as a weapon. So it was fascinating from a coaching perspective, as well. The match-ups always changed because everybody improved. Because they realised, "Oh, I have to improve." "No, I have to improve." "I lost; I have to improve." They never gave up. The level they produced, those three guys, was amazing. They all affected each other. And so they distanced themselves more and more from the other players. The other top-ten guys could only try to copy something from them. But because those three played each other in big matches all the time, they got better and better.'

As different as the three play, Vajda certainly sees similarities: 'Roger, Rafa and Novak, they have something special. Something the others don't have. This ability to feel the ball at certain moments and this absolute mental focus. I don't know if it's given or acquired by experience. You can call it what you want,' said Vajda, adding with a smile, 'I would call it balls.'

With Djokovic, something, in particular, stood out for him, said Vajda: 'He feels his body amazingly. He knows exactly how much pressure he can put on his body. He always gave me great feedback. So I could adjust the practices. I always knew if I could push more or not. He has incredible knowledge about his body, and I think Roger has too. Rafa was in a tougher position with all of his injuries. He has a different structure of the body, but he has amazing strength. And his energy is astounding.'

Djokovic became a tricky opponent for Federer, defeating him in four epic Grand Slam finals: at Wimbledon in 2014, 2015 and 2019 and at the US Open in 2015. It was impressive how he managed to stay calm or even use to his advantage the fact that the crowd was clearly on Federer's side. 'The way Novak can focus throughout the match is his biggest asset,' said Vajda. 'In the decisive moments, he was stronger mentally.' His favourite match was the 2019 Wimbledon final, when Djokovic, after saving two match points once again, won 13-12 in the third-set tiebreak. 'Maybe the quality was better in other matches. But the dramaturgy is hard to beat.'

Djokovic agrees. Asked by us during Wimbledon 2022 about the impact of Federer on him, he said: 'Of course, both of them [Federer and Nadal] have influenced my development as a tennis player a lot, probably more than any other players. The most iconic matches I have played in Wimbledon were against Roger, no doubt. The one that stands out is the final in 2019, then another two finals in 14 and 15. Luckily for me, all of those matches I won. Every time you step on the court with Roger, you feel it's not an ordinary match. There's so much more weight to everything around that match, the anticipation, the rivalry. So, of course, it's an ultimate challenge in the sport, playing Roger on grass and Rafa on clay.'

Vajda believes that Djokovic preferred to play against Federer over Nadal. 'Because there is something between them. Rafa and Novak are friends and Rafa and Roger are very good friends. But there was always a little bit of tension between Novak and Roger. They were nice and always respected each other, but there was a certain distance between them.' Which probably only spurred Djokovic on even more to succeed against Federer.

'It's been an amazing 15, 16 years,' Vajda raved. 'Looking back, everybody will probably think those three were from a different planet. We thought nobody would ever break the 14 Grand Slam titles by Pete Sampras. But three guys did it. Roger lifted the level of the sport of tennis globally. What he has done for this sport is just amazing. He triggered something that hadn't been done for decades. Those three guys are much ahead of anybody. I'm grateful that I was able to be involved in that era. I think it's a big message for the next generation. I don't think three players will dominate the sport that much again. I could well imagine there will be more changes at the top in the future.'

He always got on well with Federer, even though they were rivals, said Vajda – and added: 'And I am happy that he is married to a Slovakian lady and that she has shown him my home country a few times. So I'm proud that Slovakia is there in a way. I know Mirka, and I also know her parents.' And he is pleased that Federer's kids are learning Slovak, too. 'They have five languages in the family; that's not too bad,' said Vajda with a grin.

Mark Petchey, former coach of Andy Murray

'He took a rectangle and made curves
where there were corners'

When Andy Murray played Roger Federer for the first time, as a gangly 18-year-old with a mop of hair and skinny legs, he was surprised. It was his first ATP final, in Bangkok in October 2005, and though Murray was beaten 6-3, 7-5, he had expected to be overpowered. Instead, he found himself able to compete.

For Mark Petchey, Murray's coach at the time, it was a defining point in the career of the young Scot, which had taken off when he reached the third round at Wimbledon on his Grand Slam debut that summer.

'For Andy, the biggest take away from the match in Bangkok was that he was in the right place to beat him, ultimately,' said Petchey, a former player who guided Murray in his early days and returned to help him when the three-time Grand Slam champion came back after having a metal hip inserted. 'I think up until that point, Roger did carry a bit of a mythical kind of status amongst a lot of the players. Even though Andy knew he was good, I think Roger at that stage had just a little bit about him that you weren't quite sure if you were capable of competing with him. After the final, even though Andy lost, he came off and the first thing he said to me was: "I was surprised. I thought he would hit the ball harder. I felt comfortable out there." I think for Andy, that match was a big defining point in his own mind that he was capable of winning big events. "If Roger could do it, I think I can do it. You just need to give me a little bit more time and experience."'

Murray won six of his first eight matches against Federer, finding ways to make him uncomfortable on court, something few people before had been able to do. 'Andy's way of playing was frustrating to Roger early on,' Petchey said. 'I think if you look at the players that he's struggled with, not only have they been obviously the best players, but they've been the most consistent players. Roger got frustrated with people like Andy who could move well enough and collect enough balls at the back of the court. That was ultimately why Andy had a very good record against him.'

However, when it came to their biggest battles, Murray found Federer a very different animal. The Swiss beat him in his first Grand Slam final, the 2008 US Open, again in the Australian Open final two years later and famously in 2012, when he dashed his hopes of winning Wimbledon and left Murray in tears as he tried to address the crowd on court. It was a turning point for Murray; the country warmed to him even more through his tears and when he returned to Wimbledon a few weeks later and beat Federer to win the gold medal at the London Olympics, he became a true national hero. The following year, he won Wimbledon.

'I think Andy's achievements for me, personally, are magnified because of his losses,' Petchey said. 'You can talk about the wins but to overcome some of those gargantuan losses, catastrophic losses in his own mind – I know it's only a sport, but it isn't just a sport for Andy. It's his oxygen, it's his food, it's his nutrients. Losing those matches prior to that point, obviously winning the Olympics in 2012 and then the US Open, hurt him because he would have felt as though going into those matches tactically he knew exactly how to play. Credit to Roger for handling those big moments particularly well against Andy at the start of his career.'

Federer turned around his losing record against Murray to win 14 of their 25 clashes. In his time working as coach and a television commentator, Petchey has seen Federer on and off the court, witnessed his quality with his racquet and even his subtle ability to drop a back-handed compliment into a press conference, almost unnoticed. 'He's been unfiltered,' Petchey said. 'Not everybody likes that side to him. I've loved it. He's been super-authentic all the way through the course of his career.'

The American Andy Roddick, who lost four Grand Slam finals to Federer, once said that he had 'tried to hate this guy but I just can't'. Petchey said Federer's popularity among his peers and even his rivals gave him an extra edge.

'I think where Roger was very clever and I don't know if it was him actually thinking about it or it's just his natural demeanour, but he's very well-liked across the board by virtually everybody. And I think it helped him. I think for a long time people didn't hate him enough and didn't find enough in him that they didn't like so that they would go out there with that extra five per cent to try and beat him. I know Andy worked hard on that, worked hard on finding a reason to go out there, to not like him, to try and beat him because he was stealing all his dreams. I think Roger was brilliant at that; he is naturally an engaging person and highly intelligent and it is very hard to dislike him on any scale, but I think at that level, when you're competing against him, if you could find that reason why, it would have helped a number of those players.'

In addition to seeing him on court as a coach, and trying to find words for his genius on court as a commentator, Petchey is one of the few who has seen Federer in training, having spent time in Dubai in 2018. Working alongside the Greek player Maria Sakkari, and her coach Tom Hill, he sat in on some of Federer's practice sessions with Corentin Moutet and another Frenchman. It was a revelation.

'There were a couple of laughs here and there, but boy when the ball was in play, it was absolutely 100 per cent attention to detail, no messing around,' he said. 'I remember at one stage, Moutet and the other French guy started hitting the ball badly. They weren't messing around, but they just got tight or whatever. Roger went fucking nuts. He was like, "This is just not good enough, we're out here trying to play." He gave them a proper lecture. In a good way, I mean, it certainly sorted them out, and they got motivated and they came out, they hit the ball great. Every serve was with a purpose. It wasn't to serve for the sake of 200 serves, it was maybe 50 serves, but every single one was tight to the line. When you watch it in that detail, you go, yeah, I totally understand why he's been as good as he has and why he makes it look [easy] because behind the scenes, the work's been done every single day.'

Petchey also got a close insight into what goes on in Federer's brain when he was working for Sky Television, covering the ATP Finals in London, where the leading players sometimes went into the TV studio to analyse points on a big screen. While Novak Djokovic, Petchey said, could recall almost every point and the dynamics involved, Federer was more intuitive. He remembered points, but focused on the bigger picture. Sometimes he had set plays 'like his kick serve out wide to Novak's backhand indoors' but otherwise Federer did whatever he wanted to do. Petchey said: 'The rest of the time was very much, "I'm going to control the real estate, you're going to dance to my tune. That's why people are looking at me because I'm making it happen out here."'

Petchey was commentating on Federer's stunning win over Rafael Nadal in the final of the Australian Open in 2017, a match he considers to be one of the Swiss's best ever performances. 'It was bewildering,' he said. 'I thought he was down and out in the fifth set. Then he produces tennis that virtually no one else can and hasn't done in the past and you realise why he has become arguably the greatest showman that we've had in tennis, I would say, in terms of the way that he's played.'

Petchey was also struck by how Federer improved with age, long beyond the time when most people are long gone as a threat to win the biggest tournaments. His longevity has broken the mould, showing the way for Nadal, Djokovic and others.

When it comes to the argument about the greatest of all time, Petchey says it's about more than simply the number of Grand Slams each has won. 'For me, it's about how an athlete has made you feel,' he said. 'Michael Johnson was the greatest athlete I ever watched run. Atlanta '96 was just stunning to me. He made me feel like I was witnessing something I will never, ever see again.

'With Roger, how has he made you feel when you stepped into an arena? How has he made you feel when you've been sitting at home watching him compete and play tennis? He's one of those few athletes that can perform a sporting massacre and still you're entertained. You're still looking at it thinking, wow, how did he do that? I think from that point of view, I will say that he has been the greatest of all time in that department.

'For the majority of his career he has made the unbelievable believable. He took a rectangle and made curves where there were corners. He took a sport and defined its character, which had been built up for over a century before him, with his own personal style. Given the players who came before, that is a pretty rare achievement. It truly felt at times that the sport hadn't been played until Roger came along.'

Craig O'Shannessy, strategy analyst
'Severin said: "I'd like to talk to you about the final"'

The style and manner in which Roger Federer came out firing backhand returns in the final of the Australian Open in 2017 surprised everyone, including Rafael Nadal. For the vast majority of their rivalry, Nadal knew one thing when he served to the Federer backhand; he would get a chipped return in response. It was a tactic doomed to fail against a man with one of the most brutal forehands in history and it allowed Nadal to be comfortable under pressure, knowing what was coming.

So when Federer, having been off the Tour for six months, came out for the final against his old foe and began spanking backhand returns, everyone was surprised, most of all Nadal himself. But one person who was not surprised was Craig O'Shannessy.

O'Shannessy is a strategy analyst whose services have been used by several players, including Dustin Brown, who stunned Nadal at Wimbledon in 2015 and most notably of all, Novak Djokovic. He has written regularly for the *New York Times* and both the ATP Tour and WTA Tour, using video analysis, which only came into the game in a serious way many years after Federer had racked up a stack of Grand Slam titles.

The Australian, who worked with Djokovic from 2017 to 2019, was still in Melbourne on men's final day in 2017, long after the Serb had been stunned by Denis Istomin in the second round. As everyone there was looking ahead to the Federer–Nadal final, somehow O'Shannessy knew he was going to be in demand.

'I know Severin Lüthi [Federer's long-term coach] quite well, we're good friends,' O'Shannessy said. 'There's a certain camaraderie with coaches, when you get in a group with some of them, so that when you need some dirt on an opponent, you'll go to this guy, you'll go to this coach because you trust them and you trust the privacy and all that. So in 2017, he's got Rafa in the final and I'm still there. I know what's coming. I got a text from Severin, saying: "Craig, I'd like to talk to you about the final." On the morning of the final, O'Shannessy made his way to meet Lüthi. 'Margaret Court Arena has a coaches' locker room in there, so we went there,' he said. 'I was prepared for this.'

Nadal had only made it through to face Federer after scraping past an inspired Grigor Dimitrov in five sets in the semi-final and O'Shannessy had watched the way in which the Bulgarian had hammered backhands straight down the middle of the court against the Spaniard, rushing him and denying him an angle.

'So I'm like, that's the way to play Rafa at the start of the point for Roger,' he said. 'The problem for Roger throughout his career against Rafa is he's never known what game plan A is on the backhand side. Does he chip? Does he come over it? Does he go line, does he go rolled angle, does he go backhand cross-court? He's never had it clear and you know, he may say he's had it clear, but the proof is in the matches, the proof is in the video. Never had it clear. The epicentre is the backhand return.

'So I sat down with Severin and said, "Listen, I'm going to show you four, five or six things that you must do. But nothing matters more than coming over the backhand, Roger cannot slice." Roger has an unbelievable chip that semi-neutralises the point. They go to his backhand, he comes over it and then he finds the run around forehand and he's got you. Against every other player on the planet it's great. But against Rafa, it's a disaster because it's going to his forehand. So, do not chip one slice backhand return. Do not.'

The tactic worked to perfection, especially in the final set when, from 3-1 down, he won five straight games with aggressive, near-perfect tennis. 'In the fifth set, he committed to it,' O'Shannessy said. 'When he absolutely had to, I imagine that conversation with Severin was there. It's like, okay, you know, I've got nothing, nothing to lose now.'

O'Shannessy had coached a number of players before really finding statistics and analysis, and his Brain Game Tennis business began to take off in around 2011, when the use of video became more prevalent and more accessible. O'Shannessy used Federer, in particular, to build his profile of how a player should play.

'He's the first guy I studied,' he said. 'I looked at him more than anybody else because he was the number one player in the world. [Andre] Agassi was probably the first guy that I really studied but when I went all in, I was like, I need to know who this guy [Federer] is and what he does because I need to explain what he does and write about it. But then I'm copying, I'm studying and copying and stealing everything that he's doing because he's doing it correctly. I'm like, that's what I need to teach, the metrics of Federer. So probably more than any other player, he had the biggest impact on my coaching, journalism, analytics career. Things launched after 2010 but in order for it to launch, that 2005 to 2010 timeframe, that's when I was learning and I'm learning from him.'

O'Shannessy used Federer's statistical play in his analysis and in his coaching of other players. 'I had the absolute quintessential strategic role model, with Roger,' he said. 'This is how you play tennis. When you aspire to climb the mountain and you wonder who's sitting on top, Roger's sitting on top of the mountain. He's looking down at everybody else. And this is how you play the sport. Rafa at the time was in there, but he still had a very heavy clay-court bent, even though he was having success on hard court and grass. But it wasn't the pure origins of the tennis strategy.'

But having used Federer as a model and learned from him as he was setting up his business, O'Shannessy found himself on the other side of the battle when he began working with Djokovic in 2017. 'Nervous as hell' when they first met, O'Shannessy quickly settled down when Djokovic told him he wanted to get better in every way, including getting to the net more often.

O'Shannessy showed Djokovic how well Federer did when he went to the net and the Serb replied, saying:

'Roger's had this amazing long career and stayed away from injury and part of it is by keeping his points short.' 'I'm paraphrasing here but Novak said something like: "This is something I should copy to extend my career." So I'm finding everything that Roger does well and everything that Rafa does well and I'm infusing it into Novak's game.'

At Wimbledon, two years later in 2019, O'Shannessy was in the Djokovic camp as he took on Federer in the Wimbledon final. Federer had outplayed Djokovic from the baseline and, despite playing two poor tiebreaks, had two match points at 8-7, 40-15 in the final set. It was then, O'Shannessy says, that he made a mistake.

'I think it was 15 all and then he hits an ace down the T and another ace down the T,' he said. 'So, it's match point, just do it again! I thought it was a strategic error not to go to T again because my god you're feeling it.' Instead, Federer lost the next point and on his second match point, he came to the net off a poor forehand approach and was passed by Djokovic with a running forehand. The rest was history. 'Once it was back to deuce, it was 50-50,' O'Shannessy said.

For O'Shannessy, the debate about the GOAT is pub talk, an unnecessary debate that sparks real venom, especially on social media. For him, there are three GOATS. But in terms of who had the biggest effect on him? Of that, he has no doubt.

'Working with Novak for three years, that's certainly had a big impact,' he said. 'But I would say Roger's impact is bigger because he was the guy that I studied for a decade. The way that he came to the net, I modelled my coaching on that; if I'm teaching people the right way to play tennis, the way Roger Federer did it was better than the way Rafael Nadal and Novak Djokovic went about their business.

Because he was more the all-court player, his ability to come forward, his ability to take time away, his ability to maul you.

'Novak plays differently than that. And that's okay. And Rafa certainly plays differently than that. But Roger set my template on how I write about the sport, how I coach the sport, how I view the sport more than anybody else. There's no one more enjoyable to watch.'

Inseparable in their youth: Marco Chiudinelli and Federer as 11-year-olds.

Four medals: Danny Schnyder and Federer at the 1993 Swiss Junior Championships.

Wrestler Urs Bürgler helped Federer to find love in Sydney 2000.

A happy family: wife Mirka (centre) with children Myla, Charlene, Leo and Lenny.

Ballboy Federer: In 1994, he received the medal from Wayne Ferreira in Basel.

Always a prankster: Federer pulls the shirt of his former coach Sven Groeneveld to make him look heavy.

His most influential coach: Peter Carter (left) with Chiudinelli and Federer.

Rivals turned friends: Rafael Nadal and Federer after their 2019 Wimbledon semi-final.

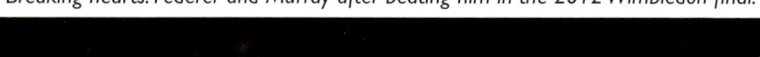

Celebrated at Wimbledon: Novak Djokovic and Federer at the 100th anniversary of Centre Court.

Breaking hearts: Federer and Murray after beating him in the 2012 Wimbledon final.

Federer inspired him to play tennis: Young Stefanos Tsitsipas with his idol.

Travelled the world for Federer: Scarlett Li is one of his biggest fans.

Thanks to Federer, she became a tennis fan: Olympic champion Michelle Gisin.

Because of Federer, she has also started a foundation: Sunita Sigtia at Wimbledon.

He made Federer's name a fixture in the UK Parliament. Former House of Commons Speaker John Bercow, after interviewing Federer for Radio 4's Today programme in 2014.

Witness to history: Former Wimbledon Committee member Michael Gradon always had the perfect seat when Federer was around.

Fun on the set: Director Luki Frieden and Federer hit it off right away.

Finding her voice: TV commentator Mary Carillo, who had to come up with words to match Federer's artistry.

Federer helped him through his toughest time: Marc Krajekian met his idol at the 2017 US Open.

Speechless: Vittoria Oliveri and Carola Pessina were surprised at home by Federer.

Hand in hand: Federer and Nadal share an iconic moment at the 2022 Laver Cup, Federer's final event. Copyright Ella Ling

ROGER, THE INSPIRATION

FROM AN early age, we look to other people for guidance, look up to them or want to surpass them. Role models drive us, make us dream and give us courage when we despair. Roger Federer was and is an inspiration for many, girls and boys alike, with his elegant play, his personality, his style. His influence in this sport will radiate far beyond his active career.

Almost all tennis players of the new generation were influenced by Federer in their own way.

Stefanos Tsitsipas wanted to play like him as a young boy and chose a one-handed backhand because of him. Later, he beat his idol at the Australian Open in their first ever encounter and became a pioneer for Greek tennis. Matteo Berrettini was impressed by Federer's ease and now also competes with him on the catwalk.

Coco Gauff benefitted from his advice for her promising career. Ons Jabeur was even called 'Roger Federer' in Tunisia as a junior because of her variation and her wonderful backhand slice. Not only role models, but also nicknames know no gender.

Federer also inspired many athletes from other sports, such as two-time Olympic skiing champion Michelle Gisin or freeskier Andri Ragettli, and even artists in other fields, such as the world-famous violinist Anne-Sophie Mutter. Federer, she says, has almost become a 'spiritual family member'. She reflects on why sport and art are so much closer than many people think. The ancient Greeks already knew.

Stefanos Tsitsipas, Greek pioneer
'He showed the world how tennis should be played'

Long after Roger Federer has laid aside his racquet, he will live on in tennis through those he has inspired. Like with Stefanos Tsitsipas. The Greek started playing tennis at an early age and discovered his fascination for the Swiss at six years old. 'I grew up with a lot of Pete Sampras, also because of his Greek heritage,' he said, while talking on a wooden bench in Aorangi Park at Wimbledon. 'My father liked him a lot. But Roger was the next up-and-coming star. Growing up, he was the perfect example for me of how tennis should be. I always wanted to be like him.'

He has been following Federer's matches on television since 2006, when he was seven or eight years old. 'I witnessed many of his battles against Nadal, against Roddick, against the young Djokovic. Roger was the reason I chose to pursue a one-handed backhand. Pete played one-handed, too. But I would mostly give it to Roger. I enjoyed watching his backhand a lot. Later, I liked [Stan] Wawrinka's backhand as well. But the first person that I saw was Federer, for sure.'

As perfect as Federer seemed to him, there was something that young Stefanos realised early on: 'It's pretty difficult to imitate the way Roger plays and the way he goes about things, it's very much unique. I don't think it's replicable. It gives you a bad perspective of how you should play because it's just impossible to imitate him. I see kids sometimes trying to be like him, but I think it's impossible to get to that level. He has a unique talent that not many people have had playing this game. It's talent at its best, and he combined it with the incredible work he has put in over the years.'

But it was not only the tennis that impressed Tsitsipas with Federer. 'As a young kid, I always wanted to dress like him, back when I didn't have any sponsors yet. His latest collections were the hottest thing in tennis. I always wanted to have the latest shoes that he had. For example, the black US Open shoes that he was wearing. Some of his red Nike collections that he wore at the French Open. I liked the way he dressed and the way he presented himself. He made the sport look more elegant, cleaner, nicer, and stylish. He introduced a different style to our game and how he carried himself on the court. His personality is unique in many ways.'

Tsitsipas did not want to imitate his idol on the court, but Federer's influence is visible in his game. 'I served and volleyed a lot when I was a kid. And I think that was also mostly because of him. My aggressive game style is definitely thanks to Roger. But I tried to develop my own technique and tried to develop my own skills on the court. I didn't try to do too much of what he did because you can probably do it a few times, but not often enough. So I went about my own thing.'

And that brought Tsitsipas a long way at an early age. Raised in a tennis family and trained by his father Apostolos, he began practising in France in 2015 at Patrick Mouratoglou's academy. He became the world No 1 in juniors and won the junior doubles at Wimbledon in 2016 with Estonian Kenneth Raisma against the Canadian duo of Felix Auger-Aliassime and Denis Shapovalov. Three of them went on to break into the top ten at the pros at a young age.

Tsitsipas remembered from that Wimbledon tournament, as well, his first encounter with Federer: 'We practised together at the match courts. It was an unbelievable experience to share that court with my idol. I remember very vividly how I put a big effort into not making mistakes. I played incredible tennis that day with him, hitting the balls clean and feeling inspired while I was hitting with him. I was very impressed by the quality of his ball, how clean his ball came down to my racquet, and how effortless everything looked. It almost felt like he was not putting any effort into the shots. And things were happening automatically. That was beautiful to watch from the other side of the net.'

At the beginning of that training session, Tsitsipas was pretty nervous, he said, looking back. 'But my nerves all went away once I started putting more and more balls inside the court. I felt much more comfortable, and I think he enjoyed the quality. The thing is that I don't feel like he had a lot of demands or he was demanding too much from me. He just wanted to go out there and enjoy his tennis and get good, short practice before his match.' Of course, they posed for pictures afterwards, and the then-17-year-old Greek was already slightly taller than his idol.

Tsitsipas established himself in the pros in no time at all. In autumn of 2017, he won his first matches on the ATP Tour; in the following year, he was already stirring things up: in Toronto, he beat four top-ten players in one week, before his 20th birthday, and he advanced to No 15 in the rankings and won the Next Gen Finals.

He faced Federer for the first time at the Hopman Cup in Perth, the national mixed team event, in early 2019. The two swung their racquets freely, and the atmosphere was relaxed; the Swiss won 7-6, 7-6 and joked afterwards that it felt like he had beaten his son because Tsitsipas played so similarly.

More was at stake 17 days later in their first official meeting on the professional Tour in the last 16 of the Australian Open. Federer had won the previous two tournaments in Melbourne, claiming Grand Slam titles No 18 and 20 there, and was unbeaten in 17 matches at Melbourne Park. But his Australian fairy tale, after his 2017 comeback, ended abruptly against Tsitsipas.

Inspired by his opponent, the Greek played the match of his life [so far] and beat Federer 6-7, 7-6, 7-5, 7-6. The amazing thing was that Tsitsipas, and not the far more experienced Federer, remained cooler in the decisive moments and fended off all 12 break points against him. Their clash was reminiscent of how the Swiss ended Pete Sampras's era at the All England Club in the round of 16 in 2001 after four titles in a row and seven in the previous eight years. Tsitsipas was as spirited in the Rod Laver Arena as Federer had been on the hallowed turf of Wimbledon and it felt like a changing of the guard.

'That was the best feeling in the world,' Tsitsipas said, beaming. 'I knew there was a chance for me to go out there and show something. I wasn't focusing too much on winning but mostly on the process of the whole thing. Try and get as many games as possible and get as close to a set as possible. Challenge him in every single set. I felt like the match was so long that I just got lost in the match. I celebrated a lot during that match; I was pumped.

It was a fantastic, memorable night with a lot of intensity at the end.'

Tsitsipas found it difficult to sleep afterwards. 'It was challenging to wrap my head around what happened that night. It took me about an hour to fall asleep. I could feel the crowd from that experience. It's almost as if you listened to a lot of music and the songs are playing in your head while trying to sleep. So that was the sensation I had and it was difficult to zone out after that match.' He reached the semi-finals that year, the first Greek ever to do so at a Grand Slam tournament.

When we talked on the day before the start of Wimbledon 2022, it had been a year since Federer last appeared on Tour. Tsitsipas said: 'Even now that he's not competing, you can feel the influence he has had not just on me, but on every tennis player. He's a big figure and his presence will always be felt. He's this unique persona on the court. He showed the world how tennis should be played. But not only is he an ambassador for tennis, but sports globally. He has influenced athletes worldwide in any other sport, pretty much.'

One more thing Tsitsipas felt essential to mention: 'Tennis has allowed Roger to be a humanitarian. It's beautiful to see the work he does with his foundation. He has helped an entire continent with education. He could be a politician, if he wanted, anytime.'

The way he plays, his behaviour on and off the court, his humanitarian commitment – Federer inspires him on many levels, Tsitsipas said. 'He does live on a little bit in me. But to be honest with you, we miss him. I wish that we could see a bit more Roger. He only brings good to our sport.'

Ons Jabeur, Tunisia's trailblazer

They called her Roger Federer

Ons Jabeur came within one set of winning Wimbledon in 2022, a victory that would have been the cherry on the cake for a woman who has set almost as many firsts and established as many records in her career as Roger Federer himself. The first Arab player to reach a slam singles final, she is also the first Tunisian and first north African player to do so. She reached the US Open final soon after made the final at Wimbledon for a second year in a row and continues to blaze a trail for Arab and African tennis wherever she goes.

Jabeur grew up as a big fan of Andy Roddick and desperately wanted the American to win Wimbledon. Having lost in three previous slam finals, two at Wimbledon and all to Federer, Roddick came agonisingly close in 2009. In the final, he had a point to lead Federer by two sets to love, only to miss a relatively easy volley, when he seemed to think it was going long and seemed about to let it go, only to make a late decision to hit it and put it wide. He was then edged out 16-14 in the final set, largely thanks to the fact that Federer hit a career-high 50 aces.

Jabeur was just 14 years old at the time, but she remembers the final well. And even though she was pulling for Roddick and wanted him to win the title, she was nevertheless happy for Federer when he snatched victory from the jaws of defeat, breaking the then all-time men's grand slam record in the process. 'I didn't want to watch the match,' Jabeur said. 'Maybe I was just 51 per cent with Roddick. But obviously, I was happy for Roger, it was his 15th slam, right?' That victory took Federer past Pete Sampras with 15 majors and the win was made even more special for the Swiss by the fact that Sampras, someone who had rarely travelled to tournaments after his retirement in 2003, had flown to London to witness the moment of history.

Despite her affection for Roddick, the name of Federer has been in Jabeur's life since she was as young as 12 years old and not just because of how often she watched him playing on television. Jabeur stood out as a brilliant junior – she won the French Open girls' title in 2011 – and her variety has left many an opponent tearing their hair out in frustration. Her slice is a thing of beauty, her drop shot second to none and her ability to first conceive and then conjure up something magical is unmatched on the women's Tour. No wonder, then, that as a junior, her contemporaries in Tunisia called her 'Roger Federer'.

'It's a great, great honour for me that they did that,' Jabeur said. 'You know, they made some videos comparing my drop shot to his and my slices to his but I am far, far from doing the best slice ever. His slice is just so perfect. And that inspires me a lot to do better. I've watched some clips of him doing some slices to get inspired and maybe be more consistent in doing that shot. I've met him a couple of times and he is such an inspiration, the way that he plays, I don't feel he stresses at all, during the match it's unbelievable how he stays calm on every shot, even if he's far [behind] in the score.'

On the Tour since her early teens, Jabeur took her time to rise through the ranks, breaking new ground at every turn. By the time she got to Wimbledon in 2021, she had just won her first grass-court title, in Birmingham, and arrived in good spirits. Those spirits soared as she became the first Arab player to make the quarter-finals at Wimbledon. It was shortly afterwards, as she was cooling down after beating Iga Swiatek of Poland to reach the last eight, that Federer came by. 'I was stretching and he was warming up for his match,' Jabeur explained, as their paths crossed at the All England Club. 'And he congratulated me. He was very funny, very nice, as usual.' Despite everything she has achieved on court, she joked later that 'I think now I'm good in my tennis career.'

Jabeur, usually one of the most effusive of talkers on the circuit, was almost dumbstruck in his presence. 'I couldn't say anything,' she said. 'I was, like, admiring and looking at him. My team wanted to take a picture with him, so he was like, "Oh, sorry, I'm interrupting your stretching." I was like, "You can interrupt whenever you want, you know."'

A lot is said about Federer's presence, the aura he possesses. It's palpable in the way he walks. And much like many of the greatest sportsmen and sportswomen in history, you can almost tell he is in the room even before you see him, people scattering out of the way as he makes his way through, laughing and joking, as he has done since he was a teenager. 'He doesn't go unnoticed,' Jabeur said. 'You can feel the energy. You can feel how great he is. And I was one of the people that just looked. I didn't even say hi. It was rude, you know, but I was speechless, like, Roger Federer is coming by. Everybody didn't say a word and he had to say hi to everyone, which was very nice and humble of him. That happened a couple of times because the way he comes by [means] everybody becomes speechless for some reason.'

Matteo Berrettini, Italy's finest
'Thanks for the tennis lesson'

When Matteo Berrettini was growing up in Rome, he dreamed of one day becoming a tennis player and emulating his favourite stars. A strong young man, he was drawn to the power of Rafael Nadal. But as a youngster building a game style, he focused on Roger Federer. 'I was a kid and I had to pick between him and Rafa,' Berrettini said. 'Rafa was lefty and Roger had a one-handed backhand. And I was like: "Oh, I like how this guy plays. It looks, like, really easy."'

Looks can be deceptive, of course. Like a swan doing all its work under water, Federer's game style is a combination of natural talent and hard work. Like all champions, Federer put the hours in off the court and on it. Then, having already been dominant, he adapted as his rivals forced him to improve. Berrettini saw that he had a gift in making things look easy. The Italian soon realised, though, that getting to that point of serenity had been a long process. As the saying goes, 'Hard work beats talent when talent doesn't work hard.'

'Growing up, I started to realise what they actually were doing to be that great, not just on court but off court and the stuff they were saying, their behaviour and everything,' he said. Berrettini continued to admire Nadal and the likes of Djokovic and Murray. 'I started to be big fans of all of them because I think when you're having such a successful career, in all senses possible, like off court, on court, you're doing so much for the sport and for the people around you, I think you're just an example for everybody. And actually the time that I got to know them, I was an even bigger fan because they are really nice guys. But then I had to switch my mind off and say, OK, now they're my opponents. So I had to feel that I wanted to beat them.'

In 2021, Berrettini reached his first Grand Slam final, at Wimbledon, with only Djokovic stopping him from clinching glory. Success came relatively late for the Italian, who, as a junior, was considered good, but not exceptional. When the Italian player-turned-coach, Vincenzo Santopadre, was asked by Berrettini's father to take a look at him as a 14-year-old, he was realistic, not promising anything. It has taken time, but as they forged one of the best coach–player relationships in tennis, Berrettini went from strength to strength.

Inspired by Federer as a teenager, his personal relationship with the Swiss began in 2015. Aged 19 and still ranked outside the top 500, he was in Rome for the Internazionali BNL d'Italia – the Italian Open – hoping to get a hit with one or two players. He struck the jackpot when he was called on to practise with Federer. It was the first time he had met him and the memory is still fresh. 'It was 2015 and I was his sparring partner for the semis and the final in Rome,' Berrettini said. 'I remember, we played probably for 25 minutes and I was sweating like I had played for three hours. For him it was really easy to do anything on the court. It was nice because his team called me back for the final. It was a nice memory.'

Four years later, Berrettini found himself in the fourth round at Wimbledon for the first time, having just broken into the world's top 20. His opponent was Federer, the first time he had come face to face with him in a competitive match. It didn't go quite the way Berrettini would have liked, his 6-1, 6-2, 6-2 defeat as one-sided as it sounds. 'Thanks for the tennis lesson,' Berrettini told Federer. 'How much do I owe you?'

It was a chastening experience but one that Berrettini believes was instrumental in his tennis education. He rose into the top ten later that year and qualified for the season-ending ATP Finals for the first time. 'That was the first time that I was playing one of the Big Three and I was probably one of the biggest Roger fans,' he said. 'That's why for me, it was really tough to play against him, not because I didn't believe that I would do it, but because I was just, I couldn't believe what was happening. You know, two years before that, I was supporting him [when he won the title for the eighth time]. And then I was the guy that was trying to beat him on probably his favourite court, so it was a lot to handle. But at the same time, I learnt so much from that situation that next time I played him or I played Rafa, I was just more ready, I guess, I knew a little bit more what to expect from that situation and what to focus on and to avoid certain kinds of thoughts. The mindset was just better, I guess.'

At the media launch of the ATP Finals in London later that year, Berrettini shared a knowing smile with Tsitsipas as first theirs and then Federer's far longer list of achievements were read out. Drawn in the same group, Berrettini was beaten by Federer again but this time it was much closer, the lessons of that Wimbledon experience already seeping in.

Federer has also been helpful off the court, encouraging him in difficult times, like when he returned from injury in the summer of 2022. 'Roger, he's a special guy,' he said. 'He texted me after Stuttgart [where he won the title] and he told me great effort on grass and the comeback after the [hand] surgery. And last year [2021] during the Laver Cup, he came and we started talking about my match and what he saw on the court. He just told me what he saw and it was really nice because he loves tennis. He loves being around and he's following everything. And I think that's one of the great things about him, he just loves this environment.'

One way in which Berrettini has matched Federer is through his love of fashion. In 2022, the Italian became a global ambassador for Hugo Boss, a deal which represented the German clothing company's first venture into tennis. Like Federer, he looks good in a suit and the deal caused some to suggest he could be the next James Bond. Berrettini said Federer has led the way, when it comes to fashion.

'I think he was one of the first to bring fashion into tennis, with Nike and his outfits,' Berrettini said. 'I remember him walking on the court with kind of a suit on. But he could do it, you know, he could do whatever he wanted. He won [Wimbledon] like 20 times. He could walk naked if he wanted to. I think it's cool when you have the chance to do something, you know, that is cool and sporty, but also a little bit of fashion.'

Coco Gauff, rising star

'Enjoy the point, enjoy the moment'

Coco Gauff was just 13 when she decided to turn professional in 2017, shortly after reaching the final of the US Open juniors. Her choice of representation was an interesting one; she became the first female player to sign up for Team8, the agency Federer created with Tony Godsick, his long-term manager. Dedicated and talented, it was an indication of where Gauff saw herself in the future.

It proved to be a smart move. Not only did Gauff get the expertise of Godsick, who has been Federer's agent since 2005 and who worked with Monica Seles before that, but she also got the ear of Federer, something few people on Tour, especially on the women's circuit, have enjoyed.

Gauff was amazed at how much time Federer would spend listening to her questions, giving her tips.

'Growing up, he wasn't like a player I really watched,' she said. 'I was really focused on the women and focused on Serena and Venus growing up. But I would say when I started playing juniors is when I really appreciated him. I mean obviously I know who he is and what he's done and what he did in the game, but how kind he was to me, even from such a young age when I was, quote, unquote, a "nobody", and this guy is like the biggest guy in tennis, and he's taking time out of his day to talk to 13-year-old me, not for just ten minutes but for a whole hour sometimes, on FaceTime calls, to talk about tennis. I think he has done it for other players as well. I'm sure other players can speak to that too.'

Gauff shot to fame when she beat Venus Williams in the first round at Wimbledon in 2018, reaching the fourth round on her debut as a 15-year-old. The American reached her first Grand Slam final at the French Open in 2022 and there is a little of the Federer about her. Honest, open and forthright in her dealings with the media, she has a presence. Seeing Federer at Wimbledon and other events has been fun for Gauff, while having the ability to spend time bending his ear has been a huge advantage. When they chat, he gives advice but what shines through for Gauff is how much Federer enjoys being around tennis and tennis players.

'I think he genuinely cares,' she said. 'And speaking to him, you can tell how much this guy loves his sport. I mean, if you ask him about a match he played, however many years ago, he probably could tell you the exact thing that happened. He loves it. And, you know, seeing somebody at the top of their game genuinely care about the future of tennis is something that I appreciate. I'm glad that tennis has icons like him representing us.'

When Federer gives you advice, you listen. Unless, that is, when you're a teenager and you have a lot of other things on your plate. In that case, you remember it later on. For Gauff, one particular tip proved to be particularly beneficial. 'I would say the biggest advice for me and honestly, I spoke to him a couple of years ago about this, but really, it didn't hit until two or three years later until really [the 2022] French Open,' she said, smiling, when we talked on the eve of Wimbledon that year. 'He told me that you're playing every week and sometimes you're going to feel like you don't enjoy it. You're going to put too much pressure on yourself about winning every week. And it's impossible to win every week on Tour.'

Successful juniors, who have been used to winning titles more often than not, often find it hard to transition to the senior ranks, where the competition is far more difficult, more physical, more intense. Federer explained to Gauff how he felt as a teenager, how he too had that feeling that you need to win all the time. He said: 'I'm going to tell you right now, it's not going to happen.' I said, 'Of course, yeah, yeah, yeah,' but, you know, I didn't really think about that until after I lost in Madrid. And I was like, you know what? He's right. You're not going to win all the time. Whatever happens, happens, just enjoy it. Enjoy the point, enjoy the moment. And I really did do that and I've been trying to just not look too far ahead. I think that was the biggest thing I was doing [before], looking too far ahead and I wasn't even enjoying what I was doing.' Less than a month later, she reached her first Grand Slam final, at Roland-Garros. Just over a year later, she won her first Grand Slam title at the US Open.

Gauff has already shown that she is a remarkable young woman, not afraid to speak up on big, political issues. The speech she made in August 2020 at a Black Lives Matter rally in her hometown of Delray Beach drew enormous praise from inside and outside the tennis world, and she has continued to tackle contentious subjects, like gun control in the United States. Billie Jean King, who recognises a kindred spirit, believes she's a leader and so it's no surprise that Federer's suggestion, during the Covid-19 pandemic in 2020, that the women's and men's Tours should merge, struck a chord with the American.

'I think it's important, having an ally,' she said. 'I mean, I can't sit here and say that we don't need men to also help and speak out about this. You can't do everything alone. So having an ally and for him to be able to push women's sports is important. I also think he's a father, so he's probably thinking about his kids, too, as well. At the end of the day, equality in general is what I think we all want, or at least a majority of us want. So having somebody like him speak about it and also push it ... it's not easy to do in his position – you can choose not to do anything and others have – it's not like he was asked about this. He kind of went out on his own terms and did it. And I think that's incredible. I just love Roger.'

Honesty and being true to oneself also means a lot to Gauff. For her, that partly explains why Federer has been able to transcend sport. 'Honestly, I feel like he's 100 per cent genuine in everything that he says and does,' she said. 'There's people who say the quote, unquote, "right" things. But I think people can feel [if] they really mean it or not. And I think with Roger, you can tell that he really means what he says. For me he always says the right things but even if it's not the right thing, you can tell that he is genuine and his heart is genuine. I think that speaks for him as a person. I will never, ever say anything bad about Roger Federer because he means a lot to tennis and means a lot to me and a lot to the world in general.'

Anne-Sophie Mutter, star violinist
'He almost became a spiritual family member'

The stage of the phenomenal violinist Anne-Sophie Mutter is the world. Prague, Moscow, Madrid, Tenerife, Gran Canaria, Milan, Berlin, Vienna, Philadelphia, New York City, Pittsburgh, Hamburg, Chicago, Washington, Lucerne and Salzburg were just a few of her concert stops in 2022. And although other musicians usually surround her, the soloist can never hide from the anticipating audience, and she always has to be ready on the spot. 'At 8pm. Not half an hour later,' she said. 'That is when you have to bring everything you have practised or trained for to the stage or the court. That requires incredible focus and great mental strength. Like the ability to completely expose yourself then.'

Mutter is talking about herself, but she is also talking about Roger Federer, to whom she sees many parallels in her profession. The musician admires the tennis artist, met him in person, rooted for him enthusiastically over the years, and travelled to many tournaments with her son Richard. She witnessed several of his Wimbledon titles on-site on the most famous Centre Court.

One could also cite the virtuosity with which they handle their stringed instruments as a common characteristic of both stars: their artistic expression, their insatiable passion. And, of course, the fact that they were both destined for great careers at a very early age. Mutter sooner than Federer, who first had to shed his horns and find his inner balance as a teenager. Her extraordinary talent was apparent when she participated in her first music competition at the age of six. At 13, she made her debut at the Salzburg Whitsun Festival Concerts under Herbert von Karajan, and the famous conductor was impressed. The following year she made her first recording for Deutsche Grammophon, the renowned classical label, an album of Mozart's Violin Concertos No 3 and No 5.

'People always ask me what I had to do without in my childhood,' said Mutter, who was considered a child prodigy at an early age. 'I always say, "Rubbish!" I did exactly what I wanted to do – I wanted to play the violin! Just like Roger wanted to play tennis. Everything else was secondary for us.'

Besides music, Mutter, who grew up in Rheinfelden, Germany, was also interested in sports, especially tennis. 'It was my eldest brother's viewing hobby. And I, as his little sister, wanted to share as many things as possible with him,' she said. 'From boxing to tennis. From Muhammad Ali to John McEnroe and Björn Borg. Then I had a slump in my enthusiasm for tennis in the mid-90s. Roger then rekindled my fire.' Or, to put it better: he started a wildfire in her.

It began in 2003 with his first Wimbledon final. Because of her Swiss mentor Aida Stucki, who had taken her under her wing when she was nine, Mutter had always had an intimate relationship with Switzerland. And when a Swiss player suddenly excelled in tennis, she felt close to him. In 2004, she travelled to London with her ten-year-old son Richard for the final against Andy Roddick. 'Oh, how I remember those rain breaks; madness! That was our first live match at Wimbledon. Richard then started to play tennis as well. From that moment on, the TV was always on when Roger played. Before the concert, after the concert. And Richard always kept me up to date with the scores, even just before I went on stage. When Roger played well, I played well. He almost became a kind of spiritual family member.'

London became the favourite destination for Mutter and her young son to watch Federer. 'We have been to Wimbledon countless times and to the ATP Finals as well. That's where we especially liked to go because you feel close to the action.' She is a hot-blooded supporter, admitted Mutter with a grin. 'I'm much more emotional on the outside when I watch Federer play tennis than when I play the violin.' Among other highlights, she witnessed the marathon final of 2009 against Roddick at Wimbledon, when Federer won his favourite tournament for the sixth time.

The following week, Anne-Sophie Mutter was present when Federer was awarded the 'Ehrespalebärglemer' in Basel, a title that honours personalities who represent Basel internationally. Film producer and multiple Oscar winner Arthur Cohn had procured the invitation for her. 'I had the great pleasure of spending the evening with Roger. I was his dinner partner.'

Federer's heavily pregnant wife Mirka was at home, and he always had his mobile phone in sight so he wouldn't miss the possible onset of labour. Myla and Charlene were born five days later by Caesarean section. That evening when she met Federer in person was a memorable experience for Mutter: 'After the starter, I said to Roger: "I am a huge fan of yours, but there is someone who is even more passionate:

my son Richard. May I change places with him?" And he then spent the whole evening talking adorably with and interested in my 15-year-old son. I found that simply incredibly sympathetic, generous, warm and natural. Of course, that cemented our enthusiasm for Roger Federer as a person.'

Subsequently, she met the tennis virtuoso from time to time at smaller tournaments like Basel or Halle, where there was not so much hustle and bustle. She took great pains to be as unobtrusive as possible. 'In the interest of his mental and physical wellbeing,' she explained, smiling. 'I know millions of people want a piece of him. And I know how unpredictably passionate fans can be. How eager they are to be noticed and spend some moments with this person they admire not only for his great performance but also for his personality. Roger is someone who really engages with the fans. That's a great talent of his. Not all of us have the patience and strength to embrace that.' Of course, Mutter is also a world star, admired by many.

As an artist, she has always been particularly fascinated by Federer because of how he plays: 'He offers the whole range of artistic mastery, of almost impossible ease and precision. He doesn't play primarily with power but with a great deal of refinement, placement and strategy and always creates surprising moments. His extremely organic, beautiful way of playing is and remains a miracle. His touch, originality and individuality ennoble him compared to those who simply play fabulously. The expansion of his technical repertoire was something that made him interesting beyond other players. I'm just thinking of his serve, for example. It's not the fastest or the most powerful, but it's incredibly precise. This subtlety of touch is something you can only admire. And that's when I think to myself: training is one thing, but talent is also not to be dismissed altogether. And when you combine discipline with talent, you get an artist like Roger Federer. His way of playing evokes a closeness to art. The boundaries are fluid. What Federer is often able to call up in tennis is of an elegance and a personal imaginative power that carries something very artistic in itself.'

How Federer takes great risks with his way of playing and with his elegance and subtlety, she sees parallels with Jascha Heifetz; for many, the most outstanding violinist of the 20th century. 'And when he succeeds, those are moments in the flow, similar to making music.' Similar to what she sometimes experiences on stage. 'The flow state can not only be experienced by a tennis player or a violinist, but also by a writer or a gardener, for example. But in addition to this being-in-the-moment, with Roger and me there is the presence of spectators or listeners. That makes it even more magical. Because space, time and people become one in a way. These emotions you share with thousands on the spot make an experience or memory valuable.'

The words pour out of Anne-Sophie Mutter. And her sentences are ripe for quotation. Like few others, she can accurately describe her fascination for Federer and the similarities to her profession: 'As a musician, as an athlete, you first have to win against yourself; against your form on the day, against your fears, against your memory, against what might have been your last defeat on this court. All the doubts that can overtake a musician before a performance, or Federer in a semi-final, have to be eliminated at that moment. It's a lifelong process, especially for an athlete who plays in front of millions and whose performance is mercilessly measurable. It also happened to Federer that he had match points that he couldn't convert. And as a fan, you had to witness how a victory you thought was certain turned into a defeat. I am convinced that he has grown from it. His great love and joy for the game remained completely unaffected. Because on the court, he can realise things that seem impossible and experience a feeling we never find in everyday life. Not even as a happy family man or a mother of two children [in my case]. There is this everyday life, and then there is life in flow. The joy of sharing that with an audience.'

But how is her great love for Federer perceived in artistic circles, where sport tends to be laughed at? 'We are all Federer fans,' she said, adding with a smile: 'In my circle of friends, no one would dare not be a Federer fan either, though.' She has to admit, however, that she has come to appreciate his great rival Rafael Nadal much more over the years. 'In the beginning, I was a very stubborn Federer fan. But you have to let others count as well.' On the other hand, she could never really make friends with Novak Djokovic.

No matter who holds which records, Federer is the greatest tennis player for her. Because he is fascinating not only as a sportsman but also as a person: 'I always found it remarkable how gracefully he wins. He loses with decency anyway. But winning, not triumphing over others, but simply enjoying his performance is a great sign of human strength and class.' She never experienced a moment with him when she thought, what a pity, so much aggression! 'Then there is his work for the foundation he established early in Africa. A remarkable commitment already at such a young age. I couldn't have imagined a better role model for my son.'

She was also inspired professionally by Federer. Even after bitter defeats and weaker performances, he focused on the positive and worked undeterred. 'You can only learn from this constructive approach. Many young musicians suffer incredibly from stage fright. The only way out of it is great mental strength, focus, the ability not to blindly put the positive of one's performance in the foreground, but also to see it in difficult moments and hold on to it.'

She sees many similarities between the performances of artists and athletes: 'Tennis, for example, has not only the athletic moment but also this ingenuity and personal imprint. In the arts, in the performance of a musician on stage, for instance, one should not lose sight of the athletic component in addition to the artistic expression, which is immediately in the foreground. In this respect, there are also great parallels. The weighting is different. But the complexity of the components that come into play on an evening, in a concert as in tennis, is present in both professions.' And it is precisely the bringing together of different disciplines that fascinates her. 'There we are with the ancient Greeks, who saw sport, music and dance as essential to becoming human. If you combine one with the other, even if it's just a hobby, it's simply a great enrichment for life.'

Unlike her son Richard, she doesn't play tennis. Could Roger Federer, the tennis virtuoso, also be a skilled violinist? 'I would enjoy giving him lessons,' said Mutter. 'And with his one-handed backhand, I suspect he could become a downright ravishing violinist.' Federer has never attended a concert by Anne-Sophie Mutter. 'I can understand that with four children, he has more interesting things to do,' she said. 'But I would be insanely happy if he came one day.

And I'm sure I'd be nervous. That would be Sneak Attack by Roger, in a completely different way.'

Andri Ragettli, freeskier
'Now do it like Roger!'

In Aspen, Colorado, it was still dark on Sunday morning, 29 January 2017, when Andri Ragettli got up in the Swiss team flat and switched on the TV. The X Games had not gone as well as hoped for the 18-year-old freeskier and he and his colleagues would be heading off to California early in the morning for the next races. In Melbourne, 16 time zones ahead, it was already evening, and Roger Federer was playing against Rafael Nadal for the Australian Open title after his amazing comeback.

Ragettli had set his alarm for 3am to join the match right in the middle. 'I could still see the last two sets. When Roger was down 1-3 in the fifth, I was thinking, "No, not again!"' But then Federer took the last five games and his 18th Grand Slam title. While his colleagues got up in a sleepy daze, Ragettli rejoiced in front of the television. 'Roger hadn't won a Grand Slam title for almost five years. I couldn't have missed this final. And the way he came back at the end was great. That's my all-time favourite match.'

The freeskier let it spur him on. Two weeks later, at the Quebec City contest, he had landed the first jump in the Big Air but didn't get the score he had hoped for. 'My memory of the Australian Open was still fresh, and I said to myself: now do it like Roger! Instead of getting annoyed with the judges, you stick with it. You've got two more jumps. Stay cool like Roger. I landed the next two jumps with a high degree of difficulty and made it to the podium.'

He is not a tennis enthusiast, Ragettli said. But he took a liking to Federer. He began following him in 2012 – when he beat Andy Murray in the Wimbledon final and the Briton took revenge in the Olympic final a month later. At the time, Ragettli was 11 and dreaming of a career as an athlete. Growing up in Flims in the Grisons mountains, however, his career would take place in the snow, not on the court.

Ragettli is convinced there are parallels between the young Roger and the young Andri: 'I think I can understand quite well what made him tick as a youngster. He was very emotional on the court, went berserk, threw his racquets or smashed them. I was the same. I didn't have racquets flying, but ski poles and sometimes even skis if I didn't manage a trick I had been practising for a long time. Or if I messed up a run at a contest. I was very quick-tempered. It was either super-good or bad; there was nothing in between for me.'

Ragettli was impressed by Federer's transformation into a Buddha, who could no longer be unsettled by anything, on the tennis court. He had not experienced his transformation at the time, he was too young for that, but he had read a lot about it. He devoured several biographies about the tennis star. 'How he became such a calm, mentally strong athlete despite his temperament inspired me, and it made me deal with the subject of mental strength at an early age.'

As a young athlete, you need role models to show you the way, Ragettli is convinced. 'You don't understand the correlations yet, why you should do what. That's why other athletes who can guide you are enormously important at this age. For me, it was Roger. He managed to channel his emotions and became very successful. So I wanted to do the same.' To do that, he worked with a mental coach and read a lot about the topic.

Today he is much better at staying calm and focused, said Ragettli. 'There are still things that annoy me. There are certainly those with Federer, too. But I have become much stronger mentally. That is extremely important for us freeskiers. If you don't land the first run at the X Games or the World Championships, the second run is your last chance. If you don't stay calm and focused, you don't even have to try again. Of course, you are not happy if you mess up the first run. But that's why you have two. So: stay calm, take a deep breath, and concentrate. Sounds easy, but it's not.'

Ragettli is now one of the best freeskiers in the world. In 2021 he became world champion in Aspen; he has also won three times at the X Games in the disciplines Slopestyle and Big Air. He has become known for his crazy videos on Instagram, how he jumps off house roofs into the snow in his shorts, from bridges into rivers or does front flips on his skis while holding a glass with a chocolate drink. Federer once wrote him a direct message on Instagram, saying his children were thrilled with his tricks. Most of them, however, are not recommended for imitation.

Ragettli became a social media star thanks to his parkour videos in the sports hall from 2016 onwards, which generated over 80 million views. His acrobatic exercises also impressed Novak Djokovic, probably the most agile tennis player. The Serb put together his course and posted a video of it. It was not quite as impressive as Ragettli's but it did show Djokovic's excellent sense of balance. Federer refrained from such feats – it would probably not have been advisable for him to copy Ragettli in the light of his knee operations.

In the meantime, the man from the Grisons already has several million followers on various social media channels and numerous sponsors. In terms of sport and popularity, Ragettli has accomplished quite a lot. Thinking big, even though he comes from small Switzerland, is something he also learned from Federer. 'As a young freeskier, I was smiled at by some, and I would never achieve greater fame, they said. But I said to myself: "Roger is also a normal person and has made it so far in the world sport of tennis, so I will also make my way in my sport."'

He learned how essential idols are through Federer, said Ragettli, who got to meet him in person for the first time in June 2022 thanks to a mutual sponsor. 'Roger was a role model for me with his mental strength. And by becoming a world star as a Swiss. I think he can inspire people in very different ways. For me, it was those two things. But each and every one takes something different away from him.'

Michelle Gisin, two-time Olympic gold medallist
Tennis helped her through her most challenging time

As a child, Michelle Gisin says she never found tennis exciting. 'My whole family watched tennis, but I didn't like it.' She discovered her love for the sport through Roger Federer when she was 13. 'By now, I'm a bit addicted,' the two-time Olympic champion in the alpine combined said. 'I have become such a tennis fan that I watch almost everything. These days, even when Roger isn't playing.'

Tennis helped the alpine skier through her most challenging time as a professional athlete in the summer of 2021, when she was struck down by another nasty virus after recovering from Covid-19: mononucleosis. For almost two months, she was so exhausted that she could almost only lie on the sofa. Even short walks became torture for a woman who is otherwise a very active person. When she thought she was finally feeling better in the morning, she fell into a hole in the afternoon and felt like someone had pulled the plug on her. 'I watched an enormous amount of tennis during that time,' she said. 'It gave me so many emotions when I felt so bad.'

It's the mental aspect of tennis that she finds so fascinating. 'I find it brutal and at the same time incredibly exciting how you as a spectator can watch how an athlete collapses but then can also catch herself again. The development of a match over hours, all the ups and downs. It is important to take it point by point, no matter what. You still have a chance even if you're down two sets and 5-0. The mental aspect makes so much difference. And then you have Roger, Rafa and Djokovic, three players who are simply on a different level than everyone else. They have won almost all the Grand Slams for almost 20 years. That's just unbelievable.'

Her favourite match? She doesn't have to study long: how Federer capped his miraculous comeback by beating Rafael Nadal in the final at the 2017 Australian Open. For hours she suffered along in front of the television. 'For me, this is his most emotional title.' Two weeks later, at the World Ski Championships in St Moritz, she could hardly believe her eyes when this same Federer stood in the finish area in a white winter jacket and watched a professional ski race on-site for the first time in his life. Two days earlier, Gisin had won her first World Cup medal with silver in the alpine combined, and on the Sunday, in only her fourth downhill race at this level, she finished in eighth place with start number 28. An amazing performance.

'I was already on a high, and then I saw Roger standing there, and there was a huge buzz around him. I thought I might say hello for a moment and take a photo with him if I'm lucky. But it got much better. He chatted with me for quite a while, telling me about the Australian Open and how he had experienced it. He still watched highlight videos of that final and got chicken skin, he said at the time. And he told me that after his pause, he had doubted whether he would return so strong again. Hearing such things from him was fascinating.' Of course, Gisin was also allowed to pose for a photo with Federer, 'and my mum too. That was very important because my mum is a huge fan of his.'

She was even more impressed when he graced the Super-G on Lenzerheide in March 2022 on his doorstep in the Grisons mountains. 'I think that was the hardest speed race of my life. I almost couldn't stay standing anyway, and then Roger was standing in the mixed zone and everyone almost fell over. Watching how the race faded into the background with the athletes was funny because everyone was just extremely fascinated and excited that he took the time for them and the race. He was there until the last runner, taking photos with everyone and talking to every athlete. I was the last one still signing autographs. And Roger was still there. It was exciting to see first-hand how he deals with this hype. You can only imagine what it's like when everyone always wants something from you. And he handles it with such calm. This calmness, modesty and relaxedness are impressive.'

For her, something stands out about Federer, the tennis player; indeed, the person in general: 'His enjoyment of the game, his enjoyment of life in other ways as well. You get the feeling that he just loves it when he goes out on the court. No matter how difficult it is. What I find incredible about Roger is how he has maintained that joy over all these years in a sport where the wear and tear are so great, which can be so frustrating, such a struggle. And it's not as if he had easy opponents; on the contrary: with Rafa and Djokovic, he had two rivals who also made history. It was the most fiercely contested era. Nevertheless, with Roger, you always had the feeling he is all about the game, about the sport itself, and everything else is secondary. I find that brilliant. How he kept that joy of playing and his looseness.'

She functions similarly to him in this respect, said Gisin. 'That joy is essential for me. I have to stand at the starting line and think: "Wow, this is the most beautiful thing in the world!" I can't stand up there and say: "Now I have to win!" Or: "Now I have to have the perfect run!" Joy is the key for me, too.' And she said she first had to find out and accept that more is not always more. 'Training, investing more and more, and then you stand at the start, you're tired, and you can't build up that joy.' Missing out on a tournament once in a while and not chasing ATP points was always Federer's strategy and an important reason for his longevity.

As different as alpine skiing and tennis may seem, Gisin certainly sees parallels. 'Both sports are very demanding in terms of coordination. It's not just about strength, endurance or speed, but everything together. It's very complex.' To illustrate the similarities, she points to Jannik Sinner from South Tyrol, who skied successfully in his youth before committing to tennis. And when it comes to mental strength, she has learned a lot from watching the best tennis players. Check off, and always look ahead. Take it one point at a time, or in her case, one run at a time. She did this excellently at the 2022 Olympic Games in Beijing when she came up with a superb slalom after a patchy downhill run to win Olympic gold in the alpine combined, just as she had done in Pyeongchang in 2018.

As for her tennis skills, they are still modest. But in the meantime, ambition has taken hold of her. 'I had tennis lessons once as a child, but since then, I've only played sporadically and not very well. But now I have retaken tennis lessons. And the nice thing about skiing is all the sports you do alongside it are good for you. It shouldn't be too dangerous, but most of it is harmless compared to skiing. As far as tennis is concerned, I thought, enough is enough; now I want to learn it properly.'

What Gisin has also firmly resolved to do is to experience the Grand Slams as a spectator on-site. 'I'm not a fan of bucket lists. But I have three things I want to experience. The most important thing is to travel to all four Grand Slams. In addition, I would like to experience the Four Hills Tournament in ski jumping and watch ski flying one day.' Her favourite Grand Slam is Wimbledon: 'I have to go there. But I want to take my time then. That's why it hasn't worked out yet.'

As a youngster, Federer rode fast in the snow but didn't want to jeopardise his tennis career and didn't ski again for more than 20 years. If he ventured back onto the slopes one day, would Gisin bring him up to speed and teach him how to carve? She laughed. 'I'm sure he'll quickly get the hang of it. It has become easier with carving skis. But I'm a terrible ski instructor. I have no patience and focus on too many things at once. But sure, if Roger wants to, I would join him any time.'

Marc Krajekian, cancer survivor
'Roger made him feel very special'

It was a gloomy Sunday in March 2016 in Charlotte, North Carolina, and the mood in the Krajekian family matched it. 'Marc had one of the worst days of chemo,' his mother Marie-Jo recounted. 'He had been so positive throughout the treatment for almost a year. But that day, he was lethargic, tired and negative.' He felt down, had no energy, said Marc himself.

The year before, the young tennis enthusiast had been diagnosed with a rare type of cancer in his right ankle: Ewing sarcoma. When the pain first appeared, the family thought it was a sports injury. But it just didn't get any better. After closer examinations, doctors diagnosed the life-threatening disease, a rare bone cancer primarily affecting children and teenagers aged 11 and up. At the time, Marc was eight. The little boy bravely submitted to the treatments. But on that Sunday, he was having a bad day.

Marc picked up a racquet at the age of four in the house's driveway for the first time. 'We got this little Wilson tennis net and started playing. And then I quickly got excited about it. So my mom put me into lessons, and I kept playing from there. And then I got into competing and got into matches and tournaments. So it meant a lot to me. I met many people with tennis, made many friends and have a lot of good memories.' Marc was so talented that tennis became more than a hobby. He trained at the Johan Kriek Tennis Academy in Charlotte, the academy of the two-time Australian Open winner [1981, 1982] from South Africa.

That Sunday in March 2016, Marie-Jo got a call from Daga, Johan Kriek's wife. She had dropped something off to them, she said. Marie-Jo went to the mailbox and saw a package from Switzerland, stamped with Swiss stamps. It was from Roger Federer. The tennis star had sent Marc signed fan articles: a headband, sweatbands for his wrist and a photo with a message: 'Get well soon, Marc, and tell me when you're ready, and I'll play tennis with you.' The Krieks, who know Federer's mother Lynette well because of their common South African origins, had asked her if Roger could send Marc a message of encouragement. 'Everyone knew we were big fans of Roger,' said Marie-Jo.

This surprise instantly blew away the sombre mood. Marc screamed with joy, ran around the house, to the neighbours, and told all his friends: one day, he would play with the great Roger Federer. 'For me, this was a big motivation to get better quickly and return to the tennis court as soon as possible,' he said. His mother added: 'I can't explain enough what this message did to us as a family and to Marc that Sunday. On a day when he was not well. What a twist of fate!'

Marc could undoubtedly use this encouragement. The major surgery was still to come for him. Together with his parents, he had decided to have his lower right leg amputated to get rid of the cancer for good. Otherwise, he would have risked the tumour spreading again. Moreover, to save the lower leg, additional operations would have been necessary to balance the two legs. Marc didn't think about it for long: 'I remember they had a little whiteboard in the hospital, and my mom was putting in two scenarios.

What would happen if I didn't amputate my leg, and what would happen if I did. And basic logic is if I cut off my leg, there will be some hard times, but over a short period, if I believe in myself and work hard, I can overcome all these things.'

On 24 May 2016, Marc said goodbye to his lower right leg and cancer. Instead of lamenting, his family and friends celebrated it as a victory. His mother said: 'We did not look at it as the day Marc lost his leg. No, that day Marc was beating cancer.' On the same day, his tennis team participated in a local tournament, and they all wore green shirts that said: 'BYE BYE CANCER!'

A few weeks after the operation, he received a prosthetic leg, and in the summer, he returned to the tennis court for the first time. And how did it feel? 'It was a bit different, but at that time, I had gotten used to my artificial leg, so it started to feel very natural. It took me a little while to get used to the movements, moving from side to side, forwards and backwards. But with time, it became natural.'

On his return to the court, he received support from Roger Crawford, the first and so far only athlete who had made it to the highest level of college tennis despite disabilities in his legs and arms. Crawford could understand how Marc must feel, as he is missing his left lower leg due to a genetic defect. Crawford also put Marc in touch with the Scott Sabolich Prosthetic & Research Center in Oklahoma City, which developed a custom prosthesis for Marc that allowed him the mobility he needed in tennis.

So Marc indeed managed to return to his former tennis team. The proud mother said: 'And really, it was a miracle that he could go back and join the same team, and he would beat kids taller than him. With this leg. And he insisted on wearing shorts and showing off to the world that with his leg, he can still compete and play.'

Meanwhile, the Tennis Channel had become aware of the story of this remarkable boy. 'The crew visited us in Charlotte and interviewed us for three days,' said Marie-Jo Krajekian. At the very end, she said, 'There's one more piece of information that maybe you'd like to look into.' And then she told of Federer's promise to play with Marc when he was back on his feet. It was fitting that Roger's former coach Paul Annacone works for the Tennis Channel. Annacone was thrilled when he heard about it and offered to arrange it if possible. He promised to approach Roger about the matter at Wimbledon 2017. Roger was in a good mood, won the All England Championships that year without losing a set, and agreed to take part.

In early September that year, the Tennis Channel crew invited the Krajekian family to the US Open, hoping the meeting would take place on the tournament's sidelines – however, without promising it. Because tennis tournaments are unpredictable. Even for Federer. On 5 September, the time had come. Paul Annacone invited Marc and his parents to the practice courts. The cameras of the Tennis Channel crew did not leave their side to capture the magical moment. Marc recalled: 'We were walking to the courts, and then I saw a big, tall guy. It was Roger. I couldn't believe it at first. We came closer and closer.' So many times he had seen the tennis virtuoso on TV, and now he suddenly faced him.

Federer was completely relaxed, even though he had later to play his round of 16 match against Philipp Kohlschreiber. He hugged Marc, chatted with him, gave him more signed fan merchandise and even played with him. One point that Marc will never forget: the two played balls back and forth, accompanied by the applause of the spectators, until Roger played a short ball and got lobbed by Marc. 'He learned that from Roger, from all the hours he spent watching him on TV,' his mother said.

'Roger was very nice,' Marc looked back. 'It was only a couple of hours before one of his matches and he gave me advice for my tennis and life. He motivated me a lot. And he even gave me one of his racquets.' His mother is still raving today: 'We couldn't believe Roger was hitting balls with Marc. No athlete in the world would do that shortly before a big match. He was so spontaneous. We savoured every second of it.' The Krajekians flew back the same evening, full of positive emotions. And Federer easily won his match against Kohlschreiber in straight sets.

After his match, Federer said about his encounter with Marc: 'I think making a dream come true for other people is something that I'm in a privileged position to be. I'm his big hero, apparently. He looked to me in difficult times. It's nice to meet these people or this little boy finally. I'm happy I was helpful without knowing it, you know. Then for me also it's a nice moment, you know, to meet someone like him. I played some balls with him, which was even better. I wanted to make sure he got the full treatment, the best experience possible. I hope he enjoyed himself.'

You can certainly say that. 'It was such a wonderful experience,' said his mother Marie-Jo. 'We spent three days in New York and met so many people even before we met Roger. We got the chance to meet all the Tennis Channel guys, Martina Navratilova, and all the presenters. Everybody was very nice. They even took Marc to where they do all the videoing. They were doing all this, trying to build up for Roger, finally meeting him. They were praying that this would happen. Paul Annacone played a vital role. He said: "I've got to make this happen for Marc because of how much he loved Roger." Marc's story got known through Roger; the admiration that Marc got through Roger was immense.'

Consequently, young Marc also came to the attention of Ivan Corretja, the brother of two-time French Open finalist Alex, who also lost a lower leg and played with a prosthesis. During the Barcelona Open, Ivan Corretja arranged for Marc to hit balls with Rafael Nadal in the spring of 2018. 'Roger was more laid-back, Rafa was more energetic. Two different personalities, but they were both very nice,' said Marc. And they both gave him the same advice: 'Just have fun playing tennis.'

Over time, however, Marc lost some joy in tennis and turned to boxing with the same dedication. He said: 'I think I did a lot in tennis, and tennis has done much for me. So it was time for a new challenge in my life. Let's see where it goes. Like tennis, boxing is a confrontational sport; it's also tough and physically demanding. In boxing, you need excellent footwork too. Tennis has helped me greatly with my hand-eye coordination and my reflexes.'

The family has since moved to Boca Raton, Florida. Marc attends high school and sometimes devotes several hours a day to boxing – with a personal instructor. 'I think that if I can become very good at a sport that is one of the most physically demanding sports, it would inspire many people that nothing is impossible,' he said. 'I'm doing things that most people, even with two legs, cannot do. So I think that's what motivates me to do that.'

He was encouraged by Roger Federer on his way to becoming the best he could be. The tennis star is aware how lucky he has been and that he can make a big difference with a small gesture. Marc's mother said: 'Roger made him feel very special, that he's not just any child that went through something difficult. He did not know this would be in the media. It was a great gesture to help a child at a critical time.'

Marc now has a clear view of his fate: 'I think everything happens for a reason. It opened many doors for me and changed my life in a good way. It taught me life lessons that I would have never learned if it didn't happen to me. I learned so many things, and it changed my mindset about life and kept me pushing forward.'

Just as Roger Federer is an inspiration to many, Marc Krajekian wants to become a role model for others: 'I think I was meant for this to happen to me. So I can show other people in the world that if you put your mind to something, nothing's impossible.'

ROGER, THE PEER

FOR THOSE who played at the same time as Roger Federer, there are two ways of looking at things; either they were blessed to be playing in the same era as one of the best ever to pick up a racquet, or it was a curse to always be compared to a man who was changing the sport in front of their eyes.

What characterises all those who played in the same era as Federer, however, is that they learned from him. Whether it be Grigor Dimitrov, who suffered from being called 'Baby Fed' in his younger days, or Thanasi Kokkinakis, who felt honoured to be asked to train with Federer in the off-season and learned from him so well that he beat him when they played on the ATP Tour.

All of his peers have seen how he conducts himself, on court and off, in press conferences and in his media and sponsor commitments, and taken a little bit from everything they've seen.

In some cases, as with the Ukrainian, Sergiy Stakhovsky, they even managed to beat him once – at Wimbledon, of all places. But what they all shared is being able to gain an insight into what made one of the greatest players of all time tick.

Seeing Federer in the heat of battle, on the court and behind the scenes, changed the way they saw themselves.

Pat Rafter, twice US Open champion

'I knew he'd be good. I didn't know he'd be this bloody good'

Pat Rafter is one of the few tennis pros who does not know what it's like to lose to Roger Federer. Rafter and Federer played three times on Tour, with Rafter coming out on top every time. It's a record the Australian should be proud of, but he admits he got a little lucky.

The first time they played was at the French Open in 1999. At the time, Rafter was the world No 3 and the reigning US Open champion. Here he was, taking on a youngster he knew little about. Thankfully, his compatriot, Lleyton Hewitt, had played Federer a lot in the juniors and warned Rafter to be on his guard.

'Lleyton just said: "This guy's pretty good",' Rafter said. 'Him and Lleyton played a lot at junior time. It was interesting just watching him play. Obviously clay's not my best surface but he was young and I was really expected to sort of give him a bit of a towel up. And, you know, I struggled. He got me the first set and then I just got in his face a bit and then he went to water. He was working with Peter Lundgren at that stage. I spoke to Peter after and he said he was really pissed off because Federer was pretty soft mentally.'

Like anyone moving from juniors to seniors, Federer was finding the transition hard. From winning most weeks, suddenly he was being beaten by older, stronger players. He was not enjoying himself. Rafter had been through something similar himself. 'I remember going through it for a couple of years as well, just dealing with losses and dealing with your emotions on the court,' he said. 'It was part of his growing up and development. I got him early when he had those limitations in his game. He was fighting his own demons on the court and how he was going to become a good player. But I remember telling some people, "This guy's going to be bloody good." I didn't know how good, didn't think he'd end up this good.'

Soon after, Rafter got to know Federer a little more. Having been coached by Peter Carter as a junior, he seemed to gravitate towards Australians and enjoyed their company. Rafter and the Aussie players accepted him and they'd share time together on Tour. 'It was just in the early days, he'd be around, if he wanted to come hang out with us and have a few drinks, he was a pimple-faced little kid who had a smile and just enjoyed people and learning the ropes on the Tour,' Rafter said.

'We had a group of Aussie guys, we had a lot of fun too. We worked hard and played hard. There was a time when he was just trying to find his little group and his own tribe as well. There weren't a lot of players from Switzerland. Whenever we saw him he was a good kid, fun. And then when I retired and I caught up with him every now and then, he'd say, "Oh, come for dinner." It was really nice, he would just take us out for dinner, myself and my wife, Lara, at the Aussie Open or overseas somewhere if we were there. Obviously, he was in a whole different stratosphere by then as well, but he's always been really grounded and really humble, in my opinion. You talk about his influence around the world. We're talking probably the top three most recognisable athletes in the world, him and the soccer players, [Lionel] Messi and [Cristiano] Ronaldo, he'd have to be up there.'

The next time he played Federer was in 2001, in the quarter-finals of the Miami Open. Federer had won his first title earlier that year, in Milan, and was improving, fast. He beat Thomas Johansson to set up a clash with Rafter but the Aussie won easily. 'He was starting to get there, but he still had too much respect for the players,' he said. 'He was still grappling with that.'

The third time they played, things had changed. 'So it wasn't until we played again the week before Wimbledon in 2001 [in Halle, Germany] where you could just say: "Oh shit, here he goes, this is when he's going to start."' Rafter won in a deciding-set tiebreak but knew things were changing. 'He had match points on me and for whatever reason, I got through all that,' he said. 'And then he beat [Pete] Sampras the next week at Wimbledon, which allowed me and Goran [Ivanisevic] to get to the final.'

Federer lost to Tim Henman in the quarter-finals, unable to come down quickly enough from the high of beating a seven-time champion in his back garden. Rafter ended up losing one of the all-time great Wimbledon finals to Ivanisevic. For him, it's the one that got away. 'I think I lost the match in the end,' he joked. 'I can't remember, I still haven't come to terms with that.'

Anyone who has seen Federer in a press conference will know how well he deals with his media commitments, how he always tries to come up with something interesting, even if he's been asked the same question a thousand times before. For Rafter, who was also one of the most honest players with the press, it's one of the reasons he's become so loved around the world.

'We know that with certain tennis players and certain athletes, you just can't really warm to them as much as other people,' he said. 'Roger, you could look at him and say, he's a little bit one-dimensional, robotic, but he has an aura and a presence about him. Because he doesn't show a lot of emotion on the court, you don't get that feedback sometimes, but he has a presence that is hard to describe. He goes about his business, he does it gracefully.

'He's humble. I think he is so articulate when he gets into the press conferences that you get that feedback as well. And you then get to know him as a person, because he gets asked curly questions sometimes. He doesn't flinch, it's not his native tongue and he can just rip something out, perfect and you go, "My God, how composed is this guy?" But he's not putting it on. It's a quick reaction. It's natural. I think being honest and being honest with yourself, that comes across pretty well in the media. I think he's always done that and maintained that. I think that's why people love him. I try and tell people that, too, if you are honest, they'll forgive you as well.'

Enormously popular in Australia, Federer would struggle to walk down a street without being accosted by well-wishers. It's a phenomenon only the very best, most charismatic and outgoing sports stars enjoy and it is an experience many shy away from. It's a big change from the early days, when he was happy to hang around with the Aussies and have a beer. 'I think probably to a degree, he might miss those times, just being another person in the crowd,' Rafter said. 'Obviously, Switzerland is a small country, there's nowhere he could go where he could be discreet. I don't know where he can escape it. But he certainly wouldn't escape it down in Australia and certainly in England, he's not going to get away from you. There's not a person in Australia that wouldn't have heard the name Roger Federer.'

How he has handled himself, in spite of the fame, has amazed Rafter. 'That's a really great reflection on his mum and his dad, I think they've done a terrific job with him,' he said. 'He's his own man with his own family, but he'll never change who he is. He'll always give time to people. There is not a degree of arrogance, there's a degree of aloofness right now, because he has to be. You just can't engage everyone that wants a piece of him. It's just part of the world that he has to live in. And I get that.

'But he's still one of those people that transcends the sport. He is his own brand, and outside of that, everyone knows the name Roger Federer. How many people can put a face to that name? I don't know, but I would say a pretty high degree of people would know who he is.'

Rafter captained Australia's Davis Cup team from 2010 to 2015 and saw Federer at first-hand when the two countries met in a play-off tie in 2011. Famously laid-back, Rafter picks and chooses his time to be around tennis but in 2017, when Federer played Nadal in the Australian Open final, he could not resist taking a sneak peek. 'I was down there doing some work and I walked down to the court and just hid in the corner and watched them walk on the court just to hear the crowd,' he said. 'It was pretty unreal. They hadn't been in the final for three or four years, here they are now playing each other, it's the hottest ticket in town, no one could get a ticket. I walked down to the court and then Craig Tiley [the tournament director] said, "Do you want to sit and watch the match?", and I went: "No, I'm going home. I'll sit and watch it on TV." I don't like sitting down to watch tennis. I like to be able to get up, grab something to eat, move around or do a stretch or something like that but I can't sit in one spot for five hours. I'll go crazy. But it was an incredible match. I really enjoyed watching those guys play.'

Having retired from tennis at 28, Rafter finds it hard to understand the motivation Federer had for playing tennis into his 40s. 'I find these guys that keep playing, beyond their best, really remarkable,' he said. 'And when you are that good, it's hard to ever write them off. The press and media, they've been writing him off for ten years. And they come back after four years and go winner, winner, winner and you go: "Holy shit, where did that come from?" It comes from being the greatest of all time. There aren't many of those people so you can never, ever write them off.'

James Blake, former US No 1

*'When I was at my best, I felt I
could beat anyone. Roger showed me
I couldn't'*

James Blake could be forgiven if he really loathed Roger Federer. In the 2000s, he was one of a group of American players coming through at the top level, all with dreams of winning Grand Slam titles. The fact that Andy Roddick, who won the US Open in 2003, was the only one of them to break through can be put down in large part to one man: Federer.

And yet Blake, who lost to Federer three times in Grand Slams, bears no grudge. 'There's so many ways to look at it,' he said. 'You know, you're so happy to be associated with one of the greats of all time. But you also know that if he had been injured for a couple of years in the middle there, then Andy and I might have gotten a couple of slams. For Andy, he got the 2003 US Open and then in 2004 Roger became Roger. If he had become Roger one year earlier, then we might be talking about Andy, the four-time Grand Slam finalist and never a winner. It's tricky, but Andy was also a couple of points away from possibly winning [Wimbledon] too and beating Roger. For Andy, I'm sure it's even trickier because those couple of points here and there really were trademarks of his career.'

Remarkably, Roddick remains the last American man to win a Grand Slam. Blake reached three slam quarter-finals, losing to Federer in two of them. His loss to the Swiss in the 2006 US Open, when he was beaten in four sets, was perhaps his best chance. 'If there was no Roger Federer in the world, I think it would have been myself and Andy in the finals,' he said. 'We had just had a three-set, 7-6 in the third thriller in Indianapolis a couple of weeks earlier and I think the US Open final might have been the same but there was Roger and he squashed both of our hopes and dreams there [he beat Roddick in the final].'

And yet Blake found himself feeling strangely pleased for Federer, even though he had dashed the hopes of a home champion again. 'If you're going to lose to someone, at least you're losing to the best and you're losing to someone that also you're happy for,' he said. 'That's the way I always felt with Andy, you know, if I'm not going to win, I hope he does. And if I'm not going to win and Andy's not going to win, I hope Roger does. He's just that nice of a person. It was frustrating to play him. But what can you do?'

For Blake, Federer was a nightmare to play. Though he did have one win over him – an important one, in the quarter-finals of the 2008 Beijing Olympics – he lost ten of their 11 encounters. 'When I retired, I absolutely would have said he's the best of all time,' he said. 'Whether or not that ends up being that way, with the results and with the slam totals and everything else, it doesn't look like it will be. But I still have him as my toughest opponent ever.'

The fact that Nadal and Djokovic will finish with more slams than him doesn't change how Blake felt when he was playing him. 'It was brutal,' he said. 'The thing people don't recognise is how much of a killer he is on the court. As much as he's nice and friendly and great off the court, you don't get to achieve what he achieved without being an absolute killer. And for me, it was tough because it was the worst match-up. That's why I think of him as the greatest, because everything I did, he did a little better. When I was at my best, I felt like I could beat anyone in the world. And then he showed me that I couldn't. He showed me there a couple of times when I could play my best and I still couldn't beat him. And I felt like, honestly, at that time, he was the only one who made me feel that way.'

Blake's affection for Federer was enhanced after he broke his neck in an on-court accident in Rome in 2004. 'When I was in the hospital, I got one note from a player,' he said. 'It was the No 1 player in the world, Roger Federer, saying, "Wish you well, come back soon". No one else really thinks about taking the time out of their schedule, when they're trying to win a tournament. He really cared about all his competitors. He cares about the humanitarian stuff he does. And he's just the kind of guy that, if he wasn't one of the most talented athletes of all time, you'd want to go sit and have coffee. He's pleasant, he's nice to everyone. And it's just really refreshing to see. And it makes it difficult, honestly, for everyone else to compete with that, because you look and there's so many excuses; No 1 in the world, he's got to be arrogant, he's got to be kind of a jerk, he doesn't have time to do this. Somehow Roger makes time for everyone. It's really incredible.'

Blake has witnessed Federer signing autographs for an hour after a practice session. He's seen how much time he gives at sponsor days, how he focuses on the people he is with and takes an interest in them. 'That's the reason as well that every sponsor lines up to be affiliated with him,' he said. 'You ask him for four hours and he'll give you six. You ask him to do an hour autograph session, he'll be there for two. That's so rare in top athletes.'

He also marvels at how Federer was able to switch from family man in the minutes before a match to a destroyer on the court. 'You can be talking to him in the locker room before you go out, saying: "What are you up to?" "Oh, Mirka and the kids, they're going to do this. They're playing nice. And what are you up to?" "I just moved here." "OK, great." And then he goes out and he absolutely smokes you. And then after the match, he's like, "Oh, man, that was a good match." I was like, "Well, for you, yeah, it was great."'

When Federer, recovering from more knee surgery, returned to Wimbledon in 2022 to take part in the Centre Court centenary celebrations, he received the loudest ovation of all. Blake was watching behind the scenes in the ESPN green room and was struck by how others perceived Federer. 'Everyone joked that James Bond was coming in,' he said. 'It's just his aura. My wife was there with us, too … she doesn't know him very well, she's met him a few times, but she said: "There is just something about him." He belongs in the Royal Box, but then he'll sit out with everyone else and he's out watching his agent's son play. He belongs in the Royal Box but he's also comfortable everywhere else. It's pretty cool.'

Jarkko Nieminen, friend and victim

A night to remember, thanks to Roger

Jarkko Nieminen enjoyed practising with Roger Federer and did so frequently. The two have known each other since they were 14 and became instant friends as talented teenagers on the junior tour. As one of the best left-handed players, the Finn has been an ideal training partner for Federer over the years to get him ready for the ultimate challenge, Rafael Nadal. They once practised at the tournament in Shanghai, and Nieminen can still remember what happened afterwards. 'Roger asked me if I wanted a ride back to the hotel with him. I always took the tournament shuttle, but the top players got a ride in a car. Of course, I gladly agreed.'

When he left the grounds with Federer and the fans caught sight of the Swiss, there was a massive buzz around him. They shrieked and tore around him; everyone wanted to take a selfie with him or get an autograph. 'You can't imagine what was going on around Roger,' Nieminen said. 'But he stayed completely calm and fulfilled all the requests. Even though everyone would probably have understood if he had cut short. When we finally got into the car and drove away, people almost climbed on top of the car. They were so excited. Those were unbelievable scenes.'

Only two weeks older than Federer, Nieminen was up close and personal with Federer's career until his retirement at the end of 2015. 'From the age of 14 or 15, I followed his career from those years on, winning everything, breaking records, playing the same tournaments as me for 20 years and becoming one of the biggest superstars in sports globally. And I still saw him as the same guy who I met in junior tournaments. He had the same great sense of humour and was still so much a down-to-earth guy. Everybody respects his achievements or takes them for granted. But I respect him even more as a person. It's awe-inspiring how he hasn't changed at all.'

How does Nieminen explain that? 'It comes down to his extremely nice parents from his values at home. I think he never valued himself based on how much he succeeded in tennis. The losses or the wins. Even though you would imagine it would be easy to do that when you are a global superstar. But he's still the same Roger, and it doesn't matter if he wins five Wimbledons or loses in the first round.'

In this respect, he was similar to Federer, said Nieminen. 'I am not comparing my career to his. But it also helped me never to measure myself as Jarkko, the tennis player. I was always the same guy, and it didn't matter if I won or lost. Of course, my confidence as a tennis player went hand in hand with how I played. But my confidence on the court is not who I am.' It's something that every psychologist today advises young tennis players: not to make their self-worth dependent on winning or losing. It sounds simple, but it's not in this sport, where victories or defeats can have severe consequences and are always personal.

After his career, it helped him a lot that he managed to separate the two, Nieminen said. 'When I finished, many people asked me: "Was it difficult?" Because it's a big change. But I didn't feel empty when I stopped. If you build your identity based on your success, you might fall emotionally into a hole. I didn't have any problems in that respect. And I guess that Roger won't have any problems after his career, either knowing that he likes to do many other things and has a big family.'

As nice and unpretentious as Federer is as a person, he knows no pity on the court. Nieminen can tell you a thing or two about that. Ranked No 13 in the world at his best, he won just one set against Federer in 15 meetings. Only David Ferrer and Mikhail Youzhny (0-17 record) have played the Swiss more often without beating him. Nieminen said: 'Roger ruined many weeks for me. When I was playing well, he came from somewhere and beat me. Sometimes in the early stages of the tournament, sometimes later, like in the finals of Basel (2007). I've never found a way to beat him.'

Although he lost most of his matches against the other top players, too, no one made it as complex for him on the court as Federer. 'Because of our playing styles, I found it easier to challenge other top players like Nadal, Djokovic or Murray. When I played well, I could keep up quite a high pace and change it up. But my high pace wasn't enough to put him in trouble in the long run. And Roger is extremely skilful in changing the pace. So when I changed the pace, he did it even better by using his slice. He took my weapons away. When I was at my peak, I played smart and in very different ways. I changed tactics and the pace during the match. But Roger is so complete that he was always able to adapt.'

Did Nieminen still enjoy these matches against Federer? 'Absolutely. My goal was to see my limits in tennis, not to win some specific tournaments. I wanted to see how good a player I could be. How high I can reach. So there was nothing better than challenging myself against the best player in the world. Even though I lost every time, I have great memories of these matches. I know Roger well, and it was always a good, fair fight with him. A good attitude from the start until the end. No playing around, no roller coaster, just tennis. I enjoyed it in many ways even though I would have wished to beat him.'

Federer did not grant him this wish but another one. Nieminen knew early on that 2015 would be his last year on Tour. 'I had two options: wait and announce that would be it. Or do it as big as possible. And then I decided tennis had given me so much since I was a little kid, so let's do it as big as possible. And what's the biggest possible dream? To play against Roger at my farewell. I don't know how many hundreds and thousands of people ask him or his manager to do this and that.' But Federer said yes, and they agreed to schedule the farewell match for 10 November 2015, in the largest multifunctional arena in Finland: the Hartwall Arena in Helsinki.

'I was a bit nervous before the tickets went on sale. Of course, Roger is huge in Finland as well as around the world. But I thought it would be embarrassing if it didn't sell out.' His concerns were unfounded: all 15,000 tickets were gone in two hours. And Nieminen believes in retrospect that they could have sold 30,000 tickets. 'It was my farewell, but most people bought tickets because they wanted to see Roger.' By the way, it was the first ever trip to Finland for globetrotter Federer.

Nieminen still raves today when he talks about that evening. 'Everything was perfect. I can't thank him enough and all the spectators that were there. It's still hard to believe that it happened.' The evening began with a doubles match with the ice hockey greats Teemu Selänne and Peter Forsberg. Nieminen is a big ice hockey fan; he has it in his blood as a Finn. Federer is also fond of ice hockey, sometimes attending a game during his time at Swiss Tennis in Biel and once meeting Selänne in Indian Wells. Nieminen played with his compatriot, and they won the set of the warm-up doubles against the pairing Federer/Forsberg.

Nieminen had never played against anyone in his professional career as often as against Federer. Would he at least let him win in his farewell match? 'We didn't talk about the score before. We just said, let's try to play good tennis. Just go full and see how it goes. Luckily I could put some balls in; the court was pretty fast. I was able to do some damage, but it wasn't enough in the end.' Federer won 7-6, 7-6, but a small triumph remained for Nieminen: 'It was the only time I could walk on to the court after Roger. Obviously, the stars come after the underdogs. I was always the underdog. But because it was my farewell, I came second. It was so strange when they announced Roger's name before mine. I was thankful I could walk on the court after him for once.'

He never seriously considered a comeback. But if he had, he could only have lost, said Nieminen. 'Because I can't think of a nicer way to finish my career.' He has remained committed to tennis, now a father of three. 'Everything is still connected to tennis, which is great. I still love the sport as I always did.' He is the Finnish Davis Cup captain and looks after the development of the biggest talents for the association. He is still on the court several times a week. He also commentates on the four Grand Slam tournaments for Finnish Eurosport – mostly from Helsinki, but sometimes he is also on-site.

Like in 2019 at Wimbledon, when he took his grass shoes, racquets, white shorts and a white T-shirt because his colleague Thomas Enqvist was commentating for Swedish Eurosport and they hoped to hit a few balls on grass. 'Luckily, I took my gear because Ivan Ljubicic came up to me before the semi-finals and asked me if I could warm up Roger for the Nadal match. He needed a lefty for that match.'

Still in good form, Nieminen did an excellent job warming up Federer. The latter beat Nadal in four sets in a high-class semi-final and had two match points in the final against Novak Djokovic. Well, the rest is history. 'But I was happy that at least Roger won that day when I warmed him up.'

Nicolas Mahut, French doubles star
'I think he was born to win Wimbledon'

In some ways, Nicolas Mahut could be considered as a rival of Federer, having played in the same era and faced him four times. But the Frenchman thinks of himself as more of a friend, someone who watched him rise from a precocious but emotional teenager into the man he calls James Bond. A year younger than Federer, he followed in the Swiss's footsteps as a junior Wimbledon champion, in 2000, and harboured hopes of translating his junior success into the biggest titles at senior level. He became world No 1 in doubles in 2016 but he will forever be remembered for being part of the longest-ever match in Grand Slam history, his 11-hour, five-minute epic against John Isner in the first round at Wimbledon in 2010. It was a match Mahut lost but one that he will be associated with whatever happens in future, having switched to a final-set tiebreak in 2019.

Mahut witnessed Federer's transition into the best player in the world. 'At the beginning he was not that, like we call it, the James Bond guy,' he said, when we chatted at Roland-Garros. 'He had long hair and was a strong character on court. He was not controlling his emotions much. He was fighting for the world No 1 junior spot with Julien Jeanpierre, so I was watching matches and it was not the good attitude he has now. And then suddenly he changed. And when he changed, he changed for James Bond.'

Mahut played Federer four times, losing all four. The first time they played, at Wimbledon in 2006, Federer was already a colossus, a three-time champion there. He walked on to court with the now-famous beige jacket, and Mahut, trailing behind, was understandably anxious.

'I was so nervous,' he said. 'I think he was No 1 at the time. I was a little bit unlucky because we played on court one. I think it's one of the few times that he didn't play on Centre Court.'

As an unseeded player, Mahut was upstairs in the clubhouse while Federer, using the seeded players' locker room, was downstairs. 'He was waiting for me,' he said. 'And then we walked and the path from the locker room to court one is very long. When you have Roger in front of you, then you start to think. You start to think, "Am I going to win a few games? What is going to happen? I don't want to watch him too much because he's Roger." And at that time, I think it was when he was walking on court with the jacket. It was very impressive.' The crowd on No 1 Court went wild for Federer, as always. 'People were just waiting for him to come, just to see him,' Mahut said. 'I mean, the goal was just to see him playing.'

The match itself was fairly tight but Mahut said he never really felt like he could win it. 'I felt like he was always in control,' he said. 'I was playing a good match. He was in control all the time. I think it was like 6-3, 7-6 and in the third set, I think he was serving for the match at 5-3, and I broke him for 5-4. I didn't see anything on his face and then he breaks back again to finish the match and close it up 6-4. Like, you feel you want to win. I was with my coach trying to say: "OK, I know Roger, I know I can play on grass. Let's see what happens." You try to believe in yourself and try to win but you can see when you have him in front of you, he's moving, he's so smooth, he's fast, he knows when to push. He knows when he has the momentum, he has an answer to everything and when he decides to accelerate, boom. On grass, that's really impressive. It impressed me a lot.'

Federer won their next two encounters easily enough. The fourth time they met was at the French Open in 2012. Into the third round for the first time, Mahut had asked to play on the slightly smaller Court Suzanne Lenglen, instead of Court Philippe Chatrier, but was told: 'You're French, you're playing Roger, there is no option.' His nerves were fraying at the prospect of playing Federer but his anxiety was then eased by a surprise request.

'That day I was really nervous to play Roger,' he said. 'And then someone from the organisation came to me and said that the former president [Nicolas] Sarkozy, who lost the election in 2012, tried to reach you. At first I thought it was a joke. They said: "No, serious." So I went to one of the offices, talked to the president and I was really nervous to talk to him. Really nervous. And then I forgot about the match for a while. And I said, well, I feel relaxed now playing against Roger. And actually it was the best match I played against him.' Sarkozy had just wanted to wish Mahut good luck for his big match. For the record, Federer won in four sets.

In his book, *Ce Sport Qui Rend Fou* (The Sport That Drives You Crazy), another French player, Gilles Simon, has a chapter called 'The Federer Myth'. In it, he says Federer hurt French tennis because coaches in the country tried to build players in his image. Mahut disagrees with

Simon's main assertion, saying that no one tried to tell Simon to play like Federer. But in another way, he sees his point. Anyone trying to emulate Federer, he said, is doomed to failure.

'I understand what he meant but I was not 100 per cent with him,' Mahut said. 'But in one way he's right because when you try to do what Roger is doing, you can't. And the thing you don't see about Roger is the way he moves on the court. Everyone is watching the technique, the ability, forehand, backhand volley, but the way he moves and the footwork is very impressive. The balance is amazing. He looks very easy. I was talking to someone about this; he said: "You want to try to do like what Roger is doing," and every time I was saying the same thing, "It's a mistake to try to do what Roger is doing." For me it was better to try to look at what [Mikhail] Youzhny was doing or even [Stan] Wawrinka was doing. I watched much more Wawrinka than Roger and even though Wawrinka is a legend, you feel like it's something he learned and you can maybe try to do it. But with Roger, it looks so easy.'

Mahut experienced Federer's popularity first-hand. In all four of his matches with the Swiss, Federer received enormous support, even in France and even when France were trying to beat Switzerland in the Davis Cup final in 2014. 'I was not in the team then but it was amazing because people were supporting France but at the same time, they wanted so much for Federer to win the Davis Cup,' he said. 'It was a little bit embarrassing as a Frenchman, to see that. But every time he's playing here, at Roland-Garros, it's amazing. He is from Switzerland, so he speaks French. Here, you feel like he's almost home. When you speak French, it's like you are half French already.'

It's not just language that helps people admire Federer, according to Mahut. 'I think why people love him is the elegance on and off the court. I think he was born to win Wimbledon, honestly. He has the perfect game style, the personality, he's a huge star everywhere. When you go to South America, he's a star; when you go to Asia he's a star. But I think when it comes to Wimbledon, for me, the greatest tournament of tennis, he is where he belongs. And when you talk about tennis, when you talk about Wimbledon, the first thing that comes to mind is Federer. You can also think about [Pete] Sampras, [Björn] Borg, but the first one to come to mind is Federer.'

One of Mahut's most precious memories is of when he played with Federer. The pair joined up one time in doubles, in Brisbane in 2014, when Federer was looking for a few extra matches in the build-up to the Australian Open. For Mahut, it was a once-in-a-lifetime opportunity that he was never going to turn down. And even though doubles was Mahut's domain, he was nervous. 'I just wanted to learn everything that he could give to me.'

He need not have worried. 'He was very kind, he was very motivating,' Mahut said of Federer. 'We played the first two matches on centre court, full houses, we won two good matches.' Federer excelled in both but when it came to the semi-final, a match played on the smaller second court for scheduling reasons, Federer's level dipped.

'It was a totally different match because Roger is not used to being on a small court,' Mahut said. 'And the level dropped so much, from centre court to court one. I was very surprised, how good he can be on centre court – even though he's not playing doubles at all, he was of course the best player on court – but once we played on court one, he felt like it was too small. He was telling me, "It's too small, I don't have any rhythm on this court." But it's a great memory. I thank him a lot again for asking me to play. It was great.'

Anyone who's ever seen Federer behind the scenes will recognise the swagger with which he walks. Mahut said it was natural. 'Maybe in the beginning he tried to show something like, I don't know, different,' he said. 'But now he's like: "I'm Roger, I have 20 Grand Slams." Not in an arrogant way, but like I said, James Bond.'

While some French players have talked about Federer getting in their way of Grand Slam glory, Mahut has loved being part of the same era. 'I'm so proud I had the privilege to play my whole career with him,' he said.

And does it matter that he has ended up with fewer slams than Nadal and Djokovic? Mahut says no. 'I think the legacy of Roger you cannot compare to anyone that I've seen,' he said. 'I would be very interested to see the TV rights before and after Roger. It's a little bit like Tiger Woods in golf. Even though Novak has 21 slams (he now has 24, as of the end of 2023], there is no way he will ever reach the popularity of Roger. And he can't, at the end of the day, because when you look at golf, Tiger is number two in terms of majors. But for everyone, he's the greatest. He's like [Zinedine] Zidane, when he plays football. He's not the greatest but when he's on the pitch you want to see him play. Roger is Zidane.'

Mike Bryan and Bob Bryan, doubles stars
'It was an honour that Roger asked us for a favour'
Very few people know what it's like to be in the locker room before a Grand Slam final. In an era when Netflix and

Amazon documentaries have become commonplace, it's one of the last areas of mystery in tennis, a place and time where the greatest players in the world gather their final thoughts before stepping out to bid for one of the sport's biggest titles. It's where players can be seen at their most raw, their nerves on show, a time when confidence can be bravado, masking the fear beneath.

For Roger Federer, though, it has been a place of relative calm. Between 2003 and 2019, the Swiss played 31 slam finals, winning 20 of them. It is usually only a player's coach and their entourage who get to witness this scene but, occasionally, a few others find themselves there at the same time, like Bob and Mike Bryan, the American twins who dominated men's doubles for most of their career. Reaching so many finals and often playing on the same days at the end of events, they got a special view of what Federer and others go through. At times, they could hardly believe what they were seeing.

'He's got no ego,' Mike Bryan said. 'I've seen him before big, big finals, because sometimes we're in there with him. It's only a few guys. And he'll be laughing with his coach like it's a Sunday at the park, you know. If you think about it, there's a lot of history on the line, there's points, there's money. And he just somehow knows how to filter it out and stay in the present.'

Mike Bryan said he watched Federer closely. 'I've just loved being around the guy,' he said. 'I've learnt tremendous things from watching Roger just inside the locker room, on the court, in life. He has a grace and ease about how he goes about things, and he's not overthinking it. He is just super-relaxed; that's tough to do in this day and age where there's a lot of stress and there's a lot of distraction. And he has more distraction than anyone, right? And the way he goes about it, he's always calm and has a sense of humour and a great perspective. He's a great dude. No one has a bad word to say about Roger. He always takes time to talk to every player, even if he's got a match coming up, he'll sit there and ask you about your family.'

Bob Bryan said it was always obvious when Federer was around. 'He was always very loud in the locker room and he was yelling,' Bob said. 'You knew when Roger was hanging around, he loves to have a good time. I think he's still got that goofy personality. He's very silly, but he's definitely matured a little bit over the years for sure.' It seems Federer also liked the odd quiz, especially if it was about his career. 'We never grabbed dinners together, but we've had awesome conversations in the locker room,' Bob said. 'He has an amazing memory. He can tell you all the matches he's played and all his wins, he remembers everything. And he always takes the time to sign autographs; we've had charity items and you never feel scared to ask Roger if he would sign it, because he'll always do it.'

Bob Bryan played Federer in singles right at the start of the Swiss's career, in Marseille in 2001. He remembers him as 'an amazing talent, but a little more volatile'. 'I think he threw his racquet,' he said. 'He tightened up his mental skills and it took him to a new level. But at that time, he seemed very fiery, very volatile.'

In doubles, as the leading pair of their generation – they won 16 Grand Slam titles together and ended the year ranked No 1 a record ten times – the Bryans played Federer on a number of occasions and usually came out on top. 'He was always so dangerous,' Bob said. 'We could take advantage of the fact that he wasn't on the doubles court a bunch. We were so sharp in those strategies and skills that he was kind of learning on the fly, but he's one of those guys that if he dedicated himself to anything he would be successful.'

It was seeing the Bryans close up and knowing how good they were that also prompted Federer to ask them for a favour, one that helped him fill one of the few blanks in his résumé. In 2014, when he was trying to win the Davis Cup for Switzerland for the first time, Federer needed some help. He and Stan Wawrinka, who had won the doubles gold medal together in Beijing in 2008, had lost four of their previous five Davis Cup doubles matches and as they prepared to face France in the final in 2014, Federer was concerned that they might struggle again.

'He came to us and asked if he could use our coach, David McPherson, in the finals,' Bob Bryan said. 'He and Stan had some losses, three or four in a row, and they knew they needed to win that match to beat France. So our coach went and gave him a couple of tips and they executed with perfection and destroyed the French team. That just shows you how much talent and ability he has.'

Some people might not have wanted their coach to be used to help another team. Mike Bryan said they had no hesitation in saying yes. 'It's an honour just to have Roger ask for a favour,' he said. 'And if he does, we'd love to help him out. He just wanted to learn more about the strategy of doubles because he goes out there and he uses his talent, his athletic ability, but there's some more nuances that he used for his advantage there. And so that was cool to watch. He wanted to win the Davis Cup. It was kind of the last thing for him to do.'

In that final, held in France, Federer and Wawrinka beat Richard Gasquet and Julien Benneteau in straight sets before Federer, who had been nursing a back injury, saw off Gasquet the following day to give Switzerland glory. Even the French crowd seemed happy. It's a situation the Bryans know well. 'When you play against Roger, you know there's not going to be a seat in the crowd and they're all going to be pulling for him,' Bob said. 'So you've just got to enjoy the atmosphere because it's definitely a unique experience.'

Together, the pair also saw the reaction he creates around the world, from Grand Slam events or at the exhibitions they played with him in countries like Mexico and China. For Bob, the attraction is his game style. 'He'll play a match and he looks like he's just walked out there,' he said. 'He plays for five hours and there's not a wrinkle in his shirt. And his hair looks the same. It's just that effortless beauty of his game, everyone can appreciate it. If you're a parent, you can bring your kid to the match and say: "Learn from this guy." He's who you want to emulate.'

For Mike, it's the fact that he managed to stay the same throughout his career. 'He hasn't changed one bit with all the fame and success and money,' he said. 'He's just so humble. It's very rare in this day and age of social media and all that attention, people building you up, to just stay the same. That's why people love him. He's so down-to-earth. He's a human being. People look at him and they can learn from his behaviour and the way he handles himself in the thick and the thin.'

Grigor Dimitrov, Bulgarian built in Federer's image
'Come on Baby Fed!' – 'Do I look like a baby?'
Some people are able to go about their life largely how they want to, out of the spotlight, relatively untouched

by external pressure. Others have expectations heaped on to their shoulders from the moment they step out into the wider world. For Grigor Dimitrov, his blessing was a curse. Gifted with enormous talent – his late coach Peter McNamara once said he had ten choices for every shot – his curse was that his style of play, in particular his serve and one-handed backhand, were eerily reminiscent of Roger Federer.

The fact that he was mentored by Peter Lundgren probably didn't help on that score. But what really loaded the pressure was when he was called 'Baby Fed' early in his career. As Dimitrov rose up the ranks, the Bulgarian accepted the compliment with grace, but the novelty soon wore off. When he played Federer for the first time, in Basel in 2013, even the Swiss was calling for the nickname to be laid to rest. Dimitrov agreed but has had to live with it throughout his career. Though it has largely disappeared, it re-emerges from time to time, and as recently as the 2019 French Open someone in the crowd called out to him: 'Come on Baby Fed,' to which he responded: 'Do I look like a baby?'

Had Federer not played on for so long, perhaps the moniker would have died its death much sooner. Dimitrov certainly would have liked that. 'I think at first it was kind of OK to hear,' he said. 'It was nice and obviously I appreciate it and all that, but it was also just nice for them to put that aside,' he said. 'I was very happy that I was able to get out of that. I think it's something that I would have loved to kind of close a little bit earlier. But unfortunately, he [Federer] dragged on for quite a while.'

That first meeting, a 6-3, 7-6 victory for Federer in the quarter-finals in Basel, left a lasting impression on

Dimitrov. 'It was just fun for me,' he said. 'I was excited. I never played him like he's my idol or anything like that. I was just excited to see where my game was at. That was something that I was just the most happy and excited with.'

Federer had the better of Dimitrov in all but one of their meetings, beating him at both Wimbledon (in 2017) and at the Australian Open the year before. But the time Dimitrov beat him, in the quarter-finals of the US Open in 2019, is a match he will remember forever. 'It was an amazing experience for me,' Dimitrov said. 'This, to me, was not about tennis. This one means something different to me. That's why when I say this, I cherish the absolute experience to play him in the best of five sets and beat him in five sets in the night session in New York. Of course [just playing the match] was already like wow for me and stuff, I was so happy and so excited at what was happening, the way I was playing mainly. But it was more, it meant something different to me than the sport itself. That's why I'm very happy that I have it as an experience.'

A junior Wimbledon champion in 2008, at the age of 17, Dimitrov was perhaps unlucky to have been born into an era when three men, Federer, Nadal and Djokovic, dominated the sport like never before. Throw in Andy Murray and Stan Wawrinka, who each won three Grand Slam titles, and the opportunities for someone else to win a major were few and far between. Dimitrov has reached the semi-finals at three of the slams: at Wimbledon, the US Open and Australian Open but never made it one step further to compete for a slam title. Djokovic stopped him at Wimbledon in 2014, Nadal edged him out in Australia in 2017 and in 2019 it was a future world No 1, Daniil

Medvedev, who dashed his hopes. Though he won the ATP Finals in 2017 and has been ranked as high as No 3, there has always been someone blocking his path to ultimate glory.

For many players, that would be a frustration. Dimitrov doesn't see it that way. 'No, I don't think so,' he said. 'It's just, you know, we often don't pick the right moments in our life. Who knows when we're going to be born and who knows what era we are going to come up with? I think that's just the case in our generation, so to speak. I mean, I'm actually ten years younger than [Federer]. I believe that it's just that generation.

'Do I feel stopped by him? No, I mean, we all have racquets in our hand, right? Yeah, some are more talented than the others, I totally understand this, but we have the control over that in a sense that we go out there to play. And it's hard. I understand. It can be frustrating, no doubt about that. It's also not the easiest generation to come up with. I mean, I even remember when I was coming up, I had to play [David] Ferrer and I had to play Rafa in such early stages and then [Tomas] Berdych. I even played [David] Nalbandian, I played [Andy] Roddick once; with these guys it was already hard enough, let alone the top three guys.'

The comparison with Federer has not been all bad, of course. It's also opened up opportunities he probably would never have imagined when he was starting out. Like when he joined Federer and Tommy Haas to sing along with legendary composer and producer David Foster (Haas's father-in-law) in an impromptu band, which they called The One-Handed Backhand Boys. The trio sang Chicago's 'Hard to Say I'm Sorry' with Foster, and though their rendition will never win any awards, they had a lot of fun doing it. As Federer said at the time, 'People had a blast over it, laughed at us, and I thought it was great.'

Dimitrov practised with Federer a number of times and also played some exhibitions with him. Off the court, he was also welcomed into the Federer family. 'I mean, I can only say good things about that and for him and his family,' Dimitrov said. 'They've always been very nice to me, very generous. And I even remember I read his kids a book at night a few times. That was a fun thing in New York. Mirka's always been very nice to me and I think everyone from his whole team has too, so I have only good to say on that.'

As a rival, albeit one who came off second best far more often than he would have liked against Federer, Dimitrov has seen what he's like on and off court, which makes him ideally placed to see what it is that draws so many people to him. While it's different for everyone, Dimitrov sees one thing in particular. 'I would say one thing that everyone [who's attracted to Federer] might have in common is his mindset,' he said. 'I mean, everybody loves a winner, right? When you win, it's great and everybody wants to get close to you.

'But for me, it's more than that. For me, it's just about your character and how you are as a person and how you carry yourself on the court and so on. I think just his mindset, the way he plays, his thought that after a point, there's another point, you know, and the next one. He's been able to clear everything up very quickly, put things behind him and go on to the next one. I think that's probably one of his biggest assets. And as a player, he simply takes your time away. And I mean, that's enough.'

Sergiy Stakhovsky, hero of Ukraine

'You realise how grateful we should be'

The first time Sergiy Stakhovsky met Roger Federer was in Doha in 2005, when the Ukrainian was still a teenager, beginning to make his way on the ATP Tour. Bright-eyed and full of hope, he was drawn to the Swiss, who was already world No 1. 'I qualified that year, so that's the first time I'd seen him,' the Ukrainian said. 'I was about 300 in the world. He was already big back then and you were coming to the matches, watching the guy playing; not playing, actually, just destroying everybody around.'

Federer was the No 1 seed, with four Grand Slams already to his name and Stakhovsky was eager to see what all the fuss was about. What he saw almost blew his mind. 'He was already described as a god-like player,' he said. 'Looking back, people really were desperate to understand how they could actually beat him or challenge him. I wanted to watch him play because it was so effortless. You watched him play tennis and you'd think: "God, this game is so easy", then you step on the court and you understand that actually it's hard.'

Watching from the sidelines is one thing; seeing him across the net was another altogether. It was six years before Stakhovsky got the chance to play Federer for the first time, in Dubai, having broken into the top 50 and reached the quarter-finals. It was a one-sided affair, Federer winning 6-3, 6-4 on his way to racking up yet another title. 'We had practised a few times in 2009, 10, 11,' Stakhovsky said. 'We did have a few hits on hard courts, almost never on clay, I guess that would be because I was not very good on clay. It was always disturbing practising with him, because he was making everything look so effortless and so easy and you're running like a dog, scraping the balls back and trying not to miss.

'I remember only one thing about that match. I remember that I had a ticket back into that match because I had a break point to come back in the second set. I hit a backhand deep on an approach shot, Roger shanked the backhand past me and then there was a late call, out [on the Stakhovsky backhand]. Then Mohamed [Lahyani] was in the chair and he, of course, in his style, [yelled] "correction" and then Roger challenged that call. Mohamed forgot that it was a late call and that it didn't actually affect the shot of Roger. Then of course the review showed the ball was good [but] Mohamed said repeat the point. I think in that match I had all of one break point, we played the point again and then it was basically ace, ace, clean winner.'

Two years later, Stakhovsky's life changed. Having beaten Rogerio Dutra Silva of Brazil in the first round at Wimbledon, he took a look at the draw and was a little despondent to see the name of Federer, then a seven-time winner and the defending champion, next to his own. 'Honestly, the mindset going into the match was not to win, it was just to do OK. Even though I had practised with Roger, the guy could hit winners from anywhere [so you think], what do you want to expect from yourself?' he said.

Exactly three hours later, Stakhovsky had pulled off the unthinkable, victory over Federer at Wimbledon. Serving and volleying, rushing Federer into mistakes, he dashed the Swiss's hopes of an eighth title at the All England Club and wrote his name into the history books.

'It was a blur, because of the moment, the emotions were pretty high,' he said. 'I remember playing the first set and I had some chances, I think I had a break, and I completely caught a rocket [from Federer] going to the fence on his backhand, on a break point. And I was sitting on the bench and saying, well, you had your chances, 7-6 is a pretty decent scoreline to have against Roger on grass in the first set. But then somewhere in the back of my mind, I was realising I didn't face a break point. And I said to myself: "Well, maybe if I'm going to be able to do what I did in the first set and serve a bit more aggressive on the second and come in a lot, I might have a chance to get somewhere deeper." And that actually is what happened.'

As he neared the finish line, though, the doubts began to creep in. Could he really beat perhaps the greatest player of all time at his favourite event? 'I was a break up in the fourth and then, of course, that moment of truth always comes,' he said. 'There were a lot of players who "could" beat Roger at Wimbledon but there is always this big "could" because at the end of the day, you still have to beat yourself, understand that now, it's your chance. And that's the worst. I said [at the time] in the wrong way, to beat Roger you need to beat his ego. It's not his ego, it's his legacy. You don't face just the guy, you face his 20 slams, you face his record-breaking. There's so many things you face and then you have a chance, it's not easy and [you think] you're not going to have another one.'

Stakhovsky barely remembers the press conference which followed but his respect for Federer was clear, admitting he would not trade a win over the Swiss for anything, but also stating that Federer was 'the greatest player we had' and just as great a person. 'He showed us that you don't have to be someone else. You can be a decent man achieving a lot of things and still be someone who everybody admires,' he said, at the time.

Years on, he still feels the same. 'I don't believe I can change my words,' he said. 'I still believe the things I said. Although maybe there is one correction, maybe a deep run in a slam – I would say getting to the finals of a slam I would trade for that win over Roger. Just because I'm older now and wiser.' The magnitude of the win over Federer was felt all over the tennis world and, perhaps not surprisingly, Stakhovsky was emotionally spent when it came to the following round, losing to Austrian Jürgen Melzer, the effects of doing so many interviews the following day leaving him flat, lacking in intensity.

Interestingly, Stakhovsky and Federer met again the following month in Hamburg, and rather than hold a grudge, Federer invited him to practise. 'We chatted a lot,' he said. 'We were both on the ATP Player Council at that time. I couldn't say that anything changed after I beat him. Maybe we practised a bit more because I was more on the favourable side [with him]. I don't want to know why, actually.'

In the few years that followed, Stakhovsky saw Federer more off the court, too, through their work with the Council, the group that represents the players' interests within the ATP Tour. Their time on the board coincided with the players securing big prize money rises from the four Grand Slam events – Wimbledon, US Open, Roland-Garros and Australian Open – and Stakhovsky has no doubt who was largely to thank.

'It was extremely good to have him because it's one thing having a Sergiy Stakhovsky or a Gilles Simon on the Council, and another when you have Roger Federer,' he said. 'It makes a lot of difference when he is negotiating or he is making a case. He was essential in terms of the prize money increases. We were going through this topic for a number of years, we had a pretty harsh time and we had a very good, solid background of the players who were willing to do something about it. And yet if it had not been for Roger and Rafa [Nadal], I doubt we would have been able to push it. I remember Roger calling us and saying we'd got the big [rise], then later on we understood why we got it. He got the deal because he said, we can either do the deal now, or you can go and talk to Gilles Simon and Sergiy Stakhovsky. It was kind of funny.'

The Federer effect also spread to how players dealt with their media commitments, Stakhovsky said. Federer was just being himself, others made a mistake in trying to follow his example instead of being true to themselves. 'He had an impact in showing what professional athletes should look like, how they should behave, and carry themselves,' he said. 'This is just my opinion but because of this, unfortunately tennis lost a bit of spark, and lost a lot of character. Because suddenly, in all the press conferences everyone wanted to be like, "Oh, the guy played great, I was just lucky." The majority of other guys are not like that. But they still understand that these are the right things to say. And because of that our sport lost some of the sparkle that Marat Safin and Goran Ivanisevic introduced after their matches.

'His kindness in his interviews, that's genuine. That's who he is and that's how he was raised. Unfortunately, even including myself, I'm not going to lie, we were all kind of copycats. We all understood that's the right thing to say, that's how the press conference should be held. In general, a lot of guys understood the concept of right and wrong [but] they were not who they are in a press conference. It doesn't bother me but I think we lost a little bit of intrigue and character through this.'

Stakhovsky was also struck by Federer's courtesy behind the scenes. 'He was always nice and friendly,' he said. 'He would always say hello, even when you're basically kind of scared to say hello to him because you're sure the guy has no idea who you are. He is basically just a normal guy. He doesn't have, I would say, enemies. He can be friends with the next generation and the old guys. Of course, because of what he is and what he became, I would say that in later years, it was pretty hard to catch him in the locker room because he understood the concept that the more he talked, the more energy he loses before matches. He started to distance himself a bit more and he was more private. Still, when he walked in the locker room he did say hi and he would chat for a bit. But he didn't spend too much time in the locker room, I would say starting somewhere in the summer 2012, 2013, 2014.'

Stakhovsky smiled as he recalled the time when Federer went out of his way to be nice to his family, too. 'I remember one year in Miami when I was already [knocked] out … my mother was in Miami because my brother's wife was giving birth and they were waiting for me in the hallway. Roger was walking by and he stopped, he greeted my mother, he greeted my sister-in-law and I could see the shock on the face of my mother, like, what's going on here? He was very polite, that's what he is. And as much as we understand, it's going to be a huge shame once he's gone. I'm very doubtful he can be replaced. It's like the era is going to change.'

Wanting to be like Federer and being like him are two very different things, of course. But following his example is something all players would be wise to do, according to Stakhovsky.

'Of course there's a huge amount you can take out of his game, the vision, how he sees the court. For me, what was remarkable was when he took his time out [in 2016, when he had knee surgery], then he came back and instead of like us old guys, trying to slow the game down because we need more time, we're getting slow, he comes in and he's rocketing the speed up. He's like, "You know what, guys, I'm going to play faster." Everybody was like, "What the hell's going on?!"

'I honestly believe that our tennis, the way it is now at this level – I know it's going to sound like I'm a Roger fan – but it's honestly my thinking and I've been carrying this thinking ... because of him, the game of tennis raised the bar so high. Because when he came, he was dominating the show because he was playing faster, he had more time, he was coming in, he had a variety of shots and everybody was getting killed.

'Tennis at the beginning of the 2000s was Safin, etc. – it was a big party, let's play some tennis sometimes and the rest you're going to party. He was one of the guys who came in and said: "Hey, you can party if you want. I am not on this wagon." So tennis changed, the mentality changed, the players started to take care of themselves more. They started to party less, drink less, smoke less, be more professional, and that, trying to chase him, it all raised the bar. I do believe that Novak [Djokovic] is the player he is now thanks to Roger.'

Stakhovsky only watched the video of his Wimbledon win over Federer for the first time in 2020, during the coronavirus pandemic, together with the former Ukraine football star Serhiy Rebrov. What he took out of it, other than that his own play was 'not too shabby', was how incredible it is to think that Federer has played at the top level so late in his career, long beyond an age when most players are retired.

'I would say that I admire what he did and for me he is maybe the reason why I'm still playing,' he said when we spoke in 2021, the year before his life changed again when, after Ukraine was invaded by Russia, he took up arms to defend his country. 'Whether you like it or not, somewhere along the way when you practise a lot, when you dedicate your life to a sport, somewhere along the way you lose the love. But when you see the guy who has a smile on his face every time he steps on the court – and doesn't matter which, clay, hard, it doesn't matter what conditions he is in, you do not see him pissed off on the court.

'That tells you a lot. You realise how grateful we should be to be able to do it, while we still can physically, and enjoy it and make a decent living, seeing the world around us, different people, to experience different cultures. It's all a part of the package. Yes, you work hard for it, you deserve it. A lot of guys are [Andre] Agassi-style, back in the day saying: "I hate tennis, I never liked it." It is just the sheer joy of his experience while he's on the court that is remarkable and actually, it gives you the spirit that this is actually something really good.'

Stakhovsky said the best quote he has ever heard about Federer came from his former coach, Fabrice Santoro. 'He told me, "He was not born for the sport. The sport was created for him." It's not far off,' Stakhovsky said. 'I remember, after his match with me at Wimbledon, everybody buried him, saying he's old, he's done, he's out.

The very next year he comes back and [later] he wins slams, wins Wimbledon without dropping a set. I understand that he works hard, I know that he does, because we practised in Dubai in pre-season, but the capability, the composure he keeps and the ability to deliver, pfff. I mean, he had some failures, like with Novak in the finals at Wimbledon [in 2019], but that's human-like. How he gets above and beyond it is also remarkable.'

Thanasi Kokkinakis, Australian rising star
'He calls me Thanaser. That's how he is'

Generosity comes in many forms. For some, it might be a word of advice in their ear, or an arm around their shoulder. For Thanasi Kokkinakis, it was the opportunity of a lifetime. A rising junior in Australia, Kokkinakis received a rare message, asking if he would like to go to Dubai to train with Federer during the off-season. It was an offer he didn't need long to accept.

'He invited me to Dubai, I think I was 18, for an off-season,' Kokkinakis said. 'He's just a super-good guy. I had lunch with his family under the Burj Khalifa [hotel], the one that they have the helipad on. Just a good guy, really fun to train with.' Kokkinakis admitted he was nervous to practise with Federer. 'You're always a bit nervous when you're playing with someone like that. But he makes you feel pretty comfortable, pretty early. You know, he's a really relaxed guy and likes cracking some jokes as well and that makes you feel a bit more comfortable. He was really, really relaxed and looks like he genuinely cares and takes interest. You're not just there to be like a sort of a hitting bitch, if that makes sense. He genuinely cares about you and your career.'

Federer has trained with many young players in Dubai over the years, from Stefanos Tsitsipas to Felix Auger-Aliassime and, more recently, young Swiss star Dominic Stricker. It's an incredible opportunity for young players, who get a rare insight into how one of the greatest players of all times practises. It was a two-way street, too. The youngsters got to train with Federer and learn how he goes about his job; Federer got to train with eager, keen players. A cynical mind might ask if there was something calculated about it; did Federer want to get a close look at the games of some of those he might meet on Tour, and perhaps gain a psychological hold over them? Well, if that was the plan, it didn't work because when Kokkinakis played Federer on the ATP Tour, in Miami in 2018, the Aussie had the temerity to beat him.

Kokkinakis doubts that Federer's invitation was anything other than generosity. 'Maybe he kind of figured out my game a little, but also I definitely felt more comfortable kind of knowing how he plays, when I was able to take the court with him and play that match in Miami,' he said. 'I don't know if he does it to suss people out – I don't think he's that in-depth with stuff like that. I feel it's more that he knows it's a good opportunity for a junior and a young guy to hit with him and he obviously wants someone that he feels like he can kind of dictate some drills with, that maybe someone older wouldn't want to do. I was very open to hitting with him.'

Anyone who has seen Federer practise during a Grand Slam event or a regular Tour event will know that his training sessions are very different to those of Nadal or Djokovic. While Nadal, in particular, plays flat out in practice, even hitting the ball harder than in matches, Federer has always been very relaxed on the practice court, never playing for too long. Kokkinakis said he had been keen to see how Federer trained when he was away from the spotlight.

'When I was training with him, he wasn't doing hours on hours on the court,' he said. 'He might have done stuff away from me, but I think all of that work, especially when you're sort of 35, 36 or something like that, all the work's done at that point. He knows what kind of makes him tick and what makes him produce the best results. For me it was kind of an hour and a half but it was intense. He'd always joke, but when it's time to train and be on court, you could tell he worked on some things and did some things that were pretty special.'

Like many who have spent time with Federer, Kokkinakis was struck by how much fun he likes to have, how playful he still is at heart. 'He's just a good guy,' he said. 'You can feel it's genuine coming from him. You can feel that he genuinely cares. And he's really a fun, outgoing type of guy. Like he loves to crack jokes, he's really relaxed and he comes up with nicknames for all of us and him and his team. It was crazy seeing his little boys in Dubai when I first met him because they literally have the same face as him and it's weird. It's just like two mini Feds running around, so it's pretty cool.'

What was the nickname? 'He calls me Thanaser,' he said. 'I don't know how he got it, but we had a joke that we just started calling everyone by the wrong name. That was the joke. For the weeks when we were in Dubai, everyone just had the wrong name. So he'd call my coach, who's Todd [Langman], something else. And I'd called Severin [Lüthi], his coach, something else. And that was just it, that's just how he is.'

Kokkinakis resisted the temptation to watch what Federer was doing on the court too closely. 'You're not emulating someone like that,' he said. 'If you try and play his game and do what he does, it's probably not going to go well for you because he's a special guy and he's probably a one-off talent when it comes to what he can do with the racquet. So if you're trying to emulate him, as a sort of an average player, it's not easy.'

What he did, though, was to soak up everything he saw, without ever asking for specific advice. Something obviously rubbed off because when they played in Miami, Kokkinakis produced the match of his life, winning in a deciding tiebreak. Federer, who was the defending champion at the time, said he was happy for Kokkinakis; for the Aussie, it was a match he continues to look back on with pleasure and to use for inspiration.

'It was crazy,' he said. 'It was a good milestone. He was defending champion in Miami. To have that win, it's something I'll never forget. I can always say I beat one of the greatest of all time and the No 1 in the world. I think I was one of the lower-ranked guys to ever do it. It was good. It almost helped my comeback [from injury], to be honest. It didn't sort of springboard me then, but when I'm down or when I'm injured or not feeling great or my body's hurting a little bit, you kind of remember those times and that win and you're like, hang on, if I put it together, I can have hopefully more of those results. It definitely gives you that inner belief.'

Federer continues to send him messages of support, like when he won his first ATP Tour title in early 2022. It's another reason he is so popular with players on Tour. 'He has no need to take an interest in me or other guys that are sort of a lot younger or nowhere near up to his standard or level,' he said. 'But yeah, you can tell he always cares and he's just one of those guys that the Tour will big-time miss.'

ROGER, THE HERO

QUEUING FOR tickets at Wimbledon is the most beautiful tradition in tennis. Those who pitch their tent in Wimbledon Park during the Championships sometimes find friends for life and always a topic of conversation: Roger. For years, he was the talk of the town, with fans travelling from all corners of the world to see him play live, to catch him on his way to practice, or to catch a glimpse of him or even a few words.

Scarlett Li from Toronto discovered her love for Federer after watching the 2008 Wimbledon final against Rafael Nadal on TV, which was heartbreaking for her. She decided to follow him around the globe, as far as her job allowed her to do so. Sunita Sigtia from Kolkata also devoted herself completely to her passion for Federer, explored the tennis world thanks to him and even had his logo and signature tattooed.

What drove them to sacrifice all their holidays and a lot of money for Federer?

For them, it's about much more than the aesthetic experience of watching him play. Their fanhood for him is also a way of life for them and is strongly linked to his character, which fascinates so many.

Thanks to John Bercow, Federer also became a recurring topic in the British House of Commons. The Speaker for ten years, he made no secret of his enthusiasm for the Swiss. Sometimes he found new allies, sometimes he offended. One thing is clear: if you ask Federer fans about their hero, you can expect a long answer.

John Bercow, former Speaker of the House of Commons

'He probably thought I was a stalker'

John Bercow is a self-confessed nerd. A Roger Federer nerd. In a good way.

Able to reel off all of Federer's opponents in his 20 Grand Slam title wins – and even some of the exact scores along the way – Bercow has been a regular fixture in the stands whenever Federer has played at Wimbledon or the ATP Finals. 'I've seen all of those matches and some of them, I must admit to you, at the risk of being thought to be a very sad anorak, I have seen more than once. And the last five games of the 2017 [Australian Open] final, I've probably seen 20 times. I am a nerd,' Bercow said.

Bercow was the Speaker of the House of Commons from 2009 to 2019 and before that was a member of Parliament from 1997. As Speaker, he held one of the most prominent roles in British politics, sparring with prime ministers and leaders of the opposition, trying to keep control of the situation. His pronunciation of 'Order' as 'Awederrr' is so iconic it led to a host of YouTube tributes.

Bercow's first love was tennis, a sport he played to a good level as a junior. A Pete Sampras fan, he first clapped eyes on Federer in 2001, when the Swiss took on the American in the fourth round at Wimbledon, a match that changed Federer's life and the life of Bercow himself.

'I think if I remember rightly, I watched it on the television in my office in Parliament,' he said. Bercow wanted Sampras, who had won the title seven times, to win, but was transfixed by Federer, who was just 19. 'He broke in the final game of the match, he was serving first in the final set, he was 6-5 up, he broke in that final game, I think to 15. And you can check the record and you'll see if it's right, but he hit a forehand return of serve down the line.'

What was it about Federer's play that he was attracted to? 'The manner of his play and his extraordinarily controlled and gracious comportment on the court,' he said. 'Now, my admiration grew and I started to see the many layers over a period of years but even then I thought, well, this is an extraordinarily versatile and dextrous tennis player. This is somebody who appears to have every shot in the book. He wasn't cocky, but he evinced an air of self-confidence and of unflappability.

'Of course, we know historically from the books that have been written about him and from what he has said that in his youth he was extremely bad-tempered. I think at least once he was told by his father, if that happens again, you're not playing again. I'm not going to keep paying for lessons and I'm not going to keep taking you to tournaments, you're not going to play if that's how you're going to behave. So eventually, a little bit like [Björn] Borg did, he came to acquire this tremendous exterior calm, whatever was going on beneath the surface.

'But it was evident even then, in 2001, this combination of self-confidence and not appearing to be remotely fazed by facing, at the time, the greatest player of his generation. And when he did have setbacks and he did have setbacks, yes, he was always ahead in the match, he was one set up, two sets to one up, but when he lost that fourth-set breaker, he just took it in his stride and stayed with Pete Sampras throughout that final set. So I thought this is a person of quite remarkable ability. The shot-making prowess was obvious, giving him the capacity to hit winners from all parts of the court. The forehand even then, I think famously described by David Foster Wallace as a liquid whip, was already evident, the backhand amazing. His service technique has changed a little bit; nevertheless, the essential rudiments, the essential components of it were there. And it was a beautiful and very unfussy service technique. He seemed to be able to hit his spots. You'll probably have heard it said many times that Roger hasn't got the fastest serve, but it is probably the best-placed serve of any player on the Tour. So it was a combination of the shot-making, the aura of calm, the quiet self-confidence, and also one other thing which grew on me more in later years – the positively balletic movement.'

Bercow was a busy man in his day job, trying to keep order in a bustling Parliament, especially in the later years when Britain was going through Brexit, the exit from the European Union. But whenever he could, he would find time to watch Federer, either live or on television, when time allowed. He first saw him play in person in 2010 at the ATP Finals and first met him in 2013, having been introduced to the American tennis coach Robert Davis, while on a trip to Burma visiting Aung San Suu Kyi, who would later become the country's leader. Davis told Bercow he knew Federer and could arrange a meeting, most likely at the ATP Finals in London's O2 in November that year. Later, Davis contacted Bercow and said could he be at the

O2 for 5.30pm, after which he would finally meet the man himself.

Bercow was delighted and excited but there was a problem. 'That day there was an address by, I think, a female president, who was speaking in the least prestigious setting in Parliament for a visiting dignitary, because she wasn't, you know, President Obama or anything, it wasn't Westminster Hall or the Royal Gallery. She spoke in the Robing Room of the House of Lords. The convention was that the two speakers always welcome such guests; I did it with Obama and others, one of us making the opening introductory speech and the other the closing speech. And it was at about 3.30pm and I must admit, I was terribly anxious – I couldn't say anything – terribly anxious that she shouldn't speak for very long.

'It finished at say 4.15 or 4.20 [so] I had time to get to the O2 North Greenwich from Westminster on the Jubilee Line, but not a ridiculous amount of time. At the end, the then Black Rod [the official responsible for controlling access to the House of Lords] – I had very bad relations with him – a man called David Leekie, a retired lieutenant general, wanted to have a debrief. And I said, "Well, you know, I'm very up for having a debrief, but I'm afraid now is not convenient. I've got to go somewhere." And he said: "May I ask, out of interest, where?" And I said: "Well, seeing as you ask, David, yes, I'm going to the O2 to watch the tennis tonight. But in particular, at 5.30 I'm due to meet my hero, Roger Federer, and nothing and nobody is going to get in the way of that, so I must go," which, to be fair, he then acknowledged. So I met Roger in the players' lounge; Robert introduced us.'

In 2014, Bercow was invited to be a guest editor on the *Today* programme, the main morning news show on BBC

Radio 4. He accepted, on the condition that he could have Federer on the programme, if possible. Federer, Bercow said, was happy to do it as long as he didn't discuss politics, not wanting to alienate any of his fans, many of whom had varying political views.

That was fine for Bercow, who didn't want to talk politics with Federer anyway. Instead, they discussed tennis for 15 minutes. 'I asked him about whether longevity was important in his assessment of the quality of a champion's career and he, in a sort of very pithy but nevertheless slightly roundabout way, he was sort of confirming that it was, he thought, important,' Bercow said. 'He actually got a headline for saying that he thought that pushy parents were a danger. And I said to him, look, I've watched 65 of your matches this year. He said: "Wow." He probably thought I was a stalker.'

It was in Parliament, though, where Bercow pushed the boundaries. If you look at Hansard, the official record of what is said in Parliament, you will find several mentions of Federer's name, thanks to the Speaker. 'Parliament can be a kind place and it can be an unkind place. It is no secret that I am something of a Marmite character. I had massively strong supporters as Speaker throughout my tenure, and I had some pretty heavy detractors, from humble ordinary employees to some very senior figures who couldn't stand me,' he said.

'I probably slightly abused my position a number of times to mention him gratuitously,' he admitted. 'I remember once when Karen Bradley, who was a government minister, was due to respond to something or to wind up some event. And I said, "Well … it's a pleasure to see the Right Honourable Lady and I'm in particularly good spirits as my hero Roger

Federer has just come back from two sets down in the quarter-finals at Wimbledon to beat Marin Cilic." Once, Ben Bradshaw, who is a Labour MP, started a question by saying, "Thank you, Mr Speaker ... sorry about the tennis." And once, Theresa May [the prime minister from 2016 to 2019] came into the chamber in 2019 after what for me was the most painful of all Roger's defeats, which I've not got over even now, and she said to me, she said, "Oh, I suspect, Mr Speaker, you're disappointed about the Wimbledon final." And I said, "Well, Prime Minister, I am, but one just has to move on." I was absolutely gutted.

'The nearest I got to a very gentle, good-humoured rebuke was when I completely took advantage of a question on the order paper about Switzerland. A member asked a question about trade agreements and Liam Fox [a government minister] answered and I said, "Yes, can I just say to the secretary of state and the House, that the best thing about Switzerland is not financial services, it's not its watches, it's not its chocolate, the best thing about Switzerland is Roger Federer." And Liam Fox said: "Well, the only thing I would say is that it perhaps seems mildly unpatriotic of you to make that observation on a day when Roger has just beaten Dan Evans." But was there sort of an air of palpable irritation? No, I think people were slightly bemused, probably.'

Federer was even able to act as a peacemaker, briefly and unknowingly, between Bercow and David Cameron, the former prime minister with whom he shared a tumultuous relationship but a love of tennis. 'David Cameron and I didn't get on terribly well, other than that we played tennis for the Commons and Lords team,' he said. 'And to be fair to David, he was a very good partner in doubles. He would excoriate himself over any error [John] McEnroe-like; I remember once he couldn't reach a drop shot and he said, "No, you fat idiot." But when I missed, he was very tolerant of my mistakes and we forged rather a good partnership around 2001 to 2003.'

The pair were discussing the upcoming ATP Tour Finals in London one year when Cameron revealed to Bercow that Federer was his favourite player. 'I must have introduced the concept,' Bercow said. 'He said that Federer was his favourite. And I agreed. This amicable moment didn't last very long. I continued, "Well, there you are prime minister, there's something we agree on." He replied, "Well, yes." And that was the end of that.'

Bercow's favourite Federer match is the 2017 Australian Open final, when he came from 3-1 down in the final set to beat Nadal, having been out of action for six months after recovering from knee surgery. 'I remember the 26-shot rally which you've probably seen on YouTube a number of times [with Federer leading 4-3, 40-40 in the final set], a quite extraordinary rally culminating in Roger's sort of half-volleyed forehand down the line, which Rafa couldn't deal with,' he said. 'The last five games were pretty spectacular.'

He readily admits he is disappointed that Federer's tally of 20 Grand Slams was passed, first by Rafael Nadal and then by Novak Djokovic. But for the former Speaker, greatness is not measured in titles alone. 'I don't think it's just a matter of stats,' he said. 'In any case, Federer's career has been and remains stellar. I just feel, I've never seen anyone play tennis quite like Roger Federer. And I think the combination of the way he plays, including the way he moves, the way he conducts himself on court, the way he discharges his professional commitments in terms of press conferences and media interaction and sponsorship commitments and charitable endeavours and so on, to me he is a class apart.

'I'm not convinced that there will ever be anybody who's admired in quite the way that he is. I think he's got a wider reach because people admire that combination of artistry, recurring athleticism and attitude. My feeling is that he retires as probably the best-remembered tennis player for most people alive today. And he's got fans in all age groups. Measured across the population as a whole, I would say, amongst tennis fans, Roger is overwhelmingly the most popular, followed by Nadal, with Djokovic way behind, and amongst a hell of a lot of people who are not dedicated tennis fans, what you might call the second tier of people, who aren't obsessives like me and wouldn't necessarily stop doing something else in order to watch a match.

'Has it made a difference to my life? It's made a very considerable difference to my life,' he said. 'When he wins, I'm elated and I go about my business with an additional glint in my eye and spring in my step. And when he loses, I'm gutted.'

Scarlett Li, world traveller
A few seconds of interaction that mean everything

Most Federer fans can tell precisely when their love story with the Swiss began. For Scarlett Li, it was the 2008 Wimbledon final against Rafael Nadal, which she watched on TV at home in Toronto. 'It just broke my heart,' said the Canadian of Chinese descent. 'Roger should have won. I blame the light; it was too dark at the end, which hurt his precision. Ever since then, I couldn't bear to watch that final again or any highlights of it. Because it would remind me of the look of sadness on Roger's face during that trophy ceremony, and it just breaks my heart again. That match drew me to him on a profound emotional level. I felt a special connection from that moment on.'

Scarlett had followed tennis before and had long rooted for Pete Sampras. But she would never have considered travelling to tournaments. She had already admired Roger's tennis as he became the world's No 1 player. But it was that Wimbledon final, which many consider the best tennis match ever, that changed her life. 'After that, I decided to go watch Roger live and started to put money aside for that. During the 2008 US Open, I cheered for him in front of the TV. I wanted him to win so badly; I didn't care about the other players anymore. And when he beat Andy Murray in the final, I screamed so loud that my mom, who was upstairs then, rushed to check on me because she thought something crazy had happened. I was just incredibly happy and excited.'

In September 2009, the time had come: Scarlett had saved enough and travelled to the US Open to see Roger live for the first time, together with her young son Benny. 'I was only planning to watch matches on Labor Day weekend. Three days, and then go back to work. But I couldn't. It's like an addiction. Once you see Roger play, you want to see him again and again. So I called my work and extended my vacation. I remember I bought two tickets for the quarter-finals, row G, lower bowl, for $475 each. That's a lot! And I was a single parent. But I just wanted to see Roger play.'

After the quarter-finals, she finally had to go back to Toronto. Her best friend was getting married, and Scarlett was the maid of honour. In her mind, however, she was also in New York that Friday when Roger played and won his semi-final against Novak Djokovic. She decided to fly back for the final, together with her son. 'I drove two hours to Buffalo and took a flight there to New York. And from LaGuardia airport, we took a taxi straight to Flushing Meadows, arriving just in time for the match. Unfortunately, Roger lost narrowly to Juan Martin del Potro. There were a lot of tennis fans on the flight back to Toronto with me that night. And most of them looked very down because Roger had lost.'

She was shocked by her exorbitantly high credit card bill back from New York a week later: 'The money I had spent was crazy. Totally out of my plan. Luckily I didn't have a husband at the time; he would have reprimanded me. And I didn't tell my mom because she would have thought I'd lost my mind.'

But she didn't let that dampen her enthusiasm for her new hobby. Or, rather, her new passion. 'Watching tennis on TV and watching in person is totally different. I had to do it again. So I immediately made plans for the 2010 Australian Open.' She planned a three-week vacation, bringing her son along. The two flew to the other side of the world in January 2010. 'It was a long, long, long journey. We were on the road for more than 24 hours, and it felt like we were changing planes non-stop. It was very exhausting, but the trip was worth it. I saw Roger lift the trophy; again, he beat Andy Murray in the final. I was ecstatic. So that's how crazy my live tournament experience started.'

Scarlett did not travel to Melbourne again; it was simply too far, time-consuming and expensive for her. But some tournaments became fixtures for her: 'I aimed at the Grand Slams and tournaments in North America. And at the World Tour Finals in London, because the flight tickets are cheaper in November.' She has been to every Wimbledon and US Open since 2010 when Roger has played.

At Wimbledon, she even developed a flair for queuing or, more precisely, camping. Her tent clearly shows which tennis player her heart beats for. It is red and white, and she has painted the initials 'RF' in gold. Attached to it are the flags of Canada and Switzerland – her home country and that of her favourite player. 'Ever since I was young, I hated camping,' she said. 'My friends always asked me to go camping with them. It's very popular in Canada. But I always said no. I think camping is so barbaric. But at Wimbledon, it's much better. You have a washroom right there. You have a coffee cart and a burger cart. It's much more convenient and cleaner. And when I get the ticket and see Roger from the third or fourth row, I feel it's all worth it. So I went every year. It's very, very special. I love Wimbledon for that. And it's much cheaper than at the US Open.'

She refers to Melbourne as her most exotic tournament destination. She has also been to Shanghai, Dubai, Basel, the Laver Cup in Chicago, Geneva, Boston and London, and the men's tournament in Canada, which alternates between Toronto and Montreal, became a must for her. And what has been her most enjoyable experience in all these years? She says, without hesitation: '2017 Wimbledon.' Of course, the first title she experienced on-site at the 2010 Australian Open was also very sweet. 'But 2017 is special because he just came back after a long break recovering from knee surgery.'

How could all this travelling be coordinated with her job? Scarlett smiled and said she once asked Roger to publish his tournament schedule earlier. 'He started to laugh, you know? And I'm like, "No, Roger, you don't understand. I mean it. I need to plan my vacation based on your tournament schedule to make sure I can go.'"

She works as a Principal Analyst in the Risk Analytics and Innovation Network team at the Office of the Superintendent of Financial Institutions Canada. It's an independent agency of the Government of Canada that supervises and regulates banks, insurers, trust and loan companies, and private pension plans. 'The good thing about federal work is we have a lot of vacation. I have 20-something days every year.' She always had to ensure that she used this time wisely and planned some of her tournament visits around public holidays. Of course, trips that had nothing to do with tennis or, more precisely, tournaments in which Roger participated became impossible.

'As a data scientist, I analyse data and work very logically,' she said. 'Following Roger around the world is the only irrational thing I've done in my life.' Working for the Financial Supervisory Authority, she refrains from strict cost control in her passion for Roger. 'I did my bookkeeping. I know how much money I put in. It's definitely over six figures. It's pretty bad in a way, some might think. But I don't regret it. I decided that's where I would like to put my hard-earned money. You see, instead of buying expensive jewellery, for example, a diamond ring, a fancy Louis Vuitton bag, or ten of them, I used the money to go to tournaments to see Roger. His tennis and the experience of watching him give me so much joy.' She adds with a smirk: 'And a lot of stress as well. Sometimes I felt like I would get a heart attack during the match because I care so much and want Roger to win so badly.'

But what fascinates her so much about Federer? First, it was his tennis. 'I noticed early on Roger's style was very different. His single-handed backhand always displayed elegance. And I am a very artistic person. I did ballet when I was young, and I play the piano and the violin. Artistic expression has always appealed to me. And Roger playing tennis is like a piece of moving art. Poetry in motion.'

Then came the fascination for him as a person. 'He has a special kind of charisma. The way that he carries himself, he always talks with a kind of serenity. You feel like he treats you as your next-door neighbour or like you're one of his friends. He would talk to you so casually and down-to-earth. You don't feel like he's a superstar you have to look up to. But then you do realise that he is that superstar.'

The brief moments of interaction with him on the sidelines of a tournament mean everything to Scarlett and many other Federer fans. 'Sometimes, we waited for hours at the practice courts. Sometimes we didn't know when or if he would show up, so we just stood there and waited. The longest I waited was at the US Open, six hours, and it was raining. They said that he wouldn't come. But we thought that he needed to get some practice in before his next match. So we were hanging out with other tennis, Federer fans chatting. When we talk about Roger, it kills time. That day, it would pay off. I remember Roger came about 6pm. They would use the towels to dry the court. And then they started practice. After that, he chatted with us for a little while. We get to talk to him a little when there are few people.'

When the crowds are large, it is essential to persevere and endure sacrifices. 'When I am first in line, I must stay there to keep my position. If I leave, someone will take my space, and I'll be in the back. So you better don't drink, don't eat because you can't go to the washroom.'

Scarlett developed her strategies to get Federer's attention in a not too intrusive way. 'When he's signing, I never yell "Roger, Roger, Roger!" I never do that. I would say, "Oh, Roger, so how's everything", or congratulate him on his great match. And then he recognises me. I will ask kind of casual questions. At one US Open, I asked him, "Do you know how to braid your daughters' hair?" He smiled and said, "Oh, no, I don't know how to do that; I haven't learned it."

'Roger is pretty good at multitasking. He would sign autographs as he listened and answered questions. I usually don't have him sign a lot of things. But I realise if he doesn't sign, he doesn't stop in front of you. So I always have something handy. And then when he signs, I'll talk to him for like a couple of seconds. And I'm telling you, everyone who gets an answer, who gets in an exchange with Roger for a few seconds, will tell you this is their best experience. They will say: "I have had my Federer moment!" So I'm fortunate that I got a lot of them.'

What she especially values: 'He always gives you eye contact. I noticed that a lot of other players are not comfortable with having eye contact with the fans. For example, I feel that Rafa Nadal is the shyer type, and I noticed many times that he looks away when he signs for fans. But Roger, on the other hand, is very comfortable. If you talk to him, he will give you eye contact and acknowledge he sees you and talks to you.' She added: 'Well, Djokovic is a little bit like that off-court as well; I just don't like his demeanour on the court.'

Federer addresses his most loyal, well-travelled fans by name during these brief encounters. And Scarlett is a familiar name to him anyway, because for the tournament in Canada, when he celebrates his birthday on 8 August, she always makes presents for his children and gives them to him. Like a Ferris wheel or a little house. She has a flair for handicrafts, like her self-made red and white earrings with the RF logo. Because of her unique outfits, she was often shown on television during Federer matches.

'A lot of people asked me why I love Roger so much. Some said to me: "Do you know he has a wife?" They're making fun of me. And I'm like, "I know, Mirka. I think she's great." Loving Roger is not the kind of love men and women have, simple as that.' Could her admiration for Federer be called a celebrity crush? 'I don't like that label,' she said. 'I never really understood when people were crazy about movie stars. Of course, George Clooney, Tom Cruise and Brad Pitt are great actors. But I never felt I would love to take a picture with them. I never saw myself as that kind of girl. I was never that fanatic. Even though I might appreciate them, they made great movies. I wouldn't call it a celebrity crush with Roger, either. But I cannot explain it rationally.'

But it is a fact that her boyfriend Vlad has to share her with Federer. 'Roger was first,' she said, smiling. 'I met Vlad in 2011. That was the year after I had started to travel around the world to chase Roger. He's fine with that; he's very supportive. He's not a big Federer fan or tennis fan. But he would travel to Wimbledon, the US Open or the Canadian tournaments like Toronto or Montreal with me; he would wear the Federer shirt and the hat I gave him and cheer for Roger because I do.'

Her mobile phone lock screen is a photo of her and Roger. And it doesn't bother Vlad that Federer is also very present in their house. 'There are a lot of pictures of Roger and me,' she said. 'And, of course, there are pictures of Vlad and me. I'm quite fortunate that he's the kind of guy who understands my passion for supporting Roger. He doesn't get jealous. I love Roger. He knows that. And he knows that I love him. It's really a different type of love. My love for Roger is more like love and care for my brother or my family, but a bit stronger, if you know what I mean.'

Scarlett has become a bit of a celebrity because of her fandom for Federer. Radio Wimbledon interviewed her about her passion for him and her unique outfits. And on Weibo, the Chinese microblogging service, she has over 100,000 followers. 'I am going to many tournaments and would like to share my experience. I post a lot about Roger; sometimes, I translate his articles into Chinese. I like to let the fans in China know more about Roger than what they see from the state-run media. China is very restricted, and people can't access Google, YouTube, Twitter, Facebook or Instagram. So I'm like the bridge to the Western world.'

Being fluent in Chinese and English, Chinese media have also asked if she would work for them as a freelance journalist at tennis tournaments. But this puts her in a dilemma: 'Of course, I would like to experience Roger at the press conferences. But being a journalist, I couldn't be a fan anymore; I couldn't openly cheer for him in the press box.'

Now Roger has retired, she will not give her heart away to any other player. Scarlett is sure of that. Roger is a once-in-a-lifetime thing for her. 'If he were to play on the Champions Tour one day, I would travel to see him play there. That's how much I love watching him.' Of course, she will miss him now that he is no longer playing on the professional Tour. But there's something good about that, she added with a wink. 'My life will be much easier, and I can go on trips again that have nothing to do with tennis.'

Sunita Sigtia, super-fan

Inspired by Roger to help the underprivileged

Today was going to be a good day, Sunita Sigtia thought when she woke up in her cousin's flat in the London suburb of New Malden. Because this Monday, the 2008 All England Championships began, and she would see Roger Federer live for the first time. Or so she thought.

She was stunned when she arrived at Wimbledon Park at around 10am to get in line. 'Thousands were already there, and I got a queue card with the number 4567. My sister accompanied me. We had to queue all day. It was already starting to get dark when we were finally allowed on the grounds.' Federer had long since finished his workday, opening Centre Court at 2pm with an easy win over Slovakia's Dominik Hrbaty. So close and yet so far from Sunita, who had travelled all the way from Kolkata to see him play live.

But she was not so easily discouraged. Two days later, for Federer's second-round match, she got up in the middle of the night. At 4am, she arrived at Wimbledon Park to queue for a ticket. But again, it was not enough for Federer. Sunita was bitterly disappointed. She went to the information kiosk to find out how to do it. 'The woman explained the whole thing to me. She said: "Do you see those tents over there? If you want to see Roger, you have to sleep overnight."'

Sunita did as she was told and spent Thursday night in the park. 'I had no tent. Nothing. I laid a mat on the grass and wrapped myself in a blanket. I was freezing in the night.' But her perseverance was rewarded. When Federer stepped onto Centre Court for his third-round match against Frenchman Marc Gicquel, Sunita sat in one of the front rows. She was so emotionally moved that she was shaking and crying. The stewards came to her to ask if she was okay. She nodded.

'Once you see Roger play live, you want to do it again and again. You get addicted to it,' Sunita said. 'When he hits the ball, the sound is different than when the other players hit it. And when you're sitting right across the net, you think, oh my God, his ball is so low, it's going into the net, but it just sails above. It's so beautiful to see. There are no words to express what he makes you feel.'

So she also spent Sunday night in the park that year to get a ticket for Federer's last-16 match against Lleyton Hewitt. That night, it was pouring with rain. Sunita sat under an umbrella to protect herself at least a little from the wet. She still did not have a tent. 'Some people came out from the other tents and asked: "Will you be okay?"' She persevered in the cold and wet. She thought she would never get another chance like this.

She was wrong.

The All England Championships became an annual must-attend event for her. From 2009 to 2018, she always camped out at Wimbledon Park to watch as many Roger Federer live matches as possible. And in the second year, she was also much better prepared; she had a proper tent and everything she needed to make the hours of waiting for Roger as bearable as possible. In the second year, and she remembers this clearly, she also got hold of his first autograph. 'He was practising on court 10. I'm not tall, and all those people were standing before me. So when he finished practising, I was screaming: "Roger, Roger, I came all the way from India! Please!" So he asked the others to make room for me so I could come to the front. After he signed my T-shirt, I jumped up and down.'

That year, she watched his matches until the quarter-finals: 'We were literally living on the camping site, and I made so many friends over there in the queue.' Sunita was relieved when he won again in 2009. She had already thought she had jinxed Roger with her appearance the previous year.

But how did she become such a passionate fan of Federer? 'In our family, we were always crazy about sports,' she said. 'We loved cricket, of course, but also tennis. I remember when I was three or four years old, my grandfather made us sit in front of the TV and watch Wimbledon. I used to be crazy about Stefan Edberg and Boris Becker.'

And then, one day, this young Swiss with the ponytail came along, beat the great Pete Sampras and gradually made his way into Sunita's heart. 'Roger just took over, and we started liking him more every year.' She and her three older sisters. When Sunita first saw Federer play live at Wimbledon in 2008, she knew it would change her life.

As a successful business owner, she is privileged to be able to indulge in her hobby. She runs a textile business in Kolkata, The Masspoint, supplying fabrics to designers all over India and the Middle East. 'Everyone knows my shop in my city,' she said. 'And even beyond. When I finished college, I started this business [in 1997] to meet the daily expenses for our family. My father was going through a tough patch. And then, by God's grace, it just grew. We try to give work, especially to the women.' She now has nine employees and works with many other women on demand. 'It was a long road for me, too,' she said.

Sunita lives alone, with one of her sisters and their children next door. Always very busy, she found her work-life balance through Federer and was inspired by him in many ways. Once a successful badminton player at university, she started swinging the bigger racquet a few years ago. Naturally, she plays with a one-handed backhand. 'It was not easy to change my grip from badminton. But in the meantime, I play quite decently.'

At the local club, just five minutes from her house, ball kids from underprivileged backgrounds pick up balls for club members for a tip or hand them water bottles. A very talented boy from the slums caught Sunita's eye, and together with some friends, she supported him financially so that he could make something of his talent.

Sunita then thought about supporting more children, following the example of Roger Federer. So on 8 August 2017, her idol's birthday, she set up her foundation: the SiiRF Foundation – which stands for: Some immensely inspired Roger (Federer) Fans. 'We are trying to help underprivileged talent in sports to realise their dreams,' she explained. 'We have supported six sports kids from humble backgrounds until now. Four of them play tennis, a girl is a karate champ, and another one is a chess player, both having represented India in international meetings. We help with equipment, training fees, tournament participation fees, travelling, food, lodging or other expenses as much as we can.'

They also help the ball kids at the tennis club. The ball boy she first supported has since made a living as a tennis instructor in Bangalore. And during the terrible times of the

Covid-19 pandemic, Sunita and her companions provided food to the needy.

The fact that Federer not only delighted his fans with his victories but also inspired them to do good deeds should make him particularly happy. Sunita printed a small booklet about her foundation and gave it to him at the tournament in Dubai. He wished her all the best with it.

Federer got to know the lively, lovable Indian personally over the years. And maybe she played a small part in his success. When Federer experienced his first prolonged dry spell in terms of Grand Slam titles, Sunita sought help from a guru in 2011. 'I asked him: "Why is Roger struggling so much?" And then he told me that Saturn is troubling him right now. And that Roger should wear something made of emerald, or at least have it near him.'

She set out to find a small emerald figurine of Ganesha, an elephant-headed Hindu god of beginnings, which brings luck. 'It was tough to find one. But thankfully, we have friends who deal in handicrafts. So they could locate one in Jaipur.' She bought the Ganesha and handed it to Federer in early 2012 before the tournament in Doha, beautifully packed in a small box and decorated with two Swiss flags. 'And then he won Wimbledon in 2012 and the silver medal at the Olympics. So I think it worked,' she said with satisfaction.

That year, she flew the 8,000 kilometres from Kolkata to London twice – first for Wimbledon, then for the Olympic Games. She was at the House of Switzerland to celebrate his medal. Sunita has witnessed over 100 of his matches live at the All England Club, the World Tour Finals, in Dubai, Doha, Basel, Halle, and even at the Australian Open. 'I spent all the money I saved on these trips,' she said. 'And in Switzerland, for example, we used the days off to travel around the country. We went to the Jungfraujoch or visited the Rhine Falls. Tennis and sightseeing, what more could you want?'

During this time, she has made many friends with Federer enthusiasts all over the globe. They can be found everywhere. 'They don't let me stay in the hotel; they always want me to stay with them. And one thing about being a Roger fan: you always have something to talk about.'

But what makes him so fascinating to so many different people? Apart from his elegance and worldliness, she says it is probably how he interacts with his fans. 'He makes you feel like you are part of his extended family. I have always felt that he understands it's not easy for me to travel the world to watch him and manage the expenses. He makes you feel special in some way. He remembers your name. He remembers incidents with you. Like in Doha 2012, when he retired before the semi-finals. There we were, just two of us waiting for him, and he said, "Sorry, I couldn't play today." As if he had to apologise to us. We were feeling so embarrassed. And then I went to Basel that year and met him for a picture for the fan club, and he said again he was sorry about Doha. He appreciates his fans. It's an extraordinary relationship. I think his fans are very, very important to him. I remember once in Basel, he was having a tough time, and Lynette [his mother] came up to us, telling us to shout louder for him. Which we did, of course.'

Sunita will never forget Federer's amazement when he met her in the players' area at Wimbledon in 2018. 'I had special guest passes from our Indian doubles players, Vishnu Vardan and Sriram Balaji. They knew me because of my foundation. So I spent three or four days behind the scenes and could watch Roger practise. He must have been wondering what I was up to.'

The fact that he knows her by name makes her proud. And his name is forever immortalised on her: in 2010, after his defeat in the Wimbledon semi-final against Tomas Berdych, she had the RF logo tattooed on her neck as a sign of her bond. In 2017, after his stunning Australian Open triumph after a six-month break, she had his signature tattooed on her right forearm. During the pandemic, Sunita watched the last five games of that epic final against Rafael Nadal almost every night – from 1-3 to 6-3. Those are 22 minutes for eternity.

She treasures every minute of her fan life, said Sunita. Not even the unpleasant moments, such as in 2008 at her first Wimbledon, when it rained cats and dogs, and she had to wait out all night, protected only by an umbrella. 'Roger has taught us so many things,' she said, 'never to give up, keep fighting. Losses and wins will come your way, but you must learn to accept every situation.'

She has long been reconciled with his career since he miraculously returned in 2017 and subsequently won three more Grand Slam titles. She has only one dream: an exhibition match with tennis greats Roger Federer and Leander Paes and cricket heroes Sachin Tendulkar and Sourav Ganguly in Kolkata. 'Who knows what the future holds,' she says. Dream big.

Vittoria & Carola, Italian juniors
'There is always a table reserved for Roger'
In February 2020, Italy was the first European country to be hit with full force by the Covid-19 pandemic. What

remains, however, are not only the terrible images but also a video that symbolises how one does not let oneself get down even in difficult times and finds creative solutions: severely restricted in their lives during the two-month lockdown, Vittoria and Carola played balls to each other with their tennis racquets from roof terrace to roof terrace in Finale Ligure on the Italian Riviera.

'We weren't allowed outside except to go shopping with our parents,' Vittoria Oliveri, who was 13 then, said. 'So we couldn't play tennis either. And if there was something we missed a lot, it was that. Otherwise, we played more or less every day. On Sundays, when our family would have a barbecue on our terrace and Carola's family were next door on theirs, it almost felt like we were eating together. After dinner, Carola and I would take out our racquets and balls and do some practice. One Sunday, my father said, "Why don't you try playing from one balcony to the other?" He said it jokingly because he couldn't stand the noise of us banging the balls against the wall anymore. But we took his suggestion seriously and gave it a try.'

Because there was an 8.5-metre-wide hole in the middle, rallies from terrace to terrace were not so easy. 'Sometimes we were a bit short, then the ball fell down,' said Carola Pessina, 11 at the time. 'But once we discovered roof terrace tennis, we played almost daily.' Vittoria adds: 'During the lockdown, we couldn't do anything, and we often stayed on the terrace chatting, enjoying ourselves.'

Because the balls kept falling as they played back and forth between the terraces, they developed a system: they attached a bag to a fishing rod, and when all the balls had fallen, someone would run down, often one of their fathers, pick them up and put them in the bag.

What started as a pastime soon created quite a buzz. To keep the more than 100 kids at the ambitious tennis school in Finale Ligure – one of the top ten in Italy – from getting out of form during the lockdown, technical director Dionisio Poggi had put together a programme of exercises for them. 'To motivate them, I told them they could send me videos of it, which I would then post on our Facebook page. So Vittoria and Carola also sent me their video, which was quite extraordinary.' In the 24-second clip, they play the ball to each other 12 times from terrace to terrace. A respectable performance.

Poggi posted the video online on a Friday evening in mid-April and then forgot about it. When he looked at the Facebook page again late in the evening, 2,500 had already seen it. The following morning it was over 20,000, and when the ATP shared it on its social media accounts, the number of views skyrocketed. 'Suddenly, I had a lot of people contacting me, journalists calling me,' Poggi said, amused. The two girls did it as a game, but it was a strong message of resilience. In Italy, we haven't talked enough about the impact of the pandemic on children.'

Carola and Vittoria became famous suddenly, both in and beyond Italy. 'A local newspaper from the province of Savona, where we live, got in touch first,' Vittoria said. 'Then we gave interview after interview, for the radio, many newspaper reporters called too. The Italian TV channel Supertennis interviewed us, and players like Stefanos Tsitsipas shared our video. Suddenly many people knew us, and we were often approached on the street after the lockdown. We discovered a new world.' Carola interjects, 'It was quite strange, though, that suddenly so many people knew who we were. They said, "Look, that's

Carola and Vittoria!" And that they wanted to take photos with us.'

Vittoria's mother, Lorenza, who made the short video, briefly joined the Zoom conversation and proudly said: 'The *New York Times* also wrote about it. *Al Jazeera* ran the story, and a Mexican journalist who usually follows the Pope covered it. It was an incredible thing.' And Italian pasta giant Barilla, which has always promoted tennis, used to work with Steffi Graf as a brand ambassador and now collaborates with Roger Federer, advertised with the two likeable girls.

When they were interviewed on the Oliveris' roof terrace on 10 July 2020, dressed in pink tennis gear, they thought it was another shot for Barilla. 'I'd like to have the elegance of Federer and the power of Nadal,' Carola says, then she sees in the corner of her eye how Federer has emerged from behind a black curtain to surprise them both. 'You have to imagine that! We weren't warned,' said Vittoria, playfully indignant. 'You should be able to prepare yourself mentally before you meet Federer. I gasped for breath; they had to stop the camera for a moment and bring me a glass of water. I felt like I was going to faint.'

The parents of the two girls, as well as tennis coach Dionisio Poggi, had known Federer was coming but had had to promise in writing to the makers of the Barilla commercial not to tell them. The grimace Vittoria makes when she first sees Federer on her terrace is priceless. The latter spent the whole day with the two girls, from 10am to 6pm. First, they played tennis from roof terrace to roof terrace – Federer alone; they were on the other side next to each other. They chatted a lot and had lunch together, pasta of course. When he drove back off by car in the evening, they waved to him from the balcony. By now, word had spread in the small town that Federer was there.

'I still get goosebumps when I think about it,' said Vittoria. Her friend Carola enthused: 'He is quite modest, nice and friendly to everyone. He didn't act like a superstar, but like a normal person.' Barilla had first suggested flying the two girls to Switzerland to meet Federer. But he wanted to join them on the roof terrace that went around the world.

Beaming, Vittoria said: 'He touched the stairs in my house! He always seems so nice on the court. You might think he's only like that when everyone's watching. But he was also wonderful to us, very approachable. He also showed us videos of him playing tennis when he was little. He told us a lot, and we asked the poor guy a thousand questions.'

For example? Carola said that she asked him how much he had to train to become so good. 'He said that it wasn't crucial how often you trained. But rather, every time you go to practice, you do it with joy and full of enthusiasm.' She quizzed him about the other players, said Vittoria. 'We wanted to know which of them was nice. We also asked him about Nadal. He spoke very highly of him. He said that they respect each other and are even friends, although they are rivals. And that their families also get on well with each other.'

Although he had no experience in rooftop tennis, Federer did quite well, the two girls agreed. 'You could tell he's been playing tennis for a while,' Vittoria said. And what about his Italian, known as a talent for languages? The girls still see room for improvement. 'We played a game and taught him some Italian vocabulary,' said Vittoria. 'Carola or I would say a word in Italian, and he had to guess what it meant in English.'

Dionisio Poggi was also there that day. 'When Barilla finished shooting the video, Roger kept playing with the girls. I had the feeling he enjoyed it,' said Poggi. 'He had all the time in the world, was completely relaxed. He is an extraordinary person, of such friendliness and closeness. For the girls, it was the nicest gift you could give them. And honestly, for me too. I am still touched today when I think about it. Even more than an exceptional tennis player, Federer is an exceptional person.'

The meeting was also worthwhile for Barilla. The pasta giant created a commercial between reality and fiction by bringing Federer and the two girls together, and it generated over 22 million views on YouTube alone.

For the girls, meeting Federer was not the end of the story. He invited them to the Rafa Nadal Academy in Mallorca for a week of training. They met the Spaniard there in October 2021 and were impressed by how normal and modest he remained, too.

That video during the lockdown turned Vittoria and Carola's lives upside down. In Rome, on the fringes of the Global Health Summit in spring 2021, they met Ursula von der Leyen, President of the European Commission. And she praised them for their initiative: 'While we try to teach our children about life, our children, in turn, teach us what life is all about. Carola and Vittoria showed that we must never let obstacles and limitations stop us, but always make the most of the moment.'

Vittoria said: 'These encounters have made us grow. They are unforgettable experiences, and I hope they benefit us in the future.' Does meeting Federer inspire the girls to strive for a professional career themselves? Carola said, beaming, 'Yes, I would like to give everything for tennis.' She trains every day and is already travelling to international junior tournaments. Vittoria injured her shoulder for a while and is now focusing more on school: 'It would be nice to become a professional tennis player. But I am realistic and know that I don't have the abilities. But I love the sport and hope to play it for the rest of my life.'

However, the dream of Roger Federer revisiting them in Finale Ligure is something the two friends dream of together. 'Roger has said he'll come by in a few years to check on my progress in English,' Carola said. She would like to invite him for a pizza at her parents' pizzeria, and Vittoria makes it clear, 'There is always a table reserved for Roger.'

ROGER, THE GAME CHANGER

WHEN ROGER Federer joined the professional Tour at the end of the 90s, the ATP launched the campaign 'New balls please'. They were worried about the future of tennis after Andre Agassi and Pete Sampras. The concern was unfounded. Federer soon took the reins, followed by Rafael Nadal and Novak Djokovic – and the Big Three catapulted the sport to unimagined heights.

Nadal and Djokovic should thank Federer, says Mats Wilander, because he started it all. And due to his variety, the sport, which had drifted in the direction of monotonous power tennis, has developed in a playful direction again. There is a bit of Federer in almost all young players, Wilander thinks. Former greats like Stan Smith and Roy Emerson particularly like his elegant play. They see him as a custodian of classic tennis, the way they used to play, and love it.

Federer was also an example when it came to locker-room etiquette. He emphasised togetherness and, as president of the Player Council, not only pushed for more prize money, but also for a fairer distribution. During Federer's time, tennis became more popular globally and more profitable than ever before – also for himself, setting new standards in marketing and establishing his own logo in tennis with 'RF'. Many followed his example.

In addition, he still found time to develop his foundation, which promotes early education in southern Africa. More than two million children have already benefitted from it. And with his manager, Tony Godsick, he set up the Laver Cup. Federer was a game changer on many levels. But what about after him? What about the future of tennis without the Big Three? The fear of the uncertain future is inherent in human nature.

Mats Wilander, tennis legend
'Roger is the only player whose shoes I would like to be in for a day'

Mats Wilander is one of Roger Federer's harshest critics and one of his greatest admirers. Does that go together? The seven-time Grand Slam champion nods in the conversation on the sidelines of the US Open: 'Yeah, of course. That's my role, right? To make sure that the game of tennis comes ahead of any player. We, the former players, have an obligation to the game to tell it exactly the way we see it, and it's not personal.'

When Wilander, one of the most prominent voices in tennis as an expert for Eurosport and as a columnist for the French sports newspaper *L'Equipe*, talks himself into the fire, it can happen that he sometimes gets carried away in his choice of words. Like after the 2006 French Open final, when he was disappointed that Federer had not risked more on his way to a four-set defeat by Rafael Nadal. At the time, he said: 'I think Roger Federer, today, unfortunately, came out with no balls. Sports are about balls and heart, and you don't find too many champions in any sport in the world without heart or balls. He might have them, but against Nadal, they shrink to a very small size, and it's not once; it's every time.' Harsh words.

Federer was not amused. Wilander noticed that the Swiss was avoiding him in the tournaments that followed. 'He didn't say hello to me for a while. Before, he had always come up to me and spoke Swedish. He had learned a little Swedish from Peter Lundgren. And being Swiss, he picks up languages easily. But I noticed he didn't come up to me anymore. I was a little worried because I hadn't meant it quite as rudely as it came across. There was a moment when I felt like, "Oh God, I feel so bad." But I knew that I was right. I'm not saying it's easy to change your game when you want it as much as he did. But I knew that he would not win the French Open against Nadal if he kept playing like that. So we meet again at the US Open for a live interview. We're talking: "How's it going?" Then he goes, "Some people think I have a Nadal syndrome." And I'm like, "Okay, Roger, I think I'm one of them." So then I said, "I want to apologise for using the words I used when I tried to make my point." Roger accepted the apology, and we never had any problems after that.'

Not that Wilander subsequently refrained from criticising Federer. For example, for the fact that he increasingly skipped the French Open in the autumn of his career, which is particularly close to the heart of the Swede as a three-time winner (1982, 1985, 1988). But it's not as if he only speaks negatively about Federer, quite the opposite. Time and again, he talks about him with great admiration. He said: 'Roger is the only player whose shoes I would like to be in for a day to feel what he's feeling. It must be incredibly fun when he's hitting the ball; his hand takes over.'

One rally, in particular, has stayed with him. One that Federer lost: his missed match point against Marat Safin in the tiebreak of the fourth set of the 2005 Australian Open semi-final. 'I'm watching in the stadium because I just coached Safin a couple of years before. So I'm sitting in the first row on the baseline, and Roger hits a tweener in front of my eyes on match point for no reason. He was running back and slowed down to hit the tweener, and he could have hit a forehand instead. Are you kidding me? On match point?' Safin won the point and later the match.

Was the choice of shot a wrong decision? Yes. But that scene taught him something important about Federer, said Wilander: 'Roger Federer probably will go down as the smartest tennis player that's ever played because of his variety. But I tell people, "You know why he's so smart?" Because he's not thinking. He's just reacting because he's so good at everything. If he's thinking, he's thinking with everything. He's thinking with his whole body. I've learned so much from watching him just playing. This is what I'm trying to teach the people I play with, the kids I play with. You're going to be as smart as possible by not thinking. The best tennis players are not thinking; they're feeling it. And Roger is the master at that.'

If you want to understand Federer's fascination, you have to watch him not only during the rallies but also in between, Wilander said. The game within the game, how he plays the ball to the ball kids on the other side after a serve is wide. 'He's like, "Give me the ball. I want to hit it and see if the guy can stand still and catch it with his hand." People don't realise that he's breaking the etiquette rules if he misses the ball kid over there. Because he's now causing a longer period between first and second serve. It's not like he can close his eyes and just hit the ball and hope that he hits the ball kid. No. He has to be focused on hitting the chip back to the kids. What kind of focus does the guy have when he's paying attention to such things that don't count? I mean, it's unbelievable. Andre Agassi used to be the opposite. When you read his book, you know what happened; he's hit too many tennis balls to love the sport. Then he learned how to love competition later in his life. Roger, on the other hand, loves to toy with the ball.'

Was he born with this playfulness? Wilander said: 'Obviously, his hand-eye coordination is somewhat God-given, but the attitude towards the sport is not; it's environmental. His outlook on life makes him excited about hitting a tennis ball. So obviously, he's got good hands. We all have good hands; the best players in the world all have good hands. Rafa Nadal has excellent hands. Most probably as good a hand as Roger. Novak has really good hands, and we never talk about that. Roger has great hands, but he also has a mind to come up with all these different little things. He took the sport to the next level with his artistry. Before Roger, tennis was heading in a very one-dimensional direction, Agassi-style. And then suddenly along comes Federer, who not only plays completely differently, but he toys with his opponents. Who hits a short slice backhand and asks the other guy to come in? It's nearly obnoxious to do that. I am not saying he would ever consider that being obnoxious, but as a tactical move, it's frickin' obnoxious.'

Wilander says that Federer's playfulness has been very good for the sport. 'He turned tennis around to what it is today – much more than Nadal or Djokovic. If Federer didn't come, if we would have had only Nadal and Djokovic, tennis would be boom, boom, boom. But because of Federer, it's back to that sort of game of feel rather than a game of power. The combination of Federer, Nadal and Djokovic is what you see when you watch Tsitsipas, Berrettini or Shapovalov. There's a bit of everybody in all these new guys, and that's so amazing; it would never have happened without Roger. He invented stuff. I've never invented anything in tennis; I was just playing. I saw Björn [Borg] and I played like Björn. Roger came up with new things. There's a genius between his brain and his hand. In that respect, he reminds me of [Diego] Maradona.'

Not only Federer's success but, above all, his playing style has benefitted tennis and helped to boost its popularity, he added. 'I've never seen people sit in their seats before the match starts at the Australian Open. But when he plays, it's full before he walks on court. That's not the case with Novak. And with Rafa, it's not the case either. If Roger plays, it's like at a symphony concert or a Broadway show where they tell you to get in your seat now because you're not getting in later. If he plays, the people sit there from the start. They don't want to miss anything. They want to see him walk on the court, which is amazing. And even watching Federer win 6-2, 6-2, 6-2 is a pleasure. Watching Nadal winning 6-2, 6-2, 6-2 is like, "Why do we still play five sets? Let's take them off the court and put the next match on." With Roger, everyone is like, "Please keep playing." That, to me, is the greatness of him.'

Speaking of greatness, how does Wilander view the debate about the GOAT, the greatest of all time? The Swede said: 'If Roger had won the most Grand Slam titles, we would have called him the greatest because he took tennis to the next level. The Big Three playing simultaneously, that's the most amazing time we've ever had in the Open Era, and we're never going to separate them. I don't think many articles will separate Novak or Rafa from Roger because Roger is the one that started it. Novak should thank Roger. And he should thank Rafa. Because Rafa said: "Wait a minute, what Roger can do, I can do too!" And then Novak said: "Okay, then I can do it too!" What Roger has unleashed is unbelievable. No one has moved tennis forward as he has. Björn Borg also lifted it to a higher level, but only for five years. Then he stopped. Roger did things with the ball that we hadn't thought possible before. Like Tiger Woods in golf. Kids grow up, see him and think, "Ah, okay, you can hit it 300 metres. Not just 220 metres. So let's try to hit it 300 metres!"'

And credit must be given to Federer for accepting the challenge of competing with Nadal and Djokovic, who are four and five years younger, respectively. 'I think people have not realised enough that he's played in two generations and dominated his generation like probably no other before. And then he's so good that he can keep up with the people that come after him that are more modern and who've grown up with a big racquet from the beginning. He somehow figured out a way to stay with the more modern way of playing tennis.'

Previously, it had always been the case that the new generation took over from the older one. Wilander was a youngster when the great era of John McEnroe was coming to an end. 'He won his last major in 1984 and when I played him, I told myself: "He's five years older than me. He's playing as they played in the 60s. I am not going to lose against him anymore. Like I am not losing against Jimmy Connors." And then suddenly comes the next generation, comes Andre Agassi. He looks at me and goes: "You don't hit the ball; you just push it all the time. So I'm just going to rip it past you." Pete Sampras did the same thing.

Federer figured out a way to stay with those guys. Yes, he got beaten more often than he won, but he still came back and won again.'

Mats Wilander nodded with satisfaction. He had to leave; Eurosport needed his assessment. To be one of Federer's harshest critics and one of his greatest admirers – yes, that goes together. At least for someone like Wilander, who doesn't just see victory and defeat but sees tennis as a universal artwork.

Roy Emerson, tennis great

'He turned and asked: "How do you get milk out of this?"'

Roy Emerson grew up on a dairy farm in Queensland, Australia. His father would have liked to hand over the farm to his son, but he had other plans. 'I said no, I'd like to leave school, play tennis and travel the world.'

So in 1953, aged 16, he left to explore the world as a sparring partner on the Australian Davis Cup team with Ken Rosewall and Lew Hoad. 'Ashley Cooper and I were the two young lads chosen to go away, we were the orange squeezers. We were happy to hit with all of them. And getting a lot of experience, particularly under [non-playing captain-coach] Harry Hopman, a tough taskmaster.' Emerson thought that if it didn't work out with tennis, he could always take over the farm. It didn't come to that.

Emerson had milked cows daily on the farm as a youngster and had a lot of experience with cattle. Unlike Roger Federer. We were sitting in the lounge of the Gstaad Palace Hotel, which towers majestically over the exclusive resort, and Emerson talked with amusement about his first personal encounters with Federer. He had a cheeky grin on his face. It was Tuesday, 8 July 2003; Federer had won Wimbledon for the first time two days before and received a triumphant reception at the Gstaad tournament. Emerson had also been called upon to congratulate him as a cow was led onto the court. 'Standing next to me, Roger said: "Goodness gracious. What am I going to do with this cow?" And I said: "Well, you have a garage back in Basel. Put it in the garage and milk it every morning and night."'

But Juliette, as Federer's 800-kilo (126-stone) living prize was called, stayed in the Bernese Oberland. That was a smart idea, all the more so as Federer was not as skilled at milking as Emerson had thought. The Australian accompanied Federer the next day to Alp Eggli, Gstaad's home mountain, to visit Juliette. 'All the photographers asked Roger, "Can we get a shot of you milking the cow?" Roger had no idea where to begin. And so he got the stool, and the cow looked at him; he grabbed a teat and squeezed it a little bit. He turned and asked: "How do you get milk out of this?" I said: "You gotta go up and down. Bring it down." We finally got a glass of milk.'

Juliette later had a calf that was named Edelweiss. In 2005 she was slaughtered because she no longer gave milk. In 2013, on his return to Gstaad, Federer was presented with another cow, Desirée.

Emerson had another story from his first meeting with Federer that he liked to share: 'I said to Roger: "I congratulate you on winning your first Wimbledon. But I congratulate you even more on what you did after you won." And he said, "What do you mean?" I said, "You stayed down on the court with your opponent. You didn't climb up into the stands and celebrate in front of a very disappointed opponent. You gave respect to him. That's the most important thing. Keep that up. Because that shows a lot of class.""

He continued: 'Unfortunately, Pat Cash had started that bad habit when he won Wimbledon [in 1987]. And it became a nice little spot for television. Everybody is doing it nowadays. But it's not showing any respect and sportsmanship to your opponent, who is extremely disappointed to watch you celebrating for five or ten minutes. But Roger said, "Believe me, I will never do that. Because I know how disappointed I would have been. And I know how my opponent feels."'

Federer kept his word. Not once did he climb into the stands after one of his 20 Grand Slam victories to hug Mirka, his coaches, his parents or the children. Emerson holds that in high regard. 'Sportsmanship was the number one thing when we grew up,' he said. 'Unfortunately, that has been somewhat lost today.' Federer upheld those values.

Emerson is convinced that the influence of his compatriot Peter Carter, who mentored Federer in his youth, played a role. Carter told him a lot about the Australian greats, Rod Laver, Ken Rosewall, John Newcombe, Tony Roche and, of course, Emerson, who knew Carter well and held him in high esteem: 'He was a really, really nice guy. Actually, he's worked with me with my tennis camps [in Gstaad]. I think Peter greatly influenced Roger on how to conduct himself on the court and also taught him the fluid way of playing tennis. Footwork, court coverage and, number one, how to give respect to your opponent. Unfortunately, the accident happened [to Carter in 2002].'

Emerson never regretted his decision to leave Brisbane Grammar School early. 'Travelling around the world is the best education you can get, and competing against different players from different countries is even better.' Ahead of his time in fitness and training methods, he became one of the most successful tennis players in history. He won 12 Grand Slam titles in singles and held the record for 33 years before Pete Sampras overtook him at Wimbledon 2000. He is the only person to have won all Grand Slams in singles and doubles.

Emerson always had a particular fondness for Federer. Because of his personality, but also because of his game: 'I always loved the fluency of it. It looked so effortless. He controlled the ball very well with spin and variety. He didn't just hit it with sheer power. He could make the ball talk. It looked like the game was easy for him. People respect him a lot for the artistry of his game. Plus, the thing that Federer showed was that if you walked into the match and didn't look at the score, you wouldn't know if he was up or down. He didn't show his opponent that he was worried or down. And that's an art. His opponents didn't know if they had him or he was in trouble, because he was always on a positive note from start to finish.'

The fact that his previous record of Grand Slam titles has now been far surpassed by the Big Three is impressive to Emerson. 'It just shows how amazing those three players are. The commitment and the training to keep the game at that high standard physically and mentally during all those years is incredible. You've got to admire the dedication to be able to keep that up. And to love the game that much to work that hard to be in top form for all those years.' His role model in terms of durability had always been Ken Rosewall, who reached the Wimbledon final for the first time in 1954 at 19 and for the last time in 1974 at 39. 'But what these three guys have done is just mind-boggling.' Emerson

217

does not like the comparisons, though, of who is the best of all time. He said you couldn't compare different eras because technology has changed the game a lot. Rosewall's dominant net play for him is still one of the most impressive things the sport has ever seen.

Emerson continued to follow the sport after his career. If only to be able to say something clever when asked, he said. With his wife Joy, he usually paid a visit to the Australian Open, while he now lives in Newport Beach, California. Thanks to tennis, he also cultivated his love of Switzerland, whose scenic beauty he was immediately enchanted by. He felt like he was in paradise, he said, when he first played in Lugano in 1954. Later, Gstaad captured his heart, where he triumphed five times at the clay tournament, and the centre court is named after him: Roy Emerson Arena. In the summer of 2023, at 86 years old, he hosted his 48th tennis camp on the courts of the Palace Hotel.

As a young boy, Emerson began playing tennis on homemade courts, made from the soil of abandoned ants' nests and with chicken wire for the net. The sport has never left him.

Mike Nakajima, former Nike tennis director
'Money and fame change people – but not Roger'

The prominent stakeholders in world tennis always rent houses near the All England Club during Wimbledon to hold meetings and welcome their athletes. 'There, athletes have a safe haven,' said Mike Nakajima, tennis director at Nike for 29 years. 'They can come and hang around and nobody asks for pictures.' Roger Federer felt very comfortable in the Nike house when he was young, liked to come over, make himself a sandwich with ham and cheese and watch Wimbledon on TV.

In 2016, as chance would have it, the Nike people on Arthur Road, on the other side of Wimbledon Park from the All England Club, were practically neighbours of the Federers. 'We had an indoor pool and we also had a tennis court in the back. It was a really bad one. We ended up resurfacing the court because we wanted to stay at that house, we put the Nike swoosh on, and everything was pretty cool.' The Nike house became the Federers' second home during the Championships. Mirka and one of the nannies went swimming with the kids and Roger played tennis with them.

'From my bedroom, I could see the tennis court,' said Nakajima. 'So I saw Roger feeding balls to his kids. It was almost embarrassing to see Roger Federer, the greatest player, playing tennis on one of the worst tennis courts. Later, he told me stories like one of the boys said; "Dad, can you get off the court so my brother and I can play?" He was on the side, and his little boys were playing together. I asked him, "Hey, Rog, when was the last time you got kicked off a court?" He just smiled. He must be fun to be around for his kids.'

Nakajima worked with many stars at Nike. From John McEnroe, Pete Sampras, Andre Agassi, Serena Williams and Maria Sharapova to Federer and Rafael Nadal. He even accompanied Serena as a shopping assistant (not his field of expertise). He first met Federer when Nike signed him as a 13-year-old. 'He was up and coming, one of the top juniors. We brought him on and I realised right off the bat that he's naturally charismatic and speaks well. And I noticed that he knew he was going to be great.'

His feeling did not deceive young Roger, and his success story also became a stroke of luck for Nike. After Sampras and Agassi, Federer turned out to be the next superstar of tennis. When Andy Roddick, under contract to competitor Reebok, won the US Open in 2003, he suspected it might be the start of the next US wave in tennis, said Nakajima. 'But it didn't happen. Europe became the hotbed of tennis, and Roger was the start of it.'

So Nike set out to popularise Federer in the US. 'I'm a little biased,' said Nakajima. 'But no one does marketing better than Nike. When you get the big Nike marketing machine behind you, that can blow that athlete through the stratosphere. Roger would have been famous on his own for sure. Even if he was playing for any other brand. But he became a lot bigger because of Nike's marketing machine. The exposure that Nike can provide to an athlete is amazing. Obviously, you have to have success on the court, which Roger had. He won a few US Opens that opened many people's eyes.'

The partnership with Nike soon expanded into new territories. 'Roger got into fashion, meeting Anna Wintour of *Vogue*, doing photoshoots for *GQ*,' said Nakajima. Federer made Wimbledon, the holy grail of tennis, his catwalk. He walked there in an old-school cardigan, a white blazer or long white trousers. He also carried matching accessories. In 2006, he wore a logo on the left breast pocket of his jacket with his last name; the following year, he wore his initials for the first time: RF.

Federer was a pioneer in tennis in this respect. Later, Rafael Nadal, Novak Djokovic and Andy Murray also had their logos created. Nakajima said: 'Many top athletes started to get signature lines because that became a bargaining chip for companies to sign them. If you sign with us, we'll create your own logo, and we will create a shoe that you'll get royalties on. Which athletes will say, "No, I don't want that?"'

The RF line was groundbreaking. 'We used to create a shirt for everybody in the world, US style, baggy, and then we realised that Europeans are so far ahead in fashion. Roger wanted it a lot more tailor-fitted. So we started creating the Roger Federer collection. That's something Mirka was very involved with. When Roger wasn't available, Mirka was. She told us this is what Roger likes, and we went by that. And we wanted to make sure that the tennis product we made, especially for Roger, became wearable as fashion. A nice polo with a little RF logo; people just went crazy over that. The RF hat was our number one seller at the US Open. A hat. It became one of the most iconic pieces we have ever created.'

Nike was lucky to have not only Federer under contract but also his rival Nadal. 'Roger and Rafa, they're very similar personalities. They are two of the nicest guys you'll ever meet on Tour. But on the court, they were completely different. Roger plays like he is walking on a cloud, light on his feet. Rafa is the opposite; his physicality is just brute force. Americans love rivalry, and we portrayed that. People love taking sides. Vamos Rafa! Allez Roger! And we had a lot of fun marketing those two.'

Speaking of marketing: Federer became the best-earning tennis player of all time, earning over $100 million a year at his (financial) peak through prize money and advertising contracts, according to *Forbes*. 'He has great marketability,' said Nakajima. 'I saw him speak four languages in a single interview and switch languages just like that. People tend to gravitate towards somebody willing to share himself and be unbashful. He's able to appeal to any audience. And people believe that he's saying the truth, whatever Roger pitches. He's that believable.'

How does he explain Federer outperforming his biggest rivals regarding marketability? 'I'm not sure Rafa wants to be the highest-paid endorser in the world. I don't think he cares. Rafa is Rafa, he has done extremely well and I don't think he needs anything else. Roger wanted to be marketed, so he appealed to different brands, audiences and consumer groups. And his management company's done an amazing job. And Novak? He could well be the most successful tennis player ever. But there's always a dark cloud around him. It's like he brings it upon himself. He hits the lineswoman at the US Open [2020] and gets disqualified? It happens, I guess. But why does it always happen to Novak? Or the whole controversy about the Covid-19 vaccination. Now, as a brand: do I want to be behind somebody who always has controversy around him? Or do I want to go with an athlete with a squeaky clean image?'

Although he became a superstar, Federer never became unfaithful to himself, said Nakajima: 'He never left his roots regarding being humble. I've had the privilege to meet so many world-class athletes. He's one of the top of my list with regards to how nice of a person he is. Yes, he's got a lot more money and a lot more of everything. But he hasn't changed. Money and fame change people a lot. I'm not going to name names, but we certainly have athletes in our sport that have changed. Money changed how they see things, act, and talk to people. Roger never did that.'

He fondly remembers the Roger Federer day on the Nike campus near Beaverton, Oregon, which must have been in 2007. 'We have Nike world-class athletes visiting the Nike campus all the time. But hardly anybody at Nike gets to work with and see athletes. So we like to create an event when they visit. Roger served coffee and doughnuts that day. He gave a gym lesson, passed out lunch, worked as a cashier, and played Wii tennis in the lobby of one of the buildings. You have to have a certain type of person to pull that off. Not many athletes are going to be OK with that. Roger was a perfect guy to do that. He's a pleaser.'

Nakajima continued: 'People love to hate successful people. They're jealous. But it always astounds me that no one ever says anything negative about Roger. Because of the way he portrays himself to others, he's loved by others. Because he treats others respectfully, he knows the audience and can adjust his conversation based on his audience. He knows how to talk to grown-ups and kids. I've had an event where he was supposed to be there an hour and was there for four hours. Four hours. Who does that? He knows that these are the people that watch him play. These are the people that are giving him sponsorships. He gets it.'

When Federer left Nike in the summer of 2018 after 24 years, moving to Japanese clothing retail chain Uniqlo on a ten-year, $300 million contract, that came as a shock to Nakajima. 'That should never have happened. For us to let somebody like that go, it's an atrocity. Roger Federer belonged with Nike for the rest of his career. Just like Michael Jordan. Like LeBron James, like Tiger Woods. He's right up there with the all-time greatest Nike athletes ever. I'm still disappointed. But it happened. I have to get over it. It wasn't my decision and I wasn't there for it.'

Nakajima left Nike in 2017 to start his own business. He founded the company BaseLine Performance Finance, which works with athletes and sports organisations. However, he remains connected to Nike, as his wife, brother and one of his three sons work for Nike. For Federer, the move to Uniqlo paid off, allowing him to become an investor in the Swiss performance footwear company On and promote its shoes. And it's all about the shoes, right?

'I'm sure everything works out for a reason,' said Nakajima. 'Roger is going to be fine. So I'm happy for him. I probably would have done the same thing if I were in the same boat. Who might have turned down a $30 million a year contract? But it should have never gotten to that point. Nike is still selling millions and millions of pairs of Jordans. When's the last time Michael played? It's been many, many years. They could have done the same thing for Roger. For years to come, they could have created shoes with an RF logo.'

Where does Nakajima see the Swiss after his career? 'I can't imagine he will be a commentator; nothing against that. But I'm sure he is thinking about other things. He's such a savvy guy; if you're a company, who wouldn't want somebody like Roger working with you? I think he'll branch out into other things. And his name will live on forever as one of the best athletes of all time.'

Stan Smith, icon

'The next time you see Roger, wear this shoe'

Stan Smith once spoke the remarkable sentence: 'Some people think I am a shoe.' The American won the US Open (1971) and Wimbledon (1972), captured 100 titles in singles and doubles and triumphed seven times in the Davis Cup. But many of today's generation are no longer familiar with him as a former tennis player but as the namesake and face of the best-selling Adidas tennis shoe. Even 50 years later, his face is still emblazoned on the tongue of the white, sleek trainer, of which more than 100 million pairs have been sold.

Time and again, there have been collaborations with celebrities to refresh the eternally stylish trainers and keep them in the limelight, like with the British fashion designer Stella McCartney. However, one collaboration Stan Smith would have liked never came to fruition: the one with Roger Federer. For a long time, Federer was under contract with Nike, and when he left the sportswear giant in 2018, he seamlessly switched to Uniqlo. 'Adidas should have signed him,' Smith said. 'We would have made a good pair.'

Federer's style has always appealed to him, Smith said. 'He's been more involved in the stuff he wears than the other tennis players. A great year was when he wore the cream blazer at Wimbledon [2006].' Perhaps Adidas could have launched a special shoe edition with Smith's face on one and Federer's on the other. Or something crazier. But that will no longer happen. Because the two are now competitors. Federer joined the Swiss running shoe manufacturer On as an investor in 2019 and co-designed a white lifestyle shoe that strongly resembles the classic Stan Smith: The Roger.

'I wasn't happy when I saw Roger wearing the shoe at the Laver Cup,' said Smith. 'Every company came up with a white tennis shoe that looks pretty close to my shoe. But maybe it's a compliment. And mine has a little bit more history.' In any case, he has nothing to worry about. Since Adidas relaunched the Stan Smith shoe in 2014, sales have exploded. Federer still has to sell a few trainers to compete with his American counterpart.

Smith has always liked Federer, not just because of his style: 'Roger has been a great ambassador for the game. He's made an incredible impact. I've always respected him as a player and as a person. He's handled himself well, in defeat as well as in victory. He's had a good perspective of playing the game. If you're the best player in the world, you tend to think you're pretty special. God has given a certain amount of talent to people. But does this make you any better than others? I don't think so. I like the way he's handled himself on and off the court. He's confident but not cocky.'

Smith, too, was world No 1 in the early 70s. He would always remind himself: 'It is essential to understand you can get injured, be finished. Suddenly, people don't invite you anymore and don't celebrate you as much. I've always felt that way. I've been fortunate to have a great wife, four children and 16 grandchildren. Those things are more important than the recognition of others.' Family man Federer would probably nod his head.

What Smith particularly likes about the Swiss: 'He has a good feel for the history of the game.' The American, who had his heyday in the 70s when you couldn't become a millionaire with tennis, is particularly passionate about this: 'I was involved in the whole process of going from amateur to professional tennis. Many of the guys before my time didn't have it as good as it is today. Guys before me were amateurs and never did turn professional. Chuck McKinley won Wimbledon [in 1963] and ended up working for a bank because he didn't earn enough in tennis to make it worthwhile. When I won Wimbledon, I won £5,000. It's great that tennis has grown; it's become a business. Today's players have a great opportunity, but many don't appreciate that as much as they should. Roger understands the history of the sport and pays tribute to it. For example, by creating the Laver Cup.'

Federer also established the link between the past and the modern era with his style of play. 'One of the reasons that the old guys like the way he plays is because he plays as we did. He's got a one-handed backhand; he can slice, top, drop shot, serve, and move his opponent around. He plays a lot as we did but at an incredibly high level.'

Smith believes that Federer would have had great success even in his time with a wooden racquet: 'I would have loved to see the Big Three and Andy Murray playing with a wooden racquet and seeing how they would do. They couldn't put as much spin on the ball, and they might have more variety. And they would come to the net more often because it's pretty hard to pass somebody with those wooden racquets. I think Roger would have handled it best. He knows how to outmanoeuvre his opponents on the court; he doesn't just overpower them. And he is a superb net player. Roger has been playing great from the baseline, and the new racquets have helped him, but he's got the full package of play.'

Federer has done tennis well by playing differently than most, Smith said. 'Roger was able to hit different shots. Some players play one-dimensional; they just stay back and hit groundstrokes. We're seeing a more homogeneous, same kind of playing style. Variety is the spice of life. It relates to tennis and everything else. That phrase I've been thinking about quite a bit. I've been fortunate in my life to have so much variety in things I've done on and off the court, which stimulates me and keeps me active. And in tennis itself, you'd like to see some variety, and you'd like to see the players not just playing power tennis.' That's why he likes young Carlos Alcaraz so much because he varies his game and plays a lot of drop shots.

As for the discussion about the GOAT, Smith doesn't want to make a definite call. 'I think the GOAT idea is fun for the game; it creates interest. My list includes the Big Three but also Pete Sampras, Björn Borg and Rod Laver. Maybe even Don Budge. He won the Grand Slam. Laver won it twice and no one's done it since. So those guys are on my list. But of course, I have Roger up there. There are so many factors to consider in this discussion. You can talk about Grand Slam victories. You can talk about the overall records, the head-to-head. You can talk about the impact on the game, about sportsmanship. That Roger's gotten this Stefan Edberg Sportsmanship Award so many times speaks volumes. All these players voted for him because he's done it in a nice way.'

Tennis fans have been very spoiled with the Federer, Nadal and Djokovic era, Smith said. 'All three of those guys are great competitors. On the court, Roger and Nadal have been a little softer, and Djokovic is a little more emotional and gets a little more negative. The fans sense that, but it's all relative. And Djokovic has handled his defeats tremendously well; he'll put his arm around a player and smile. So he's great in that sense. These three guys are all good ambassadors. And their longevity is impressive.' Even if they had all stopped playing, the last chapter was not yet written. 'I think all those guys to different levels will still make a big impact on the game. I think they will be involved in other ways.'

Apart from that, Roger Federer will continue to work on competing with Stan Smith with his shoes. Spotting my Stan Smiths – hastily added after realising that a pair of Ons would probably not go down too well – he signed the spotless white shoes with a gold, waterproof felt-tip pen and said with a mischievous smile: 'The next time you see Roger, wear this shoe and tell him I said hello.'

Heinz Günthardt, Swiss trailblazer

'He makes everyone feel: I'm madly happy to be here'

Roger Federer was not yet born when Heinz Günthardt became the first Swiss to win an ATP tournament, in Springfield, Massachusetts. Neither was his older sister Diana. It was February 1978, and the story that led to Günthardt's triumph is too adventurous not to tell. The 18-year-old had failed to qualify for the tournament when a blizzard in the north-east of the US brought everything to a standstill. It snowed for 32 hours and the snow piled metres high; thousands of cars got stuck in the white masses.

For days, the roads in Springfield were closed, and even the airport remained shut. As a result, some players could not make it to the tournament, and Günthardt slipped into the main draw as a lucky loser. With youthful exuberance, he seized his chance and won the title. In the final, he beat the heavily favoured American Harold Solomon. He became the first lucky loser ever to win an ATP tournament.

As a youngster, Günthardt had already won the junior events at Roland-Garros and Wimbledon in 1976. However, he was denied a Grand Slam title in singles with the professionals. He retired at 28 because of a hip problem that limited him throughout his career and forced him to take many painkillers. As a coach, he later led Steffi Graf to 12 of her 22 Grand Slam titles. He worked with four

No 1s – with Dinara Safina, Jennifer Capriati and Ana Ivanovic, in addition to Graf.

He would have liked to coach Federer, too, but that never happened. Nevertheless, he spent hundreds of hours with his compatriot: Federer was down on the court playing; he sat in his broadcast booth and commented for Swiss television. Even though not all Federer's matches cracked with tension, he never got bored. 'There were some matches in which it was clear he couldn't lose unless he twisted his ankle. Those matches were less of a contest and more of a solo. But the variety of shots Federer showed still made them appealing.'

He said his favourite place to watch him play was on grass, most of all at Wimbledon. 'His elegance, the beautiful grass, and spectators who behave accordingly make for a special atmosphere.' At the All England Club, he first saw the young Roger play in 1998 at the junior event. 'His demeanour was so confident; he radiated incredible self-assurance. After a few minutes, I knew: "Wow, he can play tennis!" You never know how good someone will become. But I saw his huge potential right away.'

Was Federer showered with talent? Günthardt said: 'The question is how you define talent. His athleticism, his balance and agility, the way he anticipates his opponent's shots and his variety, that's all very impressive. But probably his greatest talent is that he simply loves to play tennis. And he loves it every day. That is an enormous source of energy for him. I don't think you can teach that; that's his character. He was born to play tennis.'

That includes the big matches in the spotlight and the strenuous hours when no one is watching. 'When juniors watch clips of Roger playing a half-volley, or a drop shot and want to copy that, that's nice,' said Günthardt. 'But you don't see the 30,000 hours he's worked to be able to do that. The better you are, the more you can improvise. As Thomas Edison said, "Genius is one per cent inspiration and 99 per cent perspiration."'

His love for tennis has always driven Federer to develop his game and take on the challenge of his younger rivals Rafael Nadal and Novak Djokovic, Günthardt added. 'He is extremely interested in this sport. And the exciting thing about tennis is that you will never exhaust all its possibilities. It's similar to chess in that respect. The difference is that in tennis, you must always react. It's chaos out there, and you try to get a grip on that chaos. The way Roger took this as motivation is exemplary.'

For years, Günthardt conducted the on-court interviews at the Swiss Indoors in Basel, Federer's home tournament. Their verbal ping-pong after the matches often caused amusement, also for Federer. Like in 2007, after winning his second-round match against the young giant Juan Martin del Potro, Günthardt asked him quite innocently: 'He's only 19 and 1.95 metres tall. The day before yesterday, you played against someone who is 100 kilos. How is that? Are you starting to be one of the smaller ones in the dressing room?'

Federer instinctively thought of something other than his height and could hardly contain himself. 'I think in the middle,' he said, laughing. 'But I don't stare that closely.' It was no longer possible to think of a serious interview; Federer began to laugh repeatedly and gave ambiguous answers. The audience had a great time. In such moments, when the local hero shook off his poker face and behaved childishly, people felt a special bond with him.

One quality in particular that impressed Günthardt about Federer was his way of making people worldwide feel that he didn't want to be anywhere else at that particular time. 'That's why he's so popular everywhere. He makes everyone feel wherever he is: I'm madly happy to be here now. I'm madly happy to be in Paris. I love being at Wimbledon. I love being in New York so much. But I also love being in Shanghai. Whether that's the case, I can't say. He might also have days when he is not so enthusiastic. Still, I've never had the impression that he was in a place he didn't want to be.'

Günthardt was the pioneer who once put little Switzerland on the map of world tennis; Federer continued on this path 30 years later. But the influence of Martina Hingis should not be underestimated, Günthardt emphasised. Even before Federer made his debut on the professional Tour, she had already won four Grand Slam titles in 1997 and 1998. 'Hingis was the door opener. It no longer seemed so absurd to dominate this world sport from Switzerland. When I left for Wimbledon, I heard sentences like: "Just enjoy being part of it!" It was quite different when Roger came on the scene. And that had a lot to do with Martina. She made him believe in himself because he had seen her win big tournaments. And you can't win without that belief.'

Swiss tennis wrote an astonishing success story with 28 Grand Slam titles in women's and men's tennis through Hingis, Federer and Wawrinka, Olympic gold medals by Rosset (1992) and Bencic (2021) in singles, Federer and Wawrinka in doubles (2008) and with the Davis Cup victory (2014). How does Günthardt explain this? 'Tennis is very widespread in Switzerland. If you want to play tennis here, you can almost always reach a club nearby by bike, and that's a good starting point. In addition, we had an imported sporting culture, especially from Czechoslovakia after 1968. And at a young age in Switzerland, you automatically slide into competition through the Interclub, our popular club competition. It's a mix of many factors.'

A champion like Federer, however, cannot be produced in a factory. 'When you have such an exceptional athlete, you must create an environment where he stays motivated and plays enough tennis. That was done well with Roger. When the federation realised he was special, it pulled all the strings. But if you could produce champions, the Grand Slam nations would dominate the sport. Fortunately, there is no magic formula. You can create good conditions but ultimately the champions make themselves.'

What will be the legacy of Federer in tennis? 'Certainly the way he played. And the way he presented himself. People will continue to stand up and clap when he comes to a stadium. Even when he's not playing.' Whether the Swiss is the greatest or one of the greatest is not so crucial in Günthardt's opinion. 'The number of Grand Slam titles is a good yardstick. But do they tell the whole truth? Who played against whom at what age? You can measure the record winner, but not the greatest.'

Quite different from athletics: 'Usain Bolt is the fastest of all time. End of discussion. In tennis, you may ask: "Federer or Nadal or Djokovic?" In football: "Ronaldo or Messi?" It is this very debate that makes it exciting and helps the sport to stay in the conversation. Maybe we can agree on this formula for the time being: Federer was the greatest on grass, Nadal the greatest on clay and Djokovic on hard court.'

In any case, Federer gave Günthardt, who once set out as a teenager to be the first Swiss to leave his mark on world tennis, many an exciting hour. And many others, too.

Janine Händel, CEO of the Roger Federer Foundation

'With Roger, the children lose their inhibitions'

When Roger Federer visits a kindergarten in southern Africa, for example in Namibia or Malawi, the children don't know who he is. At least, not as a tennis player. They don't even know what tennis is. Nobody wants to take a selfie with him or get his autograph. Usually recognised almost everywhere, he is completely stripped of his role as an international star, yet he is in the middle of it all in an instant. Janine Händel, CEO of the Roger Federer Foundation, observed this time and again.

During such visits, she experienced him herself as a playful kindergartener. 'He plays along immediately, gets involved and is integrated within a short time,' she said. 'With Roger, the children lose their inhibitions. That is not a foregone conclusion. These children are not used to strangers and certainly not to people of white skin. Roger can open people's hearts and minds at the touch of a button. Children, but also adults. That is impressive for me to see.'

Usually, those children are afraid of strangers and have even burst into tears with her, said Händel. 'But Roger knows how to win the trust of the children and the kindergarten teachers. He meets everyone at eye level, and they sense that he likes and respects them. People feel taken seriously by him.'

Händel joined the Roger Federer Foundation in 2010 as CEO and its first full-time employee. With a doctorate in law and eight years in the Swiss diplomatic service, Händel was asked to lead the Foundation into a new era of professionalisation. Federer had realised that the organisation had grown too large to be run by the Foundation Council alone. Händel set up an office in Zurich's Seefeld district and proceeded to professionalise and expand it.

Federer's vague hope that he would have to spend less time through her involvement was quickly dashed, Händel said. The Foundation grew rapidly from 2010 onwards – with it, the workload for its founder and president. The money that flows into projects yearly has increased more than tenfold since then: from 0.7 to around 10 million Swiss francs per year. The Foundation has become an essential player in early education in southern Africa – in Lesotho, Malawi, Namibia, South Africa, Zambia and Zimbabwe. More than two million children have already benefitted from the programmes.

Federer never dreamed of this when he set up the Foundation on Christmas Eve 2003 with an initial capital of 50,000 Swiss francs – at the tender age of 22. The seed for this initiative was planted in his childhood: although he grew up in a middle-class family in Switzerland, he spent one or two months every summer in South Africa, the home of his mother, Lynette. So he was sensitised at an early age that not all people are as well off as they are in privileged Switzerland. He wanted to help.

The first thing his Foundation did was to finance school fees in a township in Port Elizabeth, South Africa. His visit there was an eye-opener for him at the time, as he met not only pupils but also children with cancer. Today, he frequently visits people worldwide whose last wish is to meet him. He is no longer so shocked, he once said. After all, he knows he is trying to help, and that is all he can do.

With his Foundation, Federer has remained true to the guiding principle of education in southern Africa. But it has changed a lot in these almost 20 years. For some years now, it has been focusing on school readiness in southern Africa because that is where it has the most significant possible leverage, as Händel said. 'In the previous funding strategy, we had invested about half in early education and half in primary education. Now we are linking these two levels.'

The Foundation became aware of this issue in Malawi, where it had been supporting kindergartens. 'Focusing only on the kindergarten level is not enough,' Händel realised. 'Because many children fail when they pass on to primary school. And it's important for the whole school career that children get a good start in primary school.' Because the transition is complex, as it involves different education sectors, this issue has been neglected, Händel explained. That's where the Roger Federer Foundation comes in.

Anyone who experiences Händel and hears her speak soon realises why Federer chose her: she is very goal-oriented and structured – just as he always was during his tennis career. She knows precisely what she wants and places her messages in the media in a carefully targeted way. And when a journalist asks tennis virtuoso Federer a tennis question during an interview about the Foundation's work, she gives him a frown.

The way the Foundation presents itself today reflects Federer, said Händel, a mother of two. 'When he does something, he does it right. He is involved in all important decisions, and no board meeting takes place without him.'

Despite his busy schedule on the tennis Tour, she says it had never happened that she couldn't reach him within a reasonable time when she needed him.

Händel credits Federer for being willing to go along with the new strategy of focusing on early education and school transition: 'We don't just want to do nice projects, we want to change systems sustainably. To do this, we have left the safe beaten track and depend on many stakeholders to cooperate. That is why we rely on many partnerships. Taking the risk that we can also fail in a country shows courage and a certain philanthropic maturity.'

Through his 'career as a professional philanthropist', as Händel puts it, Federer has continued to grow as a person. 'In the beginning, he just wanted to do good, but now he is professional there too and knows his influence. When he visits projects, he meets ministers and presidents. You can only do that when you have grown into that role as a personality, and as an organisation when you have developed a certain self-understanding and have a track record.'

A visit by Federer to Malawi, as in the spring of 2022, now involves much more than visiting a kindergarten supported by the Foundation and understanding how it is developing in cooperation with the village population. 'That is also very important, but new layers have been added. Equally important now is that he meets the national and international stakeholders to sensitise and mobilise them. Roger has great credibility and acceptance in his appearances. Ten years ago, he would simply visit a project. Today, he meets key people on the spot at the highest level. It almost has the quality of a state visit.'

While Federer usually stays entirely out of politics, he does become political during his visits to southern

Africa. He tries to influence early education to take on a more prominent role. The United Nations has adopted early education as a goal in its own right and formulated that every child should have attended a good-quality kindergarten for at least one year. But this is far from the case in southern Africa, said Händel. Up to 50 per cent of children fall through the cracks.

Federer has grown so much into his task that he can easily lecture and discuss his agenda on the radio for half an hour, as he did in Zambia in 2018, Händel said proudly, knowing that she had provided him with the essential information. She said: 'He is a door-opener. High-ranking politicians are well aware of his charisma, and he plays on his popularity to make a difference.'

Händel is not worried that Federer's charisma might diminish after retirement: 'Roger's reputation has long since ceased to be linked to sport. The whole package of his personality is decisive. And when he stops playing tennis, he doesn't shrug off his personality. You can take other examples like Andre Agassi with his Foundation.' The Andre Agassi Foundation for Education is dedicated to a similar theme in the USA: it helps children from underprivileged families to receive a proper education.

Federer would hardly have thought that his Foundation would take up so much space in his life while he was still an active player. This also has a lot to do with the drive and ambition of his CEO, who travels to Africa several times a year. For the children there, her boss is not Roger, the tennis player, but Roger, the funny playmate who helps. However, he benefits from the fact that he is pretty good at swinging a tennis racquet.

ROGER, THE PROFESSIONAL

NOT ALL jobs are equal. For some people, including journalists, seeing sports stars up close and personal goes with the territory. There are deadlines, difficulties, obstacles and challenges but for all that, it is a job that never gets old.

The view of a sports star through professional eyes is different to seeing them as a fan; it's more critical and more nuanced. But nevertheless, when someone like Roger Federer is conducting the orchestra, be it on Centre Court at Wimbledon or Court Philippe Chatrier at Roland-Garros, watching a master of their craft at work, close up, is a pleasure, even if it's still work.

From commentators trying to find the right words to describe a Federer performance, like Mary Carillo, who learned to let the pictures do the talking; to photographers like Ella Ling looking for the perfect shot from a man who rarely shows emotions on court, it's not always been easy.

But for all of them, including fellow players who worked with him on the ATP Player Council like Eric Butorac and journalists who needed Federer's words to enhance their writing, the Swiss was an integral part of their careers.

Mary Carillo, broadcasting legend

'Roger knows what his game does to people'

Mary Carillo has made her name on television. Ranked as high as No 33 as a player, knee injuries forced her to retire from tennis in her early 20s. That misfortune led her to move into broadcasting, where she has become one of the most recognisable faces and voices in sport. Few people can turn a phrase like Carillo.

Finding the right words to describe what we are watching is an art in itself, one made harder by the fact that it's happening in real time. What is even more difficult, she said, is trying to commentate on Roger Federer, especially when he is producing an incredible shot. 'That's why I've grown very quiet,' she said. 'Because fortunately for someone like me, I work in a visual context. I remember straining to find the words to describe what he was doing in a match. You go from saying: "That's luminous", "That's other-worldly", "That's resplendent", you start using up words and then you realise, these people are watching what I'm watching. I don't have to try so hard because what he's doing is so beautiful, so lovely. Why am I even trying to describe this indescribable, ineffable quality about this guy? I think I've done that with Roger more than anybody, where you have to get out of the way of him. You have to get out of the way of what he's doing and just let people see it.'

Carillo has tried comparing Federer to art. 'I remember the time I would have debates with the people in the booth with me; is this classical music or jazz? Is this Da Vinci or Michelangelo? I went through all of that and I went through my vocabulary.' As a student of the legendary Australian Harry Hopman, and later as a coach for him, Carillo said the best way to get across what Federer does on a court is to show them, rather than tell them. 'A lot of times I was taking a coaching look at it. We would do a replay on Roger, some long point or something, and I would say in this replay, watch his feet, watch how calm his head is, watch how steady his shoulders are. You point people to what he's doing. You can ooh and aah and say "no way" or whatever, you can make all those gasps. Or you can just quietly insert yourself and say, this is what he's doing, and you can't even tell because he's doing it on tiptoes. But watch what he does here. I'm very lucky that I work in a visual medium.'

Carillo's thoughts on Federer are influenced heavily by her upbringing. Growing up in New York, she was – and still is – close friends with John McEnroe. Together, the pair won the mixed doubles title at the French Open in 1977 and she had a bird's eye view on how McEnroe could make what was very difficult look simple. Federer, she said, has the same gift.

'From the time I was a little kid, I was watching somebody playing the same sport as me and making it look so preposterously easy,' she said. 'There was something damning about it. And it's not like he tried hard. I tried much harder than John, I practised much harder than John. I trained harder, I ate better. John followed the seasons; it was basketball season, he played basketball. He put down his racquet for the soccer season. There was something very annoying about that. But I recognised at an early age that there are some people who can make something hard look unbelievably easy. John was the first person that ever did that to me. In a way it was good for me to know that there are people like that, who can make hard things look easy. So when Roger came along, I just thought, I think I had a flashback. I remember this.'

Carillo has interviewed Federer on a number of occasions, including just after his breakthrough run at Wimbledon in 2001, when he beat the seven-time champion Pete Sampras in the fourth round before losing to Tim Henman in the quarter-finals. Intrigued at the young man in front of her, Carillo asked him an off-beat question. 'Early in the interview, I said to him: "Do you know how beautiful your game is?" And he said: "Yes." And then he started giggling and I said: "Well, do you make an effort to make it beautiful?" And he said: "Yes." It was one of those really sweet, silly conversations you could have with that guy. But he meant it. You know, he knows the effect he has on people. Roger knows what his game does to people.'

For Carillo, it's the apparent effortlessness of the way Federer plays tennis that fascinates so many people. 'You watch Roger and it looks like he's just making it up on the run,' she said. 'Plenty of people play tennis well.' 'Many people have watched tennis forever – when they see someone like him make it look like it's the easiest, most graceful, elegant thing in the world, when we all know that it could be something different from that, yes, I do think that's why people, beauty in all forms, excellence in all forms is going to get my attention. But when it's also beautiful, then you got me. Then I'm watching.'

Working for American television, Carillo has often shared a commentary booth or green room with Paul Annacone, who coached Federer to Wimbledon glory in 2012. On many occasions, the two have discussed the differences between Federer and Pete Sampras, whom Annacone also coached, including in that 2001 encounter at Wimbledon. Where Sampras wanted his major rival, Andre Agassi, to know that he was a better athlete than him, Federer has always just done things his own way.

'Is he an athlete or is he an artist? Which lane is he in? The fact is, he's in both,' Carillo said. 'He's widened the highway. The story goes that Jimi Hendrix, he used to walk around his house all day long with his guitar strapped around his waist, and he would just play it mindlessly, endlessly, just riffing, making up stuff. Roger's a river, he's like that. You could just tell that it makes sense to him in a way that doesn't make sense – people watching it think, oh my God, this guy is doing something that's much harder than you think.'

Not everything Federer has done has been universally loved. When he beat Andy Roddick in the 2009 Wimbledon final and then put on a jacket with '15' emblazoned on it to represent his record 15th Grand Slam title, some accused him of arrogance. Carillo didn't like it, either, but does not blame Federer. 'I thought that was a misstep, too,' she said. 'And I just remember when Roddick became aware of it. He's made missteps. There's no doubt about it. I think in a case like that, Nike probably said we already made these for you. And he probably said: "Oh, that's cool."'

Great champions have confidence, even arrogance at times, but Carillo said Federer is genuine, interested in the people around him and someone who made time for his family, even in the heat of a slam. 'I remember one US Open, I was working for a cable network and for CBS. And so when he sat down and said, "Who's this for?" and I said: "This is for CBS," he said: "But don't you work for USA too?" I said "Yes" and he wanted to understand. He said: "Wow, is that hard?" Like, all of a sudden, he wants to hear about my life. And again, he acts like he's got all the time in the world to do it. It's remarkable. The balance he seems to have, on and off the court, it's amazing. Paul [Annacone] would tell all these stories, like Paul would go up to his big old suite or wherever they were putting him up and he's got little kids running around and he's cooking for them, like in the middle of the US Open. It's not like he's got a separate room, you know, away from his wife and kids. He was in it. For some reason, [despite] everything that's happening to him, he seems to be able to normalise. How the hell do you do that?'

In one of Carillo's interviews, she asks Federer about the influence of his parents, Robert and Lynette. Federer tells Carillo they gave him space to breathe, to do his own thing and find his own way. They also instilled in him a sense of decency, which comes through in many ways, from the way he conducts himself on court to how he engages with his fans and how he deals with the media. Answering questions in three or four languages, Federer also uses press conferences as part of his warm-down, almost in a cathartic way. By the time he is done talking, win or lose, the match is out of his system. He even asks his coaches, occasionally, to watch his press conferences so that they know what's going on in his head.

'I think Roger enjoys it,' Carillo said. 'He enjoys that process and he usually has to do it in three languages. You know, when you listen to somebody like [Alexander] Zverev say: "I answered that question last week," like, do you know how many questions Roger has had for the last 20 years and yet somehow can maintain his patience with it? But I think he's different. I think he respects the jobs that other people are doing. He gets it. And I'm going to have to give credit to his parents for that. Be respectful, be kind.

'And again, there is something very attractive about him, he's got such an easy smile. And he smiles with his eyes, too. There's some very nice, almost childlike curiosity in his eyes, like he wants to really know what's going on. I love it when the people around him are trying to give you the old wrap-up sign. He's either ignoring it or he doesn't see it, but ... that was the beauty of his game. It never looked rushed. It looked like he had all the goddamn time in the world.'

Eric Butorac, tournament director
'He digests information incredibly quickly'

Eric Butorac worked with Roger Federer on the ATP Player Council for six years. He collaborated closely with him for two of those years as his vice-president before taking over from him as president in 2014. But before the American met Federer, he met his parents and chatted with his mother, Lynette. However, he had not intended to do so.

Butorac can't help but smile when he talks about it. It happened at the Swiss Indoors in Basel, Federer's home tournament. College graduate Butorac, a psychology major, was 25 at the time. 'It was maybe my third or fourth event on Tour. I was very new, a doubles-only player. When you enter the locker room, these people are the superstars. So it's a strange adjustment. The first time I saw Roger play was his match against David Ferrer in the quarter-finals of Basel in 2006.' It almost didn't work out, as Butorac recounts. 'I was naive to think we could take a seat in the arena and sit anywhere with a guest badge. I didn't realise that for his matches, every seat is full; there's nowhere to sit.'

But the ushers were kind enough to help Butorac and his coach Ryan Dussault. 'They told us we should try in the corporate boxes below. So we assumed that we were in some sponsor box. The people welcomed us, said they had two extra seats and were very nice, chatting with my coach and me. I was sitting next to this woman. And she was very chatty, asking me many questions about where I was from and what racquet I used. She seemed very interested in talking to me throughout the match. I had no idea who she was until after probably eight games when I asked her who they were sponsoring. And then she identified herself as Roger's mother. His father, his sister and Tony Godsick were sitting in the box, too.'

For Butorac, the rest of the match became quite distressing. 'We were quite embarrassed to be in the box. That was the last place we wanted to be; we wanted to keep a low profile. So we became quite shy and spoke less. And we tried to just politely clap and finish the match, hoping it would end quickly because we were extremely uncomfortable. But like many of his matches, it went fast and without drama.'

That episode gave him a good insight into who Federer was. 'For me, that set the tone for the person he was before I met him. His mother wasn't there to prove who she was; she was just happy to have a normal conversation. When you have that experience with someone's parents beforehand, you understand where they come from. It's the same when you maybe deal with a crazy father of a player and you understand why this player is maybe not quite as kind of an individual. And with Roger meeting his mother and father beforehand, who are also unbelievable people, you understand why he is the way he is.'

It would be another two years before Butorac also got to know Federer – when he joined the ATP Player Council in 2008 at the same time as the Swiss. 'When we started, the ten of us were all new members for the first time, and I was elected as one of the doubles representatives because I think the players knew that I was one with a college degree. And I was in the room with Roger, Rafa and Novak, and I don't think at the time I had met any of the three of them. I was looking at these three, who were already the best three players in the world at the time. And they were going on to become the greatest three of all time. So it was a unique environment to be in. I think the first few meetings, I was not speaking; I was just taking notes.'

But as time went on, Butorac took on an ever-greater role in the Player Council. Federer was the president at the time and in 2012 he became his right-hand man as vice-president. 'It was when Rafa decided to leave the Council. And I had become one of the more involved members, especially with the lower-ranked players, to try to understand the life of doubles players, qualifiers, and lower-ranked singles players. So the Council decided that I would be the right fit because you have Roger at the top who can speak in the press and understand the life of the top players. But it would be great for me to work with him to help him understand what life is like for many of these other players.'

Butorac and Federer got to know and appreciate each other better and better. 'We had a lot of conversations; they happened when we would share a car to the site sometimes, at any place around the world, in the locker room for five, ten minutes. It was at a time when we were doing some negotiating with the Grand Slams on prize money. And so much of my work was messaging everybody out here: What is the strategy? What are we doing? Because Roger didn't have time to speak to all of these players. But frankly, as a doubles guy, I did have the time, so my role was more of a messenger, acquiring information, getting it to Roger, getting it to our board members, and then bringing it back to the Council. I know that being an ATP Council member is time-consuming and mentally exhausting. And Roger has so many drains on his time that when there were things that I could pull off his plate, I would try to do that. Because it was so valuable to have him involved.'

Many people don't realise how much of a driving force Federer was behind not only increasing prize money but especially in passing it down, he said. 'The minute we got more funds committed to the players, his first comment was, "Okay, now this money has to go down. It has to go through to qualifiers, to first-round players, for a better life for them. We're okay at the top; it doesn't need to be here." So it was a selfless act in which he had put in a lot of work. For instance, in the 2021 US Open, first-round prize money was $75,000. If we looked back ten years ago, it was $20,000. That's an incredible jump for those players. And frankly, they're not the ones driving the business. The players like Roger are driving the business but it takes people like him to help the lower-ranked players. And Rafa and Novak have a similar mentality.'

How did Butorac experience the Swiss in the daily discussions at the ATP Player Council? 'He's extremely engaged, straightforward and very smart. He digests information incredibly quickly. So when you're there, you don't need to waste a lot of time; you can get to the point. And he can assess and make a decision quickly. That was what I noticed most about him. The other thing I noticed in the meetings when you're with him, you feel like you're the only person in the room. And now more than ever, I feel like you wonder now with the younger generation: are they really with you when you're talking to them?'

Butorac has a story about that, too. Working as head of pro tennis operations and player relations at the USTA since 2016, he let Federer train at Arthur Ashe Stadium one August. Even before the latter travelled on to the tournament in Cincinnati. 'So I had to lock up the facility after he left. And there was no food or anything on the site. As he had finished his practice with Jeremy Chardy, Chardy had already gone home. And he said, "Is there any food?" The cafeteria was closed; it was a Saturday and just one other person and I were in the building. My wife was coming down with my two boys at the time. And I said, "If you want, my wife can pick up some pizzas." So she stopped and took two pepperoni pizzas.'

They made themselves comfortable in the kitchen on the grounds and ate the pizzas. 'We sat there for maybe 90 minutes with Roger, Ivan [Ljubicic], my wife and my two boys. And for 90 minutes, he spoke with my wife, with me, not one time looking at his phone, never one time feeling like he had somewhere more important to be. And my wife walked away thinking she had never been with someone at this level who treated her like she was the most important person in the room. And I've seen him do that when he is with sponsors, a tournament director, or the Player Council. He's not on the phone. He's with you as a human being.'

Sometimes Butorac remembers this and tries to take Federer as an example: 'When I have many things pulling me in different directions and when I feel like I'm looking away and not doing a good job, I think back to how he is. I think that's an important quality lost with the next generation. If he can do this, I feel like any of us could learn that skill, to be very much in the moment. Wherever he is, he's there. And he doesn't seem too worried about whatever else is going on.' Today this is called mindfulness. And millions are earned with seminars and books that are supposed to convey this quality.

Butorac also remembers one encounter when his mother met Federer at Wimbledon. 'I don't know what year it was. But he was playing cards with Severin [Lüthi] and Stefan [Edberg] then. I never wanted to approach and bother him, but he seemed very calm. And I thought this was a good time to introduce my mother. She had asked me for many years. My father stayed at the table; he didn't want to go. So I just brought my mom to his table. When she met him, she had trouble finding her words. It just happened too fast. So he started to ask her questions. "Is this your first time at Wimbledon? Do you like watching him play? Do you get nervous at his matches?" I am sure he's had this happen many times that someone freezes. And so he takes over to make the other person feel comfortable.'

Butorac picks up from there: 'Generally, he asks many questions. Being who he is, he doesn't need to share. He is happy to hear about your life. He seems to genuinely like people. I think many players enjoy peace and being away. But I think he seems very happy around other people.' This trait is also evident in the locker room, where, unobserved by the public, he does not have to disguise himself. 'I think he is incredibly comfortable there and I think it's also like a safe place for him. Because once he steps out, there are people who will judge him and write about him. So I think he puts a guard up.'

Butorac ended his active career at the 2016 US Open and seamlessly switched to the other side. In addition to his role with the US Tennis Association, he rose from assistant to tournament director at the Western Southern Open in Cincinnati in February 2022. He always asks the staff to find out how the players are. 'I feel like the locker room attendants who work there really know; they know the quality of the people. I ask them all the time who is nice. And how you treat the locker-room attendant, I think, shows a lot about who you are. My locker-room staff always speak about how much they love Roger and how friendly he is.'

But because Federer, often injured in the late part of his career, was not in the locker room so often, the younger generation no longer had the same relationship with him. 'Early in my career, he was very present in the locker room. He was just one of the guys. He showed a side in the locker room that you don't see outside, high-fiving, laughing, telling jokes. Everyone loved him. He shook every hand. What I've heard in the last couple of years, the younger generation isn't as connected to him anymore. It's not his fault. It's not something he's done. He's still an incredibly gracious individual. But he's been injured and wasn't there as often anymore. That's just the evolution of life.'

But Federer has had a lasting effect on the atmosphere of the tennis Tour, said Butorac. 'I hear stories from the era of John McEnroe and Jimmy Connors that they did not treat the other players very well; they didn't care so much about the other players. I heard stories about Ivan Lendl, about Pete Sampras. Some not-so-nice things on how they would treat people and act. And then Roger comes in and sets the tone for the locker room. He cares about others and perceives the tennis community as a whole. And just as much credit has to be given to Rafa because he was right there. He has a different way about him. But the same level of integrity and caring.'

Their behaviour has rubbed off on the other players on Tour: 'And then for everybody else, whether you're 3, 5, 20, 50 in the world, it was no longer okay to be an asshole. If the top players act like this, why can't you do this? Now, you hear players talking a lot about the lower-ranked players. They don't just talk about me, me, me. And I think this started with Roger because my older friends who played on the Tour said it was not like this. The top players didn't care about number 80. They thought number 100 was lucky to be in the tournament, and they shouldn't say anything else because they're just lucky to be here. He changed the mindset, and it will live on past his career on Tour.'

Michael Gradon, former Wimbledon Committee member

'He's the unique ambassador for the Club'

Michael Gradon had the privilege to be close to Roger Federer over many years, closer than most, through his unique role on the Committee of the All England Club. In his time, a number of Committee members were assigned to work with the top 16 male and female players during the fortnight, even assisting them as a moderator during press conferences. It was a delicate, nuanced role that took time to master. Gradon accompanied Federer for more than a decade and saw how he deals with the media, and people in general, from the best seat in the house.

'I can't remember what year it was that I first [had the role] but it might well have been almost as soon as I joined the Committee,' he said. 'And that was therefore sheer luck that I was allocated to Roger and effectively did almost every single one of them [his press conferences] for the next 15 years or something, during which I think he won five times. In that sense, yes, I saw quite a lot of him, but always, of course, in a suboptimal environment, because, understandably, they want to just get in there and get it over with. I would accompany them to the main press, of course, then Roger would then have to go and do the one-on-ones with the BBC and so on and there's always a time pressure, so it is not the right moment for any form of conversation at all. So in all honesty, in those settings, my interactions were generally: "Hello, Roger. Well done, fantastic. Well played. Are you happy to go straight in [to press]?" And then at the end: "Thanks very much, Roger."'

Gradon spent more time with Federer's agent, Tony Godsick, who would accompany the Swiss at most big events. Gradon describes Federer as a 'consummate professional' and the only difficult times came when Federer lost a big match. 'It's like a funeral,' he said. 'You just don't know what is the right thing to say because almost anything you say sounds really trite. And I have total admiration for any player, but particularly for him, how they managed to endure the questioning or any form of interview when they've just lost the final of Wimbledon. And, of course, and ironically, the only one press conference that I missed in all his time was actually the 2019 final.'

That, of course, was the 2019 final when Federer held two match points, on his own serve, in the final set against Novak Djokovic but could not close it out and lost in a tiebreak at 12-12. While the anguish of that loss was sinking in for Federer, Gradon faced a race against time to get back to the media centre but was thwarted by crowds and Federer himself, who made it there faster than expected. 'I knew that was the last one I was ever going to do,' he said. 'And even though, as I say, one doesn't like to be there in those sad moments, I was desperate to do it. I went straight from the Centre Court, but it's still a battle through the crowds. And by the time I got there, he was in. I'll be honest with you, I was completely gutted in one sense – to miss any one of them, you know, would have been sad. To miss [what could have been] the absolute last one ever ...'

As a member of the All England Club, Gradon was used to seeing famous faces around the grounds, from current stars to former players like Tim Henman, who later joined the Committee himself. He doesn't seem the kind of person who would get starstruck but with Federer, it was a different story.

'I remember, the first few years I was doing his media, you would just be terrified that you would mess up in some way to upset him,' he said. 'And in fact, I did once, because this whole business of switching from English to French and Swiss German was always quite challenging, because the number of English questions would be off the charts.' Press conferences at Wimbledon traditionally last between ten and 15 minutes. 'You wanted to give them a fair run. But I didn't want to alienate the Swiss press either.

'But one of the early years that I was doing it, I completely misjudged it, I think probably because I was starstruck or whatever, but I misjudged it. We'd had a good run on the English questions. And I thought, right, well, we've still got another seven or eight minutes for the Swiss questions. And then I got this message on the monitor saying, next player waiting – sort of, get off. And so, of course, I'm then torn between alienating the Swiss press or alienating whoever's behind the scenes. Is it Serena [Williams] in the corridor or whatever? And so I allowed a couple of questions in the Swiss press and then said, I'm really sorry, our time's up. And Roger overruled me. And that, of course, made me feel like a complete idiot because I can't overrule Roger's overrule. But equally, I didn't want to have a scene with whoever was the next player. So that was an awkward moment. And in fact, one of the things I did after the first couple of years, I negotiated – originally he had the same time as everyone else – I just said: "Look, he's trying to do three languages and it's Roger," so I managed to negotiate with the powers that be that instead of 15 minutes, it was 20 minutes, but even 20 minutes was never enough either.'

Thanks to his relationship with Godsick, Gradon was able to gain an insight into Federer away from the court as well, once sitting in on a press conference in Indian Wells, to get a look from the other side. For a man who must have answered thousands and thousands of questions from the media over his career, Gradon marvelled at the way he would try to give an interesting answer to every single one. And away from the cameras and the media, Gradon witnessed a different side to Federer.

'You could hear them laughing and joking and joshing and bantering,' he said. 'That's slightly different from the public image. It's a bit like with Tim Henman; when Tim was doing interviews, he was so straight. But of course, to those of us who know him, he is one of the funniest jokers in the world. So I actually really enjoyed just listening to him chat to Tony and so on offstage or friends who came down to be around the interview area. I'd love to have known him because I could tell there was that real humour and wit.'

Gradon's most notable interactions with Federer came off the court. In Shanghai one year, after the then Wimbledon chairman Tim Phillips got a message to him, Federer came almost straight off court to sit and chat to 20 or so All England Club members, who were there for a tour. 'I thought, wow,' he said. 'Does he really want to do that? I'm sure he doesn't, but, whether it was out of respect for Tim or just because he thought it was a nice thing to do ... I think he does love the Club, to be fair, and he's everything to do with that.'

Gradon played golf in Indian Wells one year with Federer's parents, Robert and Lynette. He also used to have brunch in Wimbledon village during the Championships with Federer's father and Godsick. On one occasion, Federer and his wife, Mirka, came up to the Royal Box balcony and had dinner during the Championships, again at the invitation of Phillips. Club members sat alongside, many of them open-mouthed. 'He came in at the start and chatted to us, and at the end,' Gradon said. 'I think it was certainly a very special evening for us, just sitting there thinking, you know, there's Roger and Mirka, at their table for two outside. And there was a moment when the dregs of the crowd suddenly spotted them. They were way into their meal and were just hanging out. And, of course, this huge cheer went up and he acknowledged them, so that was really special. Just the fact that he took time for us, as it were, to chat and he didn't need to.'

As a Wimbledon champion, Federer is an honorary member of the All England Club. But the Swiss has always seemed to embody its values, so much so, Gradon said, that the Club itself was torn between being unbiased and secretly cheering Federer on. 'He's the unique ambassador for the

Club,' Gradon said. 'Always will be. I can't remember any other player who's had that sort of symbiotic relationship with the Club's values and history and everything it stands for – and to be a consistent winner, arguably probably the most popular player who's ever played, certainly in my lifetime. Equally, you don't want it to look as if he's getting some sort of special treatment. So that was always probably a subconscious challenge. It wasn't something that was ever debated but obviously, there were one or two issues with scheduling. It's very difficult not to put Roger on Centre Court because each day you look at the choice and you say, well, this may be one of Roger's last times to play and he is the person everybody wants to see. But balancing that against sort of fairness to other players ... I was always glad that I wasn't on the Committee trying to juggle that.'

One such dilemma came in 2018, when Federer found himself out on Court No 1 to play Kevin Anderson in the quarter-finals, a match he ended up losing 13-11 in the final set. Few people had expected Federer, who had won the title for the eighth time in 2017, to be away from Centre Court, and as the match wore on, Gradon had a sinking feeling. 'I actually went and sat through the vast chunk of that match, just almost to kind of will him on, but it didn't work,' he said. Gradon then sat alongside Federer in the press conference and was amazed at how he once again dealt with what must have been a huge disappointment.

'Chatting to Tony afterwards, they were very, very upset that he wasn't on Centre,' he said. 'And I can fully understand that; ironically, because he played so much of his tennis on Centre, it would be a significant disadvantage for him to be on No 1 Court. The wind moves in a different direction, the sun is in a different place. However much you say [that] the courts are identical, there must be subtleties, you know, which have got to be more known to him than me, because, of course, the rest of us don't get to see that comparison.

'I'll never forget that question, "Did you lose because you were on No 1 Court?" and immediately [there was] humour. He said: "Well, I can hardly complain about that when I had match point." I was absolutely desperate for him to win because obviously I wanted him to stay in the tournament and I just dreaded the thought, was the scheduling some part of him losing? And of course, we'll never know.'

After all his years working with Federer, Gradon said he learned to spot some of the nuances of a press conference with the Swiss. 'He's human, after all, and his patience with answering those questions was off the scale, but you could tell when he was annoyed and you could always tell, if he was being asked about his next round, you could always tell when there was a slightly subtle point being made, as opposed to just a standard answer,' he said. 'If he's on the court and he's really, really annoyed – as we all know, he had quite a temper growing up – there would just be this slight, slight shake of the head as if shaking a lion's mane. That was his sort of a slight tic … but [it was like] how he kept control on the tennis court, particularly when going through losses when having had match point.'

Luki Frieden, filmmaker

'Roger creates a family atmosphere'

Luki Frieden was rooting for Roger Federer even harder than usual on that Sunday, 6 July 2014. Written off by many the year before, Federer was playing in the Wimbledon final against Novak Djokovic for his 18th Grand Slam title. And filmmaker and director Frieden knew: two days later, he would meet Federer for the filming of a commercial for the Swiss chocolate manufacturer Lindt. He suspected that the outcome of this final would influence Federer's mood.

Federer fought heroically against Djokovic, rallying from a 2-1 set deficit and 5-2 down in the fourth set, fending off a match point at 5-4 and forcing a fifth set to the ecstatic cheers of the crowd. But Djokovic kept his cool, as he almost always did in critical moments against the Swiss, and prevailed 6-4 in the fifth set. 'When he lifted the trophy, I thought: it will be difficult to shoot a feel-good commercial with Roger in two days,' said Frieden. But the date was set; there was nothing to change.

On Tuesday afternoon, the director and his crew were waiting for the almost-Wimbledon champion at a hotel with a panoramic view of Lake Zurich, and the nervousness was palpable. In what mood would Federer show up? Downhearted? Bad-tempered? Impatient?

None of the above. Federer came to the set alone, seemed relaxed and introduced himself personally to everyone: 'Hello, I'm Roger.' He broke the ice immediately, said Frieden. 'Although he can assume that we all know him, he introduces himself to everyone. I find that incredibly likeable. He was relaxed and in a good mood, no trace of a Wimbledon hangover.'

The plan was to shoot for two or three hours. Federer said right away that he would like to put the children to bed in the evening. Two months earlier, he had become the father of twins for the second time and, of course, everything was about the boys, Leo and Lenny. But the soon-to-be five-year-old daughters Myla and Charlene also wanted attention.

'We shot a three-minute dialogue film, a Skype talk with Lindsey Vonn, who was on holiday in Miami,' said Frieden. 'Dialogue films are some of the hardest stuff. It's the most difficult discipline, even with actors, because you can't hide anything. It will be three long and embarrassing minutes if it's badly acted. I asked Roger and Lindsey to read the script only once before filming and then forget it. It was the only way to create something fresh and carefree.'

The director also ensured the two didn't see each other beforehand so he could capture an authentic greeting scene on camera. 'We shot three or four funny takes from which we edited the spot together. I took the greeting from the first one; you can't recreate the freshness of the first hello. First, the two of them talked about the Wimbledon final quite spontaneously. Those are the magic moments you look for and sometimes find. You could feel their mutual sympathy; Lindsey and Roger let their humour run free.'

Not only was Frieden happy with the film, but so was his client Lindt. So they spontaneously decided that a second one would be shot the following week when the two athletes would meet on the Aletsch glacier below the Jungfraujoch and hit a few balls on a court specially built for the day at over 3,000 metres above sea level.

The event had only been planned for PR; journalists from around the world had been invited, from Japan to the USA. Frieden did the shoot an hour beforehand, then he was flown by helicopter to Interlaken. He went to the hotel in a taxi, where an editing room had been set up, and he and his editor spent the whole night editing so that the film could be released at 10am the following day.

To date, Frieden has filmed twice more with Federer: in the summer of 2020 for the opening of the Lindt Chocolate Museum in picturesque Kilchberg on Lake Zurich; and in spring 2021, when he staged three spots for a Swiss luxury brand in a film and photo studio in Zurich, which were released during Wimbledon. 'The whole production was very challenging; we planned every tiny detail months in advance,' Frieden said.

He had great fun making the films with Federer, said Frieden: 'The playful element that characterises him on the court, Roger also lives out on the set. Be it in terms of acting but also in those moments when the camera is not running. He never waits bored for the next take or retreats; he sees himself as part of the crew, jokes with people, and takes an interest in them. He creates a family atmosphere as if they've known each other for a long time. But still, it's Roger Federer. It's not just any actor who comes to the set. Roger's whole career and history always resonate. You can feel that aura.'

Frieden recalls the following scene on set: 'Once, during a break in filming, Roger asked me how to pronounce certain first names in my Bernese dialect. He called out names, and I called the abbreviation back to him in Bernese German. He called out: "Christian!" Me: "Chrigu!" He: "Thomas!" Me: "Thömü!" He: "Andreas!" Me: "Ändu!" He: "Matthias!" Me: "Mätthu!" He was amused that most of our abbreviations end in "u". That anecdote showed his flair for languages, dialects and wordplay.'

For all his looseness, Federer knows when to be serious and focused. 'I've seen actors who are also very funny, but you can't stop them when they realise they are well liked. You then have to remind them that it's time to move on.

That is never the case with Roger. He knows: I'm here for a client and work with people who have prepared a lot – there are high expectations for this project. He's always on the spot and senses when it's not the moment to make jokes.'

Frieden comes from a tennis family, played at an early age and was the best of his age group in his region as a teenager. As a junior, he played intensively at TC Thun, the same club as Federer's coach Severin Lüthi, with whom he is friends. But then other interests intervened for Frieden. 'At 16, we started a band at school, and I was now more interested in girls and music.' Many years later, the commercials with Federer brought together two of his passions: filmmaking and tennis.

He was at ease with Federer right away, said Frieden. One self-deprecating remark from the tennis star right at the beginning of the first shoot, and he felt they were on the same wavelength. 'He comes to the set alone and is completely unpretentious. With other international stars, there is an entourage. And you sense with Roger: he likes being there. He doesn't see this simply as an assignment he must work through. He often has to say no in his life. But when he says yes, he is fully involved. He doesn't do things by halves. If he's there, he is not distracted or has to do something else besides. You always know where you are at with him. He doesn't agree with everything; he says when he doesn't like something. But I've never experienced him being moody. You can trust him fully.'

The versatility that Federer has to have on the court, in his life as a tennis pro in general, can also be felt in him during the filming. 'He likes to get involved; he's creative. It's in his genes. He loves humour and laughs heartily when any mishap occurs. I have many moments on my hard drive as raw film footage that are very amusing, but for my eyes only.'

As far as acting was concerned, he had noticed a development in Federer. When he filmed the spot with him in the chocolate factory in the summer of 2020, six years had passed since they had last met. This was an eight-hour, elaborate shoot with 11 different locations. The story: Federer shows up a day early for the museum opening and is given a tour of the building by the Maître Chocolatier, during which they get up to some foolishness. 'I was amazed at the ease with which Roger played,' said Frieden. 'He was close to the script but found his own words.' On the set, they worked out one scene spontaneously: the Maître asks him about the secret of his forehand, and he answers self-ironically, 'a bad backhand', and giggles.

Frieden doesn't know if Federer has ever taken acting lessons. But he is impressed by his naturalness and acting talent in front of the camera. 'We shot a scene in the chocolate museum where he has to do the dishes, which, according to the script, doesn't suit him at all. Roger stayed in the role for several takes, always making an annoyed face in between. Only when we left the kitchen again did he drop the grumpy role. This is a technique that actors use. Some even stay in character for weeks during an entire film shoot, even after work.'

For the commercial in the chocolate factory, Frieden wrote a funny alternative version while working on the script: Federer is not caught off guard by the Maître but by a caretaker with Spanish roots. 'He's a huge Nadal fan and wants to find out everything about his beloved player. "What's Rafa like in private?" he asks. In the end, he asks Roger to sign a Nadal autograph card. I think

Roger would have found it funny. But we decided on the Maître Chocolatier because it fits the brand better.' By the way, Frieden can confirm that Federer is a chocolate ambassador by conviction: 'He likes to eat chocolate. But as a professional athlete, he is far more disciplined than I am. I indulge much more uninhibitedly.'

Frieden graduated from the teachers' seminar in Thun, came across an advertisement for the New York Film Academy in the weekly newspaper *The Village Voice* during a trip to New York and studied to become a screenwriter and director. He directed award-winning feature films (*November*, *A Thousand Oceans*, *Our Child*) that deal with unfulfilled longings and disruptions in life. Seen in this light, a feature film about the success story of Roger Federer would probably not have been so exciting for him, would it?

Frieden thought for a moment and said: 'When Roger won everything, he would have been too successful for my films. There was too little drama. But when he had to fight harder for his victories and began to lose more, he would have become more fascinating as a protagonist. A victory becomes much greater when you also experience defeat. Otherwise, his comeback in 2017 would never have been so emotional. This up and down makes life interesting. Only in difficult moments does one's true character reveal itself. When you're a winner, it's easy to be nice. In defeat, you can sometimes lose your composure. Or break down because of it. Roger never has.'

Federer is now quite experienced in front of the camera, with over a dozen advertising partners and about a week of shooting days a year. Frieden said: 'You notice: he has been filming a lot and understands how the cinematic language works, making many things easier. He has a quick grasp on the set. He is simply an intelligent person. After a shoot with him, in the evening, you go home with a smile. The days of shooting are strenuous, the tension is great, a lot is expected, and the spots with Roger go around the world. You can't afford a bad film with him, even less than usual. You have to work to the point; time is money.

'In the evening, the tension is gone, but you feel melancholy because you think: maybe this moment will never come again.'

Ella Ling, photographer
'My favourite shots of him are of his backhand'

Ella Ling's first look at Federer came in 2001 when he played Sampras at Wimbledon. Back then, she was watching as a fan. Later, in her job as a photographer covering the Tours all year round, she saw him through a professional lens.

Ling began her career in 2005, by which time Federer was already well established as world No 1, dominant on the world stage. The first time she saw Federer in action for work was at the Australian Open of 2006, the year he beat Marcos Baghdatis to win the title for the second time. While Federer was the darling of the crowds, for Ling, it was a different story.

'I was not a fan of Federer, at all, as a photographer, because I love photographing players who show a lot of emotion, maybe smash a racquet or two, they make better pictures,' she said. 'But Federer was almost perfect, too perfect. On the court he didn't really show any emotion. He broke a racquet once in Miami and I was there for that. Apart from that, he just doesn't get angry. I think at that age I was pretty young, obviously inexperienced.

I didn't really appreciate the style that he played, how unique he was.'

By the end of 2006, Federer had already won nine grand slam titles and while Rafael Nadal was emerging as a threat on all surfaces, not just clay, he was virtually untouchable. That made for some stunning tennis but not always for great photographs. 'He was completely dominating and I just found it a bit dull,' Ling said. 'He was winning everything. I was too young to appreciate what he was, even photographically, I was so into; the sort of players showing their emotions and maybe some sort of quirky action as well, whereas he was just (perfect). I mean, now, I look back and it was just incredible to have him.'

Timing is everything in tennis and photography. The great photographers find the right shot even when under pressure, just like a great tennis player. It's tiring and stressful. 'I think a lot of people would never think about photographers' point of view,' she said. 'A lot of my friends just say: "Oh, sitting in the sun all day watching tennis, what a life." But I literally cannot tell you what a single point looked like during a match. I couldn't tell you anything about the quality of the match. You're just focusing on the player. You're focusing on circumstances, the light, obviously the scoring, you've got to focus on the scoring because on a big point, you know you're going to get something, a celebration or a racquet smash. But it's not exactly enjoyable. It's certainly not relaxing because you're on guard all the time.'

With Federer, who often showed little emotion during a match, that feeling is exaggerated. 'You know that if it's a tight match, he will (show something) and there will probably be one point during the whole match where he'll do a cele, we call it, a celebration. It's so quick, like blink and you miss it. You do have to be on the ball to catch that moment because those moments are really rare. If you miss it, you know, you're going to be upset.

'In an easy match, you could literally go the whole match without a single emotion shot, nothing. In a match that's more competitive, you might get a very calm fist pump at the end of a set or break point. And if it's a really tight match and a really good match, then you're going to get, it could be a jump, fist pumps and "come on", or whatever he says in Swiss German, looking towards his box. But you don't really get any anger. If you get an angry picture, it's like wow, because it's so rare. I think actually, as his career has gone on, he's possibly showing a bit more emotion but I'm not really sure.'

One of Federer's most iconic poses is when he's looking down at his strings after a forehand, long after the ball has left his racquet. For Ling, though, that's not a shot that often works. 'It doesn't really come out in a photograph very well, that point, when he's just hit the ball and is still looking at the strings,' she said. 'Normally you'd try to get ball on strings and then the full follow-through, or the take-back. Obviously when he's just hit the ball and the ball is sort of a few inches away, he's still looking at the strings. I wouldn't say that's something we really focus on.'

Ling met Federer when he was finalising his move from Nike to Uniqlo in 2018. 'That was an interesting one because I was one of, God knows, like six people to know that he was going to Uniqlo,' she said. 'They contacted me about five days before the start of Wimbledon and said: "We still haven't signed him, but we're hoping to, and we've got a photoshoot with him. Are you available?"'

Heavily pregnant at the time, Ling organised for the shoot to be held in a studio in Wimbledon, where security and secrecy had to be maintained. 'No one knew about it, so he had to be smuggled in because there was an Adidas shoot and something else going on at the same venue at the same time,' she said. 'So they put this black curtain around him while he was getting out of the car and coming into the studio. All the windows were blacked out. I did the shoot with him. That was pretty much the first time we actually had any kind of conversation, but there was nothing about photography, it was all about me being pregnant. And he was telling me about his kids and stuff like that.

'He was extremely professional from start to finish. Normally you might need to direct the player to pose in a certain way but not with Roger. He was so cool, composed and clearly experienced. He led me. And at the end when he had to sign some shirts, he knew exactly how to pull the clothes tight so that we could get the best autograph. I think that absolutely reflects his personality. A perfectionist to the end.'

For Ling, there is a knack to getting the best photos of individual players. Each has their own style; for some, a celebration shot is best; for others it's about the way they play. 'You've got a choice of positions on the court at most events,' she said. 'You know certain players will photograph well from courtside, some will photograph well from the catwalk at the Australian Open, for example, or the concourse – those are the three main spots you've got. So for example, Federer is sort of an all-rounder because you'll get something from all angles. Some players, you know you're going to get a lot of emotion – then I'd want to be courtside to get close to those reactions – whereas other players might be more athletic, energetic, so then you want to be up top. And maybe if it's a sunny day, you get lovely shadows with them jumping around.'

Ling's favourite photos of Federer come when he's in shadow, almost in silhouette, in Madrid, where the Caja Magica creates unique shots. 'In Madrid you've got the shadows, which look awful on TV, but for us, that's like gold dust,' she said. 'The shadows at the back of the court just literally touching the baseline, so that the rest of the court is in the sunlight, and he's serving. Actually, it's not just the serve, his backhand has a beautiful follow-through. So he was on that baseline doing a backhand, the background is completely black – I was shooting from up top – and the background is completely black. You expose it for the light. So the background's completely dark and he's side-lit, so he's in the light and you've got the shadow of him on the court and the background is black. You've got the shape of his backhand, which is very balletic. And it just looks really stunning. I think my favourite shots of him are of his backhand. It's just incredibly beautiful, and it's really unlike anyone else's. If you wanted to teach a single-handed backhand, then that would be it.

'There are some matches where especially with that type of player, you know there's possibly just going to be one really beautiful shot from the whole match. You know the lighting conditions are perfect for that, and then it's just sort of almost a matter of luck where he is, what he is doing at a certain time, the shadow moving all the time as well. He's got to be in a really specific place to get that shot. And chances are you won't get it. But that day he was in the right place at the right time.'

One of the toughest defeats of Federer's career, his loss to Rafael Nadal in the 2008 Wimbledon final, was also a difficult moment for Ling. As the match descended into darkness, the chances of getting a great photo, especially of the winning moment, were slim to none. 'That was pretty early on in the digital camera era, so when you lost the light, you had to really ramp up the ISO, which allows more light in, but you lose the quality of the picture. So if you look back at any of those pictures, they'll be so grainy. Mine were. And dark. Basically, horrible to look at. We could hardly shoot.

'Nowadays it would be much easier because the cameras have improved so much, you can allow more light in and still retain the quality. And obviously, you're not allowed to use a flash. I remember one photographer on match point, as soon as Rafa was down on his back, ping, he got it. As a result, we got some interesting pictures, with his flash in the background. I just remember hating that match so much because it was so long. And my bum hurt because I was sitting there for five hours. Because you can't leave, just in case. So as photographers, there's nothing worse than a five-set match. Which is sad, but true.'

If ever there was an example of what makes photography so special, it came at the Laver Cup in September 2022, when an emotional Federer was soaking up the applause from the crowd at London's O2, shortly after his last ever professional match, a doubles with his biggest rival and old friend, Rafael Nadal.

As Ellie Goulding was singing her lungs out in the stadium, Federer and Nadal were sitting courtside. Nadal was trying everything not to cry, while Federer could not stop himself. When the match finished, Ling had been high above the court, on the concourse level, but she had rushed back to the court, realising she would have more chance to take a good shot from close-up and found the pair 'sitting on the bench together with the rest of the team standing around, framing them really nicely'.

Once she found a spot, Ling's view began to be obscured by a TV cameraman who was inching his way into her shot. It was then that Ling decided to move, a choice that may just have been one of the best of her career.

'I think that was why I got this picture, because I actually made an effort to move, because obviously I wasn't going to get anything if he was inching into the frame,' she said. 'At the point where I took that frame, I was right down at the end of the court in the corner, past Ellie Goulding and had a good view towards them. It was quite amusing because Rafa was just – you don't really see him cry that much – he was really trying to hold it all in and he couldn't look anywhere. His head was down looking the other way, just desperately trying not to cry. But Roger didn't care, he was just going for it, he was crying, he was letting it all out.

'I think as the song went on – you listen to music and it was quite a powerful, emotional song, it brings out the emotions even more – it all got to him. He put his hand over and gave Rafa's thigh a squeeze, which is the shot that I missed. But then as he put his arm back, he placed his hand on Rafa's hand and gave it a little squeeze. It was literally like half a second or something. And luckily, I managed to get two or three frames from that whole sequence.'

At first, Ling was not sure she'd got the shot, let alone knew the significance it would have. 'I didn't even have time to look back at the camera during that,' she said. 'It was only when I got back to my desk and opened up all the pictures on the computer, I found that one and I was like: 'Oh, wow, this is something different, it's a really beautiful image. I'd like to share that one online with people after doing all my work."

'I knew I'd hit the shutter button and I hoped I had it. I probably did glance, literally glance, just to make sure it was there. But I didn't look in any detail until I got back and then, the expressions on their faces were brilliant, and the actual hand-hold, it looked like they were sitting there just holding hands. That's the beauty of photography. They weren't, it was a sort of a split-second thing. But if you're able to capture that moment, that's priceless. It's there forever and it summed up that whole feeling of the night. And that's why I love photography.'

The image of Federer and Nadal holding hands, even for a split second, quickly went viral. 'It was completely surreal,' Ling said. 'I never expected that in a million years. I like the image, but I just didn't think it would get such a following and become so popular.'

Things began to escalate when Jon Wertheim, a well-respected journalist for *Sports Illustrated* and a broadcaster for CBS's *60 Minutes*, retweeted a version of the photo, without knowing who had taken it. Ling put him right and after the pair exchanged messages, he posted the photo again, explaining who had taken it, later going on to suggest it should win 'sports photo of the year'. Famous names, including Piers Morgan, retweeted the photo and the image almost took on a life of its own.

Ling was interviewed on CNN, which made her nervous. 'I'm not very confident doing these things,' she said. 'I've had very little experience talking about (photography). I'm good at taking pictures but I'm not good at talking about it. I was so hesitant. It actually went really well and I was happy with the outcome. A lot of people said nice things about it, which is really good.'

Ling produced a number of limited edition prints of the photo and as a freelance, the publicity was invaluable. Strangely, the image has lost some of its lustre for her, however. 'I can't even look at that picture now,' she said. 'I don't know if you know this feeling, but when you look at something a lot, too much, it becomes abstract to you and you lose that initial reaction to it. When I took it, I knew I really liked this image and that it would be the image that I posted to sum up the feeling of that moment of that evening. But I've lost that initial feeling towards it now. It just feels like too much. But it is completely surreal. I think that is the main word. I'm obviously over the moon that people really, really like it, and it's stirred a lot of emotion in people. To have an iconic picture, it stays with you for life, doesn't it? Sort of puts your name on the map.'

What Ling is also proud of is the message the photo sends.

'I think that's another part of why it's become iconic in some people's minds,' she said. 'For me, that is such a beautiful thing to see. The fact that they don't mind just sitting there, completely open, raw. It's such a pure image. They're unafraid to be vulnerable. They're completely vulnerable in that moment, sitting there crying, completely letting go of their emotions. Two very strong, masculine men who don't show that emotion, on the whole.

'In sport in general, men don't cry. They're meant to be tough. That's the image they're meant to have. That's why it's so impactful, I think, because, again, these two big rivals have suddenly become amazing friends. And I think they've shown to society that it's OK to cry, no matter who you are. It's a really beautiful thing. You should let your emotions out, don't keep everything inside. I think that will help a lot of people around the world, seeing that.'

Ling's appreciation of Federer has grown over the years. Seeing him become more vulnerable has made him seem more human. 'I think when he stopped dominating and then when he was obviously getting older and we all knew that he'd have to retire at some point, then he becomes sort of like a precious commodity,' Ling said. 'I began to appreciate the way that he played and aesthetically, how he looked through the camera. I began to appreciate that way more. I just realised how unique he was and no other player – you're probably not going to find another player ever like that.'

A WORD FROM THE AUTHORS

Simon Cambers, British journalist

*Perfection, honesty, generosity: Federer set
an example for everyone*

With Roger Federer, I've gone through many phases. When he first broke through on to the world stage, I was as captivated as anyone, in awe of someone who could play like he did, seemingly without breaking a sweat. It was effortless, yet brutal, the way he dismissed opponents.

When he was utterly dominant, especially in 2006 and 2007, I must admit I found myself a little bored, yearning for someone to step up to compete with him, to stop each Grand Slam from being a procession. Outside of Roland-Garros, he was more or less unstoppable and though his genius was obvious, writing about him and talking about him became more difficult, with no one to even push him hard enough to break a sweat, away from Rafael Nadal on clay.

It is in later years that I've really grown to appreciate what Federer has meant to tennis. In the four and a half years between his 2012 Wimbledon win and his next Grand Slam victory, at the Australian Open in 2017, many players in his situation would have looked at Nadal, Novak Djokovic and Andy Murray and thought that the writing was on the wall. But Federer never gave up, he was always knocking on the door and when he came back from knee surgery to win in Melbourne in 2017, he was arguably better than ever, at the age of 35.

As journalists, we are privileged to see the players behind the scenes, sometimes in the corridors between interview rooms, in player lounges and when they're relaxing after matches or preparing for their next match. Some players shy away from journalists in those situations, avoiding eye contact. Others, like Federer, are unfailingly polite. He walks with a unique swagger but he always says hello and gives you a smile as he carries on his business, making you feel like he knew who you were. It doesn't sound much – and Nadal is similar – but a little common courtesy goes a long way.

I remember one Australian Open, it must have been 2016 because that's the only time we travelled to Melbourne as a family, that I, or more accurately, my son, who was then two and a half years old, had asked me if we could get an ice cream. It was a couple of days before the Australian Open was due to begin and my wife, also a journalist, and I were taking it in turns to do the parenting while we ran around getting our remaining interviews with various players. Walking down the corridor toward the old media rooms, we passed the player restaurant, always a hive of activity in Melbourne. Inside, I could see Federer, who had his back to me, sitting with his manager, Tony Godsick. I acknowledged Tony and knelt down next to my son. Pointing to Federer, I told him that he was looking at the best player of all time. Godsick nudged Federer, who duly turned round and gave my son a wave. My son's response? No wave back, just a request: 'Can we get an ice cream now?' I don't think Roger realised what was going on; if I'm brave enough, one day maybe I'll explain the unwitting snub.

I was at Wimbledon for Federer's famous, breakthrough victory over Pete Sampras in 2001 but I can't remember being on court for it. I was, though, in Halle, Germany, in 2003 for Federer's first grass-court title. Three weeks later, he won his first Grand Slam title, beating Mark Philippoussis in the final at Wimbledon. From then on, he never looked back.

The best tennis I ever saw live, in terms of a single, pure performance, was at the US Open in 2004 when Federer took on Lleyton Hewitt for the title. Hewitt had been a real problem for Federer early in his career, winning their first three meetings and seven of the first nine. But this was 2004, as so many people have said, the year Roger became Roger. Hewitt had not dropped a set on his way to the final but he had absolutely no chance. Sitting courtside, I watched Hewitt, as good a competitor as there has been, win just five points in the first set, which took 18 minutes. To be honest, he was lucky to get five points.

Though the second set was tight, Federer winning it on the tiebreak, the third set was an annihilation again as he sealed a 6-0, 7-6, 6-0 win. At times, the tennis was so perfect, it was almost ridiculous.

There are many other moments that stand out: his victory over Andy Murray at Wimbledon in 2012 when he dashed home hopes again; his victory in Australia in 2017 when he played five astounding games to finish off Nadal; and other difficult moments to watch, too, none more so than at Wimbledon in 2019, when he had two match points to beat Djokovic in the final, only to falter at the final hurdle. That would have given him the title at the age of 37 and it must have been incredibly hard for him to take, but when we next saw him, at the US Open, he accepted it and said he'd moved on. Champions do that.

You never know when a champion is going to play his last big match and so at Wimbledon in 2016, when he went two sets down to Marin Cilic in the quarter-finals, I ran out to get a seat on Centre Court, thinking this might be the last time I saw him play. Of course, Federer duly came back for victory and anyway, I should have known better than to write him off. I remember him saying when he was about 26 that he wanted to play on at the top until at least 35, and me thinking he was deluded. Again, what did I know?

In some ways, Federer's presence at the top of the game for so long was a huge bonus for all tennis journalists. Newspaper editors loved Federer's style throughout and always responded to any pitch involving him. That's partly down to the incredible job Federer did off the court in understanding both the needs of the press and what it can do for him. As a young player, he decided to be honest with the media and treat us as equals, which was a masterstroke. Honesty and integrity mean everything to a player's image and the thing about Federer is that when he says something, you believe him. He is genuine.

His ability to hear a question and even realise what you might be looking for is unparalleled in tennis. No one has had to answer as many questions as Federer, who does it in three languages. Yet, though a large percentage of them may have been similar, he has always found a way to be thoughtful and offer an interesting answer. What's more, he even learned to use them for his own purposes, getting matches out of his system faster than he might otherwise have done.

I think we will only really appreciate how much Federer did for tennis as we come to terms with his retirement.

Simon Graf, Swiss journalist

My idea of the idealised Federer made me a better person

Roger Federer was not my first love in tennis. He was too young for that (or I was too old). It was Mikael Pernfors. The Swede with the crew cut impressed me right away when he made it to the final at Roland-Garros in 1986 as a little-known college boy. No one played passing shots as calmly, and topspin lobs as precisely as he did. And above all, he seemed incredibly cool. He looked like James Dean, I thought. From then on, I pranced like Pernfors on the return, and I desperately wanted the same tennis clothes as him. But they weren't available in the shops, and you couldn't just order anything online.

At that time, Roland-Garros was still my favourite tournament (later, it became Wimbledon) because the matches could drag on for five hours or more. I loved to spend whole afternoons in front of the television and watch Mats Wilander put every ball into the court without ever committing an error. There was something immensely calming about that. Pernfors and Wilander – my first tennis idols were Swedes. There was still no thought of a Swiss Grand Slam champion in the men's game.

Then came Federer and I became a tennis reporter while he joined the pros. Timing as perfect as Federer's on his forehand. I was filled with pride when I walked from the press centre to Wimbledon's Centre Court for the first time on the first Monday of the Championships in 2002.

The year before, Federer had dethroned the great Pete Sampras, and now he was about to take over. And I would accompany him as a journalist. After two hours and three lost sets against Mario Ancic, I walked back to my desk in consternation and sorted out my thoughts and sentences.

But I was to experience one or two of Federer's triumphs later. Of course, the first Wimbledon title in 2003 always remains unique, even if the final against Mark Philippoussis was not memorable. Afterwards, a group of us Swiss journalists celebrated the day for tennis history in an Italian restaurant in the London district of Hammersmith until well into the night. The owner of the restaurant seized the opportunity and put a bottle of grappa on the table, the contents of which we immediately put to its intended use. Then we had another one. The bill turned out to be lavish.

As we returned to the hotel at two or three in the morning, my colleague René Stauffer looked at his mobile phone and saw a message: 'Mirka has texted me. We can do our one-on-one interview with Roger tomorrow morning. Before the official press appointment.' We had been asking for a while but Federer had felt under pressure after another debacle at the French Open and had not granted any longer interviews. Now he had shown it to everyone and was willing to talk. Back at the hotel, we had a quick shower, put our heads together downstairs in the lobby and brainstormed some clever questions. Then a short sleep for an hour or two.

Federer couldn't help but laugh when he saw us early in the morning in the garden of his rented house at 10 Lake Road. We probably looked even more tired than he did. He said then: 'Winners stay, losers go away. Winners and losers are so close and yet so far apart. What makes true champions is simply that they win.' What might have sounded arrogant was the unadorned truth. And Federer felt at the time that he would not stop winning soon.

For us Swiss tennis reporters, he became a blessing. He played as regularly as Swiss clockwork and provided us with pleasant planning security. From Wimbledon 2004 to the Australian Open 2010, he reached the semifinals of a Grand Slam tournament 23 times in a row. So we no longer had to stay in Hammersmith during Wimbledon but rented a house not far from the All England Club for a fortnight during the Championships. There was little danger of us having to leave early because all the players from Switzerland had been eliminated in the first week.

Federer was a stroke of luck not only because of his success and beautiful game but also because of his approachability. He became the most interviewed athlete on the planet – yet he thought of a clever answer to practically every question. A German colleague once told me that Steffi Graf won her match in 37 minutes and was angry afterwards because she had dropped two games and was therefore brief in the press conference afterwards. A one-sided match and hardly any quotes, what an arduous task for journalists.

Federer was the complete opposite. He always gave us enough material for stories, even if his matches sometimes didn't offer much. As abstruse as the question was, he always tried to put himself in the reporters' heads. He thought about what kind of story they wanted to write and how his answer could help. Even when, in the autumn of his career, he had grown a bit tired of being questioned by the international media, always focused on the three-way battle with Rafael Nadal and Novak Djokovic, he always remained very accessible in Swiss German.

What always amazed me: he knew very well which journalists asked which questions, when and where. Once, after an interview on the sidelines of the Davis Cup in Geneva in 2006, which we had conducted in his hotel suite, he asked me why a certain Swiss reporter at Wimbledon always sat in one of the last rows during the press conferences and never asked a question. Federer likes to keep track of things and has an excellent memory for people.

As much as he revealed about himself and as masterfully as he played, there was also a time when it was not so easy to put Federer's fascination into words. Because by then, it had become almost expected that he rushed from victory to victory. We journalists clung to statistics, figures, records and comparisons with greats from earlier times to explain why it was not normal. And when he lost, it was almost a state affair in Switzerland – unless it was at Roland-Garros against Nadal, because people had become used to that, too.

Federer's Grand Slam victories in the times after his great dominance – like at Roland-Garros and Wimbledon in 2009, at Wimbledon in 2012 or the Australian Open in 2017 – felt even sweeter to many than those before. Most Federer fans now cite his miraculous return in Melbourne 2017 after his six-month break and the epic final against Nadal as their most defining Federer moment.

Coincidence and our geographical proximity meant that I bumped into Federer every now and then away from tournaments. Like in 2019, a few days after Roland-Garros, when he brought his two daughters to swimming lessons at the indoor pool in my home village, we chatted for almost an hour in the cafeteria. I tried hard not to ask tennis questions. My then seven-year-old daughter Lavinia was also there; we had gone swimming together and had intended to hit a few balls. But of course, I didn't want to miss this opportunity to talk to Federer. And he caringly looked after my daughter when he noticed that she was getting bored. He asked her what she liked to do, and at one point, he took her by the hand and bought a cake with her at the buffet because she didn't want to go on her own.

Sometimes in my private life, I think, 'How would Federer have reacted?' For example, when I'm annoyed with my daughters. And I then imagine how he would have remained completely calm and smiled. It may well be that I have an idealised image of him as a private person. He probably also gets annoyed when his children don't want to get out of bed in the morning, when they don't listen or when they only leave half of their dinner and then search the cupboards for sweets. But my idea of the idealised Federer helped me, and it made me a better person.

The Roger Federer effect was very pronounced and direct for me. For more than 20 years, the tennis virtuoso enriched my professional life and probably made me grow as a journalist. Because, thanks to him, I experienced more, got around the world, looked for new angles for stories and built an international network.

And last but not least, at the time of Brexit, it led to a Swiss-British cooperation with my namesake and highly esteemed colleague Simon Cambers for this book. It was a pleasure!

INDEX

INDEX

THE AUTHORS

Simon Cambers

Simon Cambers has been covering the ATP and WTA Tours for well over two decades. After starting his career with *Bloomberg News*, he later became a freelancer and is a regular contributor to a number of publications worldwide, including *The Guardian*, *Glasgow Herald*, ESPN, the *New York Times* and *Reuters*. He has interviewed all the biggest stars in the game and you can also hear him working as a commentator on Radio Roland-Garros and Australian Open Radio. He lives on the south coast of England with his wife and young son.

Simon Graf

As a journalist for the Swiss newspapers *Tages-Anzeiger* and the *SonntagsZeitung*, Simon Graf has covered Roger Federer and the ATP and WTA Tours for the last 20 years. Graf has a master's degree in history, German literature and linguistics. He lives with his wife and two daughters in Kilchberg by Lake Zurich, where he occasionally meets Roger at the Indoor Swimming Pool or the tennis courts nearby. He is the author of several sports books in Switzerland. His biography about Roger Federer, published in 2018, has been a bestseller. It has been translated into English, Italian, Japanese and, most recently, Arabic.